D0000845

ADVERTISING DIVERSITY

ADVERTISING
DIVERSITY

*Ad Agencies and the Creation of
Asian American Consumers*

SHALINI SHANKAR

DUKE UNIVERSITY PRESS

Durham & London

2015

© 2015 Duke University Press
All rights reserved
Printed in the United States of America on
acid-free paper ♾
Typeset in Chaparral and Myriad by Tseng
Information Systems, Inc.

Library of Congress Cataloging-in-Publication Data
Shankar, Shalini, 1972–
Advertising diversity : ad agencies and the creation
of Asian American consumers / Shalini Shankar.
pages cm
Includes bibliographical references and index.
ISBN 978-0-8223-5864-0 (hardcover : alk. paper)
ISBN 978-0-8223-5877-0 (pbk. : alk. paper)
ISBN 978-0-8223-7561-6 (e-book)
1. Advertising—Social aspects—United States.
2. Asian American consumers—United States.
3. Asian Americans—Race identity—United
States. 4. Stereotypes (Social psychology) in
advertising—United States. 5. Advertising
agencies—United States. 6. Minorities in
advertising—United States. I. Title.
HF5813.U6S53 2015
659.1′042—dc23   2014040371

Cover art: Illustration based on a photo by
the author.

For Roshan and Anisha

CONTENTS

Different paths led me to undertake this research and write a book about advertising. I had watched many ads with youth and their families during fieldwork for my book *Desi Land* in Silicon Valley, on satellite and cable television channels and programming blocks that were explicitly made for and aimed at South Asian American audiences. I wondered who made these ads, whom they thought they were reaching, and where this advertising fit in the broader American commercial media landscape. As a long-time viewer of live televised sports, I had also become attuned to how ads had changed over years, especially the increased inclusion of minorities in ads that previously featured mostly, if not exclusively, white talent. The appearance and speech styles of some actors suggested their ethnic or racial identity, while others seemed intentionally difficult to place; corporations seemed to deliberately shift brand identity to foster a broader range of consumer identification.

I decided to pursue this project about advertising development and production because of my interest in race and representation as well as media and consumption. Advertising brought these concerns together, and a production-based perspective allowed me to consider the cultural and linguistic semiotics of the process. I began fieldwork for this book in the spring of 2008, when the effects of the financial crash were becoming a new economic and social reality, when the United States was on the verge of electing its first black president, and when smartphones and social media claimed their place as a household presence. My position as a university professor made most people I met favorably disposed to my research; it evoked a level of respect that I did not have to earn but did have to maintain. I did this in large part by being as inconspicuous as possible and respecting whatever boundaries were drawn for me. The limits of the data I was able to collect, as well as that which I am able to discuss, are evident throughout the book.

This is a book about the complex dynamics of imagining and representing diversity in advertising development and production. I focus on Asian American advertising but also consider general market and other multicultural markets and explore connections between the social dynamics of agencies and the finished products of advertisements. Writing about American advertising was unexpectedly challenging. As a linguistic and cultural anthropologist, I never felt completely at ease in corporate America and found the banter of marketing and networking events awkward, as I was not looking to get ahead in the business world; I continue to be critical of capitalism and the social and economic inequalities that it engenders and renews. Advertising is designed to be capitalism's biggest cheerleader, creating need and desire for goods and services. Advertising executives are archetypal middlemen, selling themselves to corporations as much as they sell products and services to consumers. But middlemen, as I learned, come in a wide range of political beliefs and subjectivities. I came to respect and appreciate their efforts, the long hours they worked, and the sometimes harsh criticism they endured when defending their creative and production work. Their own social status rarely mirrored the idealized worlds of their ads, and the marginalization some contended with owing to their race, gender, immigration status, accents, and limited social networks was intense. So too was the success they enjoyed when they challenged white hegemony with their counterimages of Asian Americans and their ambivalence about furthering particular stereotypes of themselves or others.

This is not a book about exposing advertising executives as racists or illustrating that all advertising is racist. Rather it is an analysis of the interaction between entities such as the U.S. Census, advertising agencies, market researchers, and the goods and services industries, focusing on those individuals who offer products and services for sale (clients, advertisers, marketers) and those who create messaging to promote them (advertising executives). Theirs is the day-to-day work that produces the sometimes spectacular, sometimes offensive, but often just forgettable mass-mediated versions of an America in which race, ethnicity, gender, sexuality, class, nationality, and citizenship are carefully rendered. That race and ethnicity continue to matter in ads stands in direct opposition to the claim of conservative media and corporate America that we are in a "postracial" era in which racism is no longer a social ill. In this world ethnic and racial difference is called "diversity"—a surprisingly cheerful term because it acknowledges difference but none of the inequalities that can underpin it. Yet racism persists in corporate America as well as in America more broadly, from everyday remarks masquerading as humor to violent crimes of hate and xenophobia. As I completed this manuscript, America made sense of the "not guilty" verdict in the trial of George Zimmerman, the acquitted killer of the black teenager Trayvon Martin, and acknowledged the one-year anniversary of the Oak Creek, Wisconsin, Gurdwara shooting. Most recently, the events in Ferguson, Missouri, provide gruesome new evidence linking racism, police brutality, and the inequities of everyday life for African Americans and other racial minorities. These and myriad other events in which ethnic and racial difference as well as dynamics of privilege and inclusion come to the fore confirm that America is in fact not in a postracial era, despite claims to the contrary.

The continued relevance of race and ethnicity, especially in light of demographic predictions that America will be a "majority minority" nation by 2042, is quite beneficial for advertising, because representing difference makes money. The advertising industry cares about diversity because it makes good business sense, and addressing diversity is necessary to remain relevant to clients and compliant with regulatory agencies. Diversity matters in everyday interactions among ad executives, in their personnel decisions, and in their creative and production work; it has come to shape notions of what ad executives highlight as being "normal" about the United States. I focus my discussion on the development and production of ads themselves, but I do so in ways that do not simply critique the work of advertising as contributing to racialized capitalism or by praising Asian American advertising for producing ethnically and linguistically specific ads that disrupt white corporate hegemony. Rather I present my version of the world I observed, filled with racism and inequality as well as attempts to address these issues in workplaces and in creative work, and I consider what may be learned about the formation and reproduction of these dynamics in corporate America.

Each chapter in *Advertising Diversity* begins with a vignette containing a portion of an advertising account intended to highlight various parts of the development and production process. The account unfolds from start to finish to offer glimpses into the inception, growth, vetting, and making of an advertisement, as well as its plan for circulation, with names and other details modified for confidentiality purposes. Although development and production can unfold in a number of ways, aspects of the process are found in most advertising and marketing activities. Taken together the segments illustrate the broader process of advertising pitching, creative development, and production and complement the structure of the book.

If you can recall an ad that you thought was really funny but public outcry deemed it racist, or have been told to lighten up when you think an ad is racist, or just cannot escape the ads you would rather ignore on live television, framing the pages of your newspaper, in your glossy magazines, on flat screens in taxis, preceding your YouTube video, waiting to greet you on airplane tray tables, showing up on your Facebook newsfeed, or as they replay in your mind when you would rather be thinking about anything else, then read on to find out how some of them came to be.

The Pitch

At 6:20 p.m. on a warm evening in May 2008, ad executives trickled into the agency's large conference room. Open windows let in the sounds of Manhattan traffic along with a refreshing breeze. Projected on the wall was the PowerPoint presentation the Asian Ads account team had sent to the client for a new business pitch. They had worked well with this client over the years by developing and producing insurance and financial services ads for Chinese American audiences. Today they were presenting their ideas for a brand launch into markets designated as "Asian Indian" and "Korean" by the U.S. Census. Ad executives who worked on the pitch gathered around the speakerphone in the center of the conference table, speculating about the location of the client based on the unfamiliar area code the account executive was dialing. "Indiana! Wow. I didn't expect that," one creative exclaimed as she looked over the brand-awareness print creative concept. An automated voice greeted them from the pod in the center of the large conference table. "Please wait for the moderator of your conference," requested the pleasant female voice as the account executive hit "mute" and the team reviewed their plan for the presentation. The account executive began to quiet down her colleagues when the automated voice finally announced, "Your moderator has arrived. Welcome to the Allied Country conferencing center. Please enter your pin code followed by the pound key." A larger than usual group had assembled for this new business pitch, each ready to contribute if needed. Sunil, an account executive who had already worked with this client, remained reserved and deferred to his colleague Kew to make the presentation. In past accounts Sunil had begun presentations in a lighter tone with more jovial openings, like "They are gonna sell their concept to you today, if you will buy it!" Exposing the artifice of the work being done, he delivered the line with just enough affect to draw a chuckle from his clients, warming them up so that his creatives' work would be well received. Today, however, he remained quiet, not wanting to jeopardize the possibility of new business in a down economy. "I'm very excited about this presentation," creative director An Rong told his team as they awaited connection to the conference call. He reminded them, "This is the first phase: branding." The client finally arrived in the virtual conferencing center: the vice president of marketing, George, and his colleague Nadine. Turning on the charm, account executive Kew warmly welcomed them and began making small talk. Without the benefit of presenting in person and entertaining the client, their performance via speakerphone along with the visuals they had sent had to do the work of "selling it in," as some account executives called it. Kew began, "We have two concepts for you, each that sells your brand, cultural insights, as well as incorporates your logo. How are we selling all three in one package? Let me show you with Concept One."

Over the past century or so, the American advertising industry, like advertising globally, has undergone dramatic shifts, rifts, controversies, and reconceptualizations. It has created beloved jingles, produced deplorable caricatures, and become absolutely inescapable. It has been thoughtfully and stylishly explored through such dramatic renderings as AMC's award-winning drama *Mad Men* and served as a more casual backdrop for other fictionalized dramas and comedies. It has even survived the dreaded digital video recorder that allows television viewers to fast-forward through commercial breaks. Indeed the cost per second for ads during the Super Bowl has steadily risen, even after the 2008 recession. And no matter how charming Don Draper can be and how much *Mad Men* fans relish his creative presentations, most of us are still annoyed at the commercial breaks during this show about advertising. Despite this, advertising is a seminal part of our shifting media landscape. Currently, when television, radio, social media, and the Internet converge in ways that make the boundaries that separate them increasingly less important, the work of advertising is far less straightforward. Creating brand identities, generating aspirational imagery, and building a growing consumer base still remain paramount, but catchy creative alone cannot accomplish this. Multiple platforms, regional tactical events, and promotional tie-ins with other retail and media outfits make advertising today so much more than generating and executing a commissioned creative vision. Brands are managed from above, co-opted from below, and appropriated in unforeseen ways. Advertising's role is to stay ahead of consumers by creating aspirational imagery, while it also strives to be sure audiences identify with the representations they circulate. Especially as the U.S. population changes in its ethnic and racial composition and who counts as a coveted consumer, ways of staying current and relevant are sites of ongoing contest and competition.

AIMS AND OBJECTIVES

Advertising Diversity investigates processes of racial and ethnic representation in various segments of the American advertising industry. I look at the day-to-day work of development and production, the people doing the work, the broader corporate constraints in which this work is based, and how all of these areas shape mass-mediated commercial representation. I consider the role of this work in bringing about particular representational shifts while sometimes reproducing racism and the modalities through which it does so. If we pose the question "Why does race still matter so much?" with regard to advertising, the reductive answer would be "profit."[1] If advertising's role is to create aspirational imagery and brand identification for consumers, then people in ads should look something like their intended U.S. audience, in which one out of three people identify themselves as African American, Hispanic, Asian, Native American, or some other nonwhite minority. Advertising reflects but also creates difference, and both these strategies are intended to further brand identities and consumer identification. *Niche advertising* does this in specialized ways, by targeting subsections of the population, creating ads that address them specifically, and placing these in media that is thought to appeal to them. *Multicultural advertising* is one type of niche advertising; it targets ethnic and racial minorities through *in-culture* and *in-language* messaging. Beginning with Jews and blacks in the 1960s—groups that were sometimes reached by departments within general market agencies—and Hispanic and Asian consumers from the 1970s onward, multicultural agencies attempted to reach audiences from these groups through strategies that differed from mainstream advertising.[2] Yet large, multinational *general market* agencies, as they are called in industry parlance, have also sought to reconceive of the mainstream in ways that more centrally include minorities.

Defining Normal

Consumers identify with brands on many different levels, but I argue that race and ethnicity remain central to constructions of brand identity and consumer identification in the United States. As each U.S. Census provides new data about minority populations, marketing has followed suit and attempted to reach these consumers as directly as possible. Since the 2010 Census especially, the inclusion of minorities in general market advertisements in ways that are not disparaging or mocking has increased, allowing general market advertising executives to display their expertise in reaching African American, Hispanic, and Asian audiences. Using the corporate-friendly term *diversity*, they represent what marketers call the "new normal" as marked by difference, conceived in inoffensive and sometimes ambiguous ways. Another reason why race still matters so much can be found in a consideration of the people who make ads and how their own subjectivity intersects with client expectations to shape this work. The New York City Human Rights Commission and other entities have alleged that the American advertising industry has made minimal progress in diversifying its ranks in the past forty years. If this is the case, how does this predicament bear on creative work in multicultural advertising aimed at minorities, often made by minorities who are expected to embody the differences they represent? How might it play out in general market advertising, where a broader culture of whiteness pervades agencies and creative renderings of what is normal and taken as objective fact?

Over the course of this book I will argue that the American advertising industry, like much of corporate America, has been shaped by economic and political shifts during the past several decades. These shifts, marked by the civil rights era, multiculturalism, and currently the notion of a "post-racial" United States, have led to changes in discourse about ethnic and racial difference. Capitalism and race have long been intertwined, and the current iteration of this relationship is evident in corporate America's ver-

I.1 Best Buy Super Bowl spot starring Amy Poehler and Jake Choi (2013).

sion of diversity, a formulation that recognizes ethnic and racial difference as decoupled from inequality and prejudice. Diversity, however, is anything but apolitical; it contains tensions that arise from geopolitical concerns of U.S. militarized conflict, relies on biopolitical ways of tracking migration and counting bodies and their consumer trends through the U.S. Census, and furthers capitalist networks that link individuals and industries in different locations. Such a conception of diversity furthers the culture of whiteness that pervades corporate America and shapes its notions of normal while it also makes invisible the work that normal does to obscure racism, discrimination, and prejudice.

The highly subjective concept of normal is differently understood by those who work in the corporate world of advertising and those on the outside looking in. One thing this book will show is how different normal can look depending on where one stands within corporate America, especially when it comes to race, ethnicity, and language. Elizabeth Povinelli has provocatively suggested that "the ordinary" does not simply exist; rather it is a projection of numerous statistical ordinaries.[3] In advertising the notion of normal can be considered a collection of *aspirational* norms—how diversity looks in an ideal world and how that world can be rendered without looking like an advertisement. One of the processes I investigate is how certain values come to be considered normal and what the consequences are of having that version prevail in commercial media. It remains to be seen whether multicultural agencies that render ethnicity and language in highly specific ways or general market agencies that have sought to increase the overall inclusion of nonwhite actors in their ads will win out, but the competition certainly seems to be on. The stakes are clear: there are over 100 million minorities in the United States, and reaching them through advertising has become a top priority. By looking at everyday interactions among advertising executives and between them and their clients I consider how agencies full of smart, educated people, many of whom are minorities or otherwise espouse liberal, progressive politics, can still make ads that are publicly called out as racist.

A broader aim of this book is to see the potential of advertising for furthering a politics of antiracism, even while the advertising industry's goals are of course very different. Millions of people labor for corporations worldwide, and academic critiques of them fall within a double bind of ethical complexities when offering an account of the positive and negative work they do.[4] Unlike the investment bankers and hedge fund managers who epitomize corporate America in cities like New York, most advertising executives I met saw themselves as working in a different echelon of corporate America, one premised on the unending social promise of doing good creative, of empowerment through consumption, and of bringing humor, originality, and small bursts of fleeting pleasure. Although drawn from a very different context and literature, James Ferguson's "politics of the 'anti-'" is useful here. Ferguson argues that it is somewhat predictable for anthropologists and the Left to rail against neoliberal forms of governance but not suggest any viable alternatives. He urges anthropologists to think creatively and imagine the possibilities of recent transformations in government and spatial organization, to find the contemporary possibilities of what we actually do want to see.[5]

When considering Ferguson's challenge in this light, how can we think about commercial media in ways that do not immediately condemn it for its superficiality, its reductive imagery, and its potential to reproduce stereotypes? If we could see it doing something different, what would that look like? I realize that Ferguson's discussion about governmentality, aid organizations, and pro-poor activism in Africa takes on issues of a different order and purpose, but the questions he raises can be adapted to the subject of advertising: What would we like to see advertising do, if what it is doing now is not to the liking of critical scholars and media-literate consumers alike? Barnor Hesse has written, "It is not simply the postracial horizon that confounds the theoretical critique of racism, but it is also the concept of racism itself that confounds the critique. This is now the vital phase of the so-called race question."[6] To apply this line of questioning to

I.2 Nissan Chinese American spot featuring in-language voice-over and Chinese American family (2013).

the advertising industry, I ask, What makes commercial communication racist? Is it exclusion based on certain characteristics? Is it discrimination? Or is it the unequal reliance on certain individuals for intellectual and white-collar labor that ultimately shapes social values at a societal level? Put another way, if advertising executives do not want to be racist, and the clients who fund the advertising do not want to be racist, and the media outlets do not want to be racist, then what would need to happen in corporate America to bring an antiracist agenda to the forefront of advertising development and production? My approach is to deconstruct the idea of normal as an objective social fact in advertising and consider how naturalized versions of race and ethnicity, what might be called normal, come to be. *Normal* is a term I heard routinely among ad executives in ways that rendered subjective notions of social life and difference as commonly held beliefs shared by all. Throughout this book, and especially in the conclusion, I return to the politics of the anti- to see what can be learned from analyzing the broader dynamics of capitalism, race, and media that govern the advertising industry and how economic and political ideologies that come to bear on cultural and linguistic choices ultimately constitute diversity.

Categories and Terms

By considering the advertisement from an industry perspective—that is, a fifteen- or thirty-second film, soundscape, or work of art that strives to tell a story, be entertaining, and be authentic—I consider what culture and language mean in the context of advertising diversity. I do so by focusing on Asian American advertising as a part of broader processes of commercial media production, representational strategies, and capitalist agendas. Asian American advertising is a product of more than the advertising industry; it emerged from the "new immigration" that occurred after 1965, the postwar rise in consumer and youth culture, multicultural ideologies that celebrate heritage languages and culture, and a corporate world that welcomes racial minorities who are willing to do cultural and linguistic work for hire. That Asian Americans—especially the five largest groups, Chinese, Korean, Filipino, Asian Indian, Vietnamese, and, on the West Coast and Hawai'i, Japanese and Pacific Islanders—constitute a viewing public is a claim that many general market advertising agency executives find spurious. Numbering just over 15 million (alone or in combination) in the 2010 U.S. Census, they constitute barely 5 percent of the total U.S. population. Unlike Latinos, who at 50 million constitute 17 percent of the overall U.S. population and have at least two full-time television channels that feature original content, Asian Americans have a handful of satellite television channels that pull content from Asia, weekly program blocks on local access cable, and various print media with relatively small circulations. So why bother to target them at all? If we are to believe the ad executives who pitch their services to potential clients, it is because this group is believed to have the highest purchasing power and per capita income of any group, including whites. These statistics have been qualified and even contested, as I discuss in chapter 1, but remain valid and apparently quite influential.[7] Major challenges, however, oppose these enticing statistics. With several different languages and orthographies, not to mention nationalities, religions, and colonial pasts, the Latino advertising approach of using one variety of Spanish and downplaying ethnonational differences simply does not work for Asian American advertising. Rather, Asian American advertising continually grapples with how to create and produce messaging aimed at specific Asian ethnic groups that is broad enough to index the category of Asian American.

The ethnographic examples presented in this book are drawn from my fieldwork in advertising agencies. In most cases, unless I am describing

I.3 Mercedes-Benz in-culture and in-language print ad for Filipino American consumers (2004).

the history of a specific agency (mostly in chapter 1), and in sections of this introduction, chapter 1, and the conclusion in which I discuss the growth and development of marketing approaches to diverse audiences, I have changed the names of people, agencies, and brands. Real names generally include a surname as well as a title, to differentiate them from pseudonyms. All of the excerpts from meetings and creative conversations are from one Asian American agency based in New York City, and interviews and observations are drawn from fieldwork in Asian American agencies in New York, Los Angeles, and San Francisco, as well as general market agencies in New York. Most of these Asian American agencies are founded, owned, or operated by individuals of Asian descent; some are currently owned by a larger media conglomerate. The individuals who develop and produce these ads are predominantly Asian American and perform this category in a variety of ways for their clients, for their colleagues in the advertising industry, and among themselves. Their performances of affect and identity offer a glimpse into the minute negotiations of creative concepts, intricate choices about language varieties and translations, and finer aspects of casting individuals and directing them in print, television, and radio ads. Taken together, the corporate work of commercial media production and the representations they yield provide a window into intersections of race, capitalism, and the products of its labor in the twenty-first-century United States.

Before I elaborate on the theoretical concerns of the book, I offer glosses on some of my terminology. *Ethnoracial* or *ethnorace* combines the terms *ethnicity*—referring to differences of nationality, religion, language, and cultural heritage that can be defined by institutions such as the U.S. Census and put into social practice, or by communities and societies in ways that may or may not eventually get recognized by more formal entities—and *race*, referring to U.S. Census categories under which ethnicities are grouped.[8] These are not mutually exclusive and sometimes overlap; for example, the category Hispanic can be classified as white Hispanic or non-white Hispanic. With the Asian category, there is less ambiguity about race, as Asian constitutes a single racial category with various ethnicities as well as "Other Asian" listed within it. The term *ethnorace* was not prevalent in advertising agencies; they preferred *ethnicity*, which they used to refer to specific groups, whether racial (i.e., Asian or Asian American) or ethnic (Chinese, Korean, etc.), or the term *diversity* when referring to social difference in general. Usually *diversity* indexed differences associated with race or ethnicity, but it could also be used to refer to LGBT (lesbian, gay, bisexual, or transgender) issues, differently abled individuals, and other underrepresented groups. In those contexts where ethnoracial difference was made explicit—usually in multicultural advertising—advertising executives most commonly used the terms *African American* or *black* for populations living in the United States, *African* for recent immigrants from North Africa, *Hispanic* for Latino or Chicano, and *Asian* for Asian American (a term they also used to talk about Asia the continent).

Within the category of Asian, ad executives generally dropped the "American" and simply referred to groups as Chinese, Vietnamese, and so on. They also used the U.S. Census–derived term *Asian Indian* for Indians and did not include individuals from other regions of the subcontinent in this designation. I retain their usage when quoting or paraphrasing but also use the more common academic terms in my analysis, such as *Asian American* and *South Asian American* when addressing categories broader than just Indians. Terms such as *corporate America* and *whiteness* are defined in contexts of use, and their use is not negative; rather they are intended to conjure a broader setting and collection of practices in which advertising is developed and produced. Finally, I use the term *racialization* to consider how certain social meanings become linked to particular racial categories and how these meanings are vetted and sometimes transformed in everyday encounters. I look at this process in activities such as creative brainstorms, in which ad executives conjure particular cultural attributes of Asian Americans, as well as in interactions between ad executives and their clients in which they embody and perform this category as a marker of authenticity and legitimacy for the work they produce. Racialization in the advertising industry, as in other sectors of corporate America, operates such that individuals act as diversity experts based on their ethnic and linguistic heritage rather than formal skills or knowledge they may have acquired. This wide range of terms signals the separate but overlapping agendas of advertising executives and clients, as well as my own as an academic, of putting into words the work of advertising.

THEORETICAL ORIENTATIONS

Several literatures have influenced my cultural and linguistic anthropological conception of these ideas, including critical race theory, critical ethnic studies, Asian American studies, and media studies. One of the approaches I foreground in particular is to bring critical ethnic studies into conversation with linguistic anthropology. I am certainly not the first to do this, as Jane Hill, Michael Silverstein, Bonnie Urciuoli, and others have talked about language and racialization in U.S. media. My goal is to use these literatures to analyze the ethnographic examples that follow. There are admittedly some stumbling blocks to this approach; most apparent are method and scale. Linguistic anthropology tends to focus on microlevel interactions, while critical ethnic studies tends to apply broader theoretical claims in the analysis of texts (literature, film, television, advertisements, etc.). An ethnographically informed analysis of the development and production of ethnoracial representation is bound to be less neat and orderly than analyzing completed texts. Bridging scales of inquiry is an ongoing challenge, and the book accordingly toggles between different levels of analysis.

Assemblages of Diversity

A central concept I employ to do this bridging is "the assemblage," beginning with Gilles Deleuze and Félix Guattari's introduction of the concept and the numerous ways it has been analyzed and applied in the years after its introduction in the mid-1990s. Deleuze and Guattari describe the assemblage as a "field of multiple maneuvers," as temporally achieved and open to transformation as it endures and circulates. They emphasize the "expressive potential" of the assemblage in ways that can accommodate change without structuralist causality.[9] Assemblage is a useful analytic to understand advertising development and production as spatially and temporally delimited events. The concept allows me to illustrate the intersection of competing interests and vantage points at a particular moment in American history, global capitalism, and communication. Ben Anderson explains that assemblages are "provisional unities that may themselves have 'emergent' or 'complex' causality that is irreducible to their component parts," while Jasbir Puar develops the Deleuzian notion of an event as "an assemblage of spatial and temporal intensities, coming together, dispersing, reconverging."[10]

The assemblage has been productively used in a number of disciplines; for anthropology, George Marcus and Erkan Saka suggest that it holds great potential as well as challenges for ethnography precisely because it allows for the discussion of social formations that do not endure across time and space. Such an application is tricky for ethnography because how assemblages come into being and how they are perceived can be somewhat open-ended. Marcus and Saka write, "Assemblages are thus finite, but they have no specific or distinctive life-span; they do not have a specific temporality. Furthermore, assemblages have no essence. . . . The assemblage is productive of difference (non-repetition). It is the ground and primary expression of all qualitative difference."[11] Extending this conception of assemblage, which seems quite immaterial, I am interested in the materiality of assemblages and their construction. I use the concept to consider how temporally and spatially circumscribed meanings of race and ethnicity intersect with semiotics of language use and visual culture, and the ways these are vetted between entities and produced and circulated through media. I use the concept to focus on the actual assembling that happens in the advertising process, beginning with how certain types of politically informed demographic data collected by the U.S. Census are used to justify the creation of certain types of marketing efforts, like multicultural marketing; how these inform planning and strategy of an ad campaign; and the way a particular ad looks, sounds, and feels.[12]

While most formulations of assemblage do not attend explicitly to language, at least not beyond referential meanings, I would like to extend assemblage to bring together different levels of signification. Assemblages also allow me to examine finer aspects of advertising messages vis-à-vis bodies, sound, and affect that are all carefully selected, vetted, and finalized and how ethnoracial difference is managed in media contexts toward the end of profitability. My approach is semiotic, giving attention to both the linguistic and the material dimensions of the advertising process. Jillian Cavanaugh and I have termed this emergent field *language materiality* to draw attention to the material in linguistic signification, a dimension that had been somewhat overlooked in discussions of language and context, political economy, and language ideology.[13] Elsewhere I have looked at the power of commodities as they interact with narrative and their shifting social meanings as they circulate, as well as at broader intersections between language and materiality, with special attention to authenticity and value.[14] By *materiality* I mean the properties of ads beyond language or the commodities they may feature. I am interested in sound and substrate, in thinking how elements interact as qualities and properties to assemble into something social that would index diversity. In other words, I do not want to reduce my concern with materiality to a reification of ourselves as "subject, social relations, or society," as Daniel Miller has cautioned.[15] This will be carried out in a number of ways, including explorations of linguistic materiality, or considering language in the same frame as the material dimensions of advertising, such as how language and culture are objectified, how language takes on material qualities in advertisements, and the ways metalevel creative and production activities enable particular types of semiotic work. These concepts allow me to bring to life this material and discursive world and enable me to more fully illustrate contests of expertise, authenticity, and ethnoracial assemblages.

Thus my agenda for using the concept of assemblage is threefold: first, to demonstrate spatial, temporal, and semiotic contingency in ways that historicize and make politically relevant the cultural and linguistic ideologies that underpin advertising development and production; second, to investigate modes of production and questions of circulation, including the politics of creative concepts, trademark, ownership, and reinscription; third, because reception is not limited to any one semiotic plane, to consider the linguistic, visual, material, affective, and sensorial dimensions of developing and producing an advertisement in ways that can accommodate all these modalities. Considering diversity in advertisements as ethnoracial assemblages offers insight into why ads look and sound the way they do, how they circulate, and the intended and unexpected ways they are consumed. The creation of assemblages can be seen in the everyday work of advertising development and production, as well as in negotiations and contests about representation. These can take the form of broader cultural concepts and ideological assertions about particular ethnoracial groups, such as that Chinese Americans value kinship or that

1.4 MassMutual Asian Indian American in-culture print ad featuring a Diwali *rangoli* (colored powder) design (2011).

South Asian Americans tend to rely on the recommendations of their social networks for certain goods and services. They can also be found in the minutiae of semiotic details, such as the wording of the ad, the accent in a voice-over, and the precise look of the visuals. How assemblages are interpreted temporally and spatially by different parties underscores their contingent nature and the work they do to further particular notions of racialization, antiracism, activism, and social transformation.

Diversity and Capitalism

"Diversity is not to be good, diversity is not to be fair, diversity is not to be liked by different people. Diversity is business. And if you want to conduct business with people, you can't ignore them. You can't insult them. You can't talk down to them. You've got to talk **to** them," Douglass Alligood, one of the first African American men to work in general market advertising, said to me.[16] As Mr. Alligood's decades of experience have shown him, the importance of diversity has steadily increased since the 1960s, and the climate of corporate America has shifted to accommodate diversity in light of economic and political shifts. Neoliberal ideologies of capitalism shape how differences of ethnicity, race, gender, and sexuality are given market values and have become the basis of profit-making and mass-mediated representation in the new economy.[17] The theorist Michel Callon, with others, has remarked that "value" is not merely an economic fact but is also a social achievement, contingent on cultural as well as material processes.[18] I extend this inquiry to look at what types of economic as well as social values are accomplished through cultural, material, and language-based processes, attending especially to the social and linguistic interactions and actors that underpin them. I build from Kris Olds and Nigel Thrift, who have identified "cultural circuits of capital" as "able to produce constant discursive-cum-practical change, with considerable power to mold the content of people's work lives as well as produce more general cultural models" that affect society on a broader level.[19] In this book I look at how cultural circuits of capitalism—as evident in certain profit-generating enterprises such as advertising and marketing—are involved in the production and circulation of racial and ethnic formations. In my first book, *Desi Land*, I started to look at how broader movements of capital and technology shape everyday lives, and I have since turned my attention to advertising as a different set of cultural and linguistic formations that have also emerged from new configurations of capital.

Focusing on the work of capitalist businesses rather than the movement of capital itself allows me to analyze the production of racial and ethnic meanings in a variety of commercial media projects and how they affect the lives of individuals involved in their making. Capitalism has relied on changing desires and needs as much as technology, and here we see both at work. What is useful about anthropological approaches to the new economy is that they offer counterpoints to economic analyses that naturalize the forces of the market and instead investigate the social and cultural relationships that underpin them.[20] As part of her ethnographic study of capitalism, Karen Ho focused on how the experiences of investment bankers are "thoroughly informed by cultural values and the social relations of race, gender, and class." Her agenda was to "portray a Wall Street shot through with embodiment, color, and particularity."[21] Likewise I aim to capture how notions of diversity are gauged through a capitalist lens and how social meanings about ethnicity and race emerge from capitalism as well.

The ideology of neoliberalism has been shown to bring about numerous changes in how we assess value, accomplishment, productivity, and social meanings in corporate contexts. Neoliberalism is an economic model in which markets determine value with minimal state intervention. David Harvey has traced linkages between deregulation and loan-making practices to account for the rise of the market as a force of social power and how market forces can determine the value of individuals and their work.[22] Within this realm, I am most concerned with a dynamic that Povinelli has identified as follows: "Neoliberalism works by colonizing the field of value—reducing all social values to one market value—exhausting alternative social projects by denying them sustenance."[23] If diversity has a market value, as Mr. Alligood and numerous others in advertising suggested, then representing it becomes a competitive arena. The notion that the "best" approaches will be rewarded by market forces underscores that "neoliberalism is not a thing but a pragmatic concept—a tool—in a field of multiple maneuvers among those who support and benefit from it, those who support and suffer from it, and those who oppose it and benefit from it nevertheless."[24]

Race is instrumental to capitalism, as Manning Marable and others have argued, such that "racialized capitalism" draws attention to the specific ways that labor is parsed according to racial difference.[25] Neoliberalism and racialized capitalism shape not only financial decisions but also how people talk about and represent race. Neoliberal ideologies are evident in how diversity is conceived and operationalized in corporate work environments and in creative work about ethnoracial difference. Here assemblage illustrates how diversity is created, circulated, and reformulated for commercial purposes, but it alone does not tell the story. Affect is very important as well, and the affective labor of talk and embodiment are integral to how certain agendas get accomplished while others are not as easily executed. Bonnie McElhinny elaborates on "the new regimes of self associated with neoliberalism," including adults being responsible, autonomous, self-sufficient, and entrepreneurial.[26] Such processes are "multimodal" and span different domains of interaction;[27] they affect how people are expected to communicate, the stances they take, and how they challenge or accommodate one another communicatively. I am interested in the "soft" or "people" skills that are conveyed through affective performance and participation in shared modalities of interaction.[28]

Diversity as Qualisign

Ethnoracial assemblages and performances of affect shape diversity in corporate America, but diversity remains elusive as a concept. Sara Ahmed has written that diversity is difficult to pin down because it has no clear referent; it does not point us to "a shared object that exists outside of speech or even necessarily create something that can be shared."[29] Urciuoli rightly observes that people mean different things when they use the terms *diversity* and *culture* and that the same words have been recruited into different registers that each glosses differently.[30] Her point is that they may seem interchangeable but actually can index different meanings and histories. Given this elusiveness, I find qualisigns helpful in understanding how referents are defined and meanings are generated in ways that take on normative values. In her widely cited work on the Gawa society, Nancy Munn conceives of value making in terms of qualisigns of value. Building on the semiotic approach of the American philosopher Charles Sanders Peirce, Munn identifies qualisigns as useful because "they exhibit something other than themselves *in* themselves."[31] Qualisigns are iconic signs, in that they bear a resemblance to that which they represent, yet they only signify when "bundled" with material forms to convey socially relevant meanings. Munn masterfully illustrates how the Gawa community "creates itself as the *agent of its own value creation*."[32] Her analysis relies on both material and linguistic elements to illustrate qualisigns, and in this book I consider how diversity can act as a qualisign of linguistic materiality. Diversity is bundled with other qualisigns of race, ethnicity, or simply non-whiteness, as well as with certain uses of language varieties, accents, and other signs, to make meaning in specific ways. Indeed even individuals can be regarded as qualisigns of diversity, embodying the ethnoracial difference for which they are valued.

What constitutes diversity in corporate America, who embodies it, and what work it is imagined to do among ad executives and in advertisements draw attention to the complexity of this concept as well as how this complexity can be reduced to better fit corporate ideals and norms. Analogous to Ahmed's observation that nonwhite individuals in university settings are told, "You *already* embody diversity by providing an institution of whiteness with color," I found a similar management of ethnoracial difference in ad agencies.[33] Corporate America is a rarified world with numerous barriers to access. Physically protected and ideologically guarded, it discloses little about its composition or practices unless required by regulatory agencies. It offers an illustration of George Lipsitz's insightful argument about how meanings of race are "enacted physically in actual places . . . [and how] race is produced by space, that it takes places of racism to take place."[34] By equating what is normal to whiteness, advertising worlds remain a largely white space in which diversity must conform to those norms of whiteness.

When marked ethnoracial difference is acknowledged and represented in advertising, it is done in consultation with a minority voice, either by someone compelled to serve as an expert on that group or with the assistance of a multicultural agency. At some agencies there was an individual "in charge of Diversity and Inclusion,"[35] while at others there were "Diversity Councils." Diversity was formalized to the extent that I was often told to contact certain individuals — the head of a diversity council, the head of a unit responsible for diversity research — to learn more about a new division explicitly focused on culture. In this marked form, diversity was rarely thought to be something the average ad executive could address. Rarely was it thought to simply be part of the everyday fabric of the agency as an institution; no one ever suggested that I contact "anyone" about diversity, because it lay outside the normal activities and environment of the agency. Such a conception keeps in place a "white spatial imaginary," to use Lipsitz's term, and diversity exists outside of it. The way token minorities factor into creative work is very important, something I discuss in chapter 3, regarding how claims of expertise are made and challenged about creative strategy. Often one or two minority individuals were assembled as ad hoc focus groups or asked to comment outside of their areas of training and expertise, solely on the grounds of their race and ethnicity.

These token few notwithstanding, whiteness thrives in American advertising in large part because it is embedded in the notion of a "colorblind" or "postracial" America. Evelyn Alsultany notes that the postrace idea began after the Civil War, as a way of marking progress since the times of slavery. Some mark the election of Barack Obama as America's first black president as the ascension of postrace, but arguably multiculturalism did some of this work as well, as Jodi Melamed has outlined in her concept of "neoliberal multiculturalism."[36] These are admittedly different terms, but they seem to accomplish similar ends. In studying the production and circulation of marketable images of Latinos, Arlene Davila identifies the importance of color blindness to the rise of neoliberalism and its role in constricting dialogues about inequality.[37] Instead there is a greater emphasis on marketability and which aspects of diversity may prove to be profitable. Indeed, as Davila argues, "the use of sympathetic representations to create the illusion of a postracial era is how racism operates now, through a denial of itself."[38] White characters remain at the "center of consciousness," and minorities are respectfully included in ways that do not threaten U.S. exceptionalism.[39]

In this sense corporate America has long been coded as a white place, one that does certain work in openly addressing racism while perpetuating it in new packaging. Similar to Daniel Hosang's argument that whiteness stays dominant in state politics because white politicians don't speak "as whites" but present themselves as racially unmarked, so too is whiteness in American advertising racially unmarked.[40] Critical race theorists have noted the centrality of blackness and black bodies to this ascension of whiteness as the mark of modernity.[41] Stuart Hall has cautioned against such essentializing, as it "naturalizes and dehistoricizes difference, mistaking what is historical and cultural for what is natural, biological, and genetic."[42] Yet this approach actually works best in advertising because ad executives want to represent difference with as little controversy as possible. The concept of diversity here leads to a departure from more critical terms by acting as shorthand for inclusion, and confrontations about racism are avoided at all costs.[43] This approach is in line with what the linguistic anthropologist Jane Hill has so deftly illustrated in *The Everyday Language of White Racism* and the sociologist Edward Bonilla-Silva has contended in *Racism without Racists*. Racist ideologies and discourse are couched in the language of joking, humor, or simply business, and because no one intends to be racist, they are absolved of any offense they may inadvertently create. Allegations of racism are downplayed as misunderstandings about good-natured fun or are counterbalanced with evidence of nonracist work and collegiality with minority coworkers. Especially because racism in ads, as well as in the advertising industry, incurs negative publicity, clients work hard to steer clear of anything that would cross the line from being "edgy" to being "controversial," as ad executives explained it. I present evidence of these dynamics in the development and production of the creative work of ads and in interactions between Asian American ad executives and their corporate clients to illustrate how racialization happens and how norms of whiteness are maintained, despite good intentions to respect ethnoracial difference and minority individuals.

The reduction of racism to the figure of the racist allows structural and institutional forms to become obscured.[44] Having met over two hundred industry professionals during the course of this project, I did not find a single one who performed the role of racist openly. I did, however, find environments pervaded by whiteness and the use of the term *diversity* to emphasize anything outside of it. The type of political correctness that emerged alongside multicultural agendas was quickly defined as oppressive and even absurd, and color blindness was an ideology that ad executives in general market agencies seemed to embrace. In my view interrogating whiteness as economic and social advantage is quite different from condemning white people. As long as racialized spaces are maintained—in this case, diversity being treated as a special interest—single actors do not need to decide to discriminate in order for racism to persist or, as Lipsitz puts it, for "space to be racialized and race to be spatialized."[45] In such spaces, as Hall and others point out, liberal-minded individuals may "inadvertently participate" in reproducing racism.[46] Multicultural advertising executives participated in this cheerful conception of diversity but were not always able to avoid racist unpleasantness. In chapters 1 and 3 I consider how advertising executives manage their affect to preserve the pleasant tone of diversity, regardless of racial or ethnic tension. Performing alacrity in the face of racist jokes, reframing a client's cultural ignorance as an educational moment, and embodying the difference they are asked to produce in their ads are just a few of the affective strategies I will discuss.

Biopolitics and Racial Naturalization

Dimensions of the ethnoracial assemblage that I am especially attuned to are the geopolitics of how Asia and, by extension, Asian America has shifted and continues to change according to U.S. global policy and militarized conflicts and the biopolitics of how the U.S. population is divided and counted by a Census Bureau that redefines categories of race and ethnicity as it sees fit. The ways these processes are influenced by advertising and marketing, and the reciprocal effect the latter may have on the former, are both relevant to making sense of ethnoracial assemblages. Biopolitics, in bare terms, refers to intersections of human life and politics. Foucault's writings about biopolitics and biopower have been instrumental to understanding governance, knowledge production, new technologies, genetics, and other areas that "illuminate the relations between life and politics."[47] Census Bureau categories are deeply influenced by social and political formations, as evidenced by the fact that immigrants from Asia had lived in America for over a century before the term *Asian American* came into parlance. Biopolitics evident in the counting and categorizing of the U.S. population is the foundation for multicultural advertising, and Asian American ad executives point to census figures such as income and population concentrations to further their own work. Two loosely connected questions of biopolitics emerge from these dynamics and are considered in various portions of the book: How might the ways advertising executives conceive of groups and populations shape these categories on upcoming U.S. Census counts? How do forms of digital surveillance, enabled by smartphones and other GPS technologies, track the physical bodies of Asian American consumers as they move through space and in particular places?

Much has been written since Henri Lefebvre theorized that individuals manipulate and interact with space, represent it, and code certain spaces with socially constructed meanings.[48] Neil Smith and Setha Low discuss the restructuring of public space in the twenty-first century;[49] arguing that public space has been reprioritized, they build on Lefebvre and investigate what is currently encompassed in what he termed the "production of space" to consider how people experience spaces. In a different vein, Sharon Zukin has discussed the social spaces of shopping and how consumption opportunities transformed public space.[50] Developing strategies based on how they imagine consumers will interact with signs, digital promotions, and experiential, place-based marketing, advertising agencies stand to further transform places as well as the actual spaces through which branded messaging can circulate. Spatial concerns of managing technologies of power and production are also important, in that they create new ways of linking space with consumption practices, ways that ultimately aid in more effective marketing strategies in areas densely populated by Asian Americans.

Contests of who is best able to represent America's diversity are evident throughout the book, especially in the interactions Asian American advertising executives have with their clients and how they defend their work in an industry that does not uniformly see the value in their targeted approach. Like Mr. Alligood, numerous ad executives were quite blunt about diversity being about money and that displaying diversity in advertisements and within agencies was about generating an awareness that is called for in the contemporary United States. Displaying expertise about diversity has accordingly become a site of intense competition. Multicultural advertising, consisting of agencies catering to Asian Americans, African Americans, and Latinos, competes for clients with general market advertising. Especially since the 2010 Census, these large agencies have become far more explicit about their ability to offer clients "cross-cultural" and "total market" strategies that address diversity; I discuss their specific approaches further in chapter 4 and the conclusion.

How individuals are counted, grouped, and characterized as consumers with particular education and income levels, as well as their "purchasing power," suggests how biopolitics works in advertising and how it shapes racial and ethnic assemblages. Here my goal is consistent with the argument of Inderpal Grewal, who connects biopolitics, or ways of classifying and organizing bodies, with the geopolitics of how national boundaries are drawn.[51] She and others contend that American state imperialism has been replaced by globally decentralized sources of power and that America has used international and domestic practices of exceptionalism as a way to circumvent the policies to which it holds others accountable while it continues to wield its influence through regimes and technologies. I am interested in how American advertising conceptualizes life in the United States, how that conceptualization is accounted for and tallied in the census, and how these are put together for capitalist production and consumption. Grewal shows that these configurations have a major effect on diasporas and consumer culture, and this book similarly offers analytic lenses through which to understand how ad executives invoke Asia, how Asians in America are grouped and enumerated in the census, and how these contribute to knowledge production about difference in agencies and in ad-

1.5 "SF Hep B Free," a public health campaign aimed at Asian Americans for preventative hepatitis B screening (2010).

vertisements. While most campaigns target a single Asian ethnic group at a time, also significant are the ways individual executions are grouped together by agencies to constitute the broader category of Asian American.

I view aspects of Asian American creative work as well as professional interactions through the framework of racial naturalization. As I have explained elsewhere, racial naturalization refers to the work advertising does to transform Asian Americans from "model minorities" to "model consumers" and the use of consumerism to make claims of legitimacy and national belonging.[52] Once existing outside the bounds of the nation-state, as Claire Jean Kim illustrates, Asian Americans are slowly and selectively being brought into the fold of U.S. citizenry as model consumers who are no longer "forever foreigners," to use Mia Tuan's term.[53] Racial naturalization involves the conversion of social and cultural capital into economic forms, a process Pnina Werbner has illustrated with Asians in the United Kingdom and Junaid Rana with Asians in the United States.[54] Devon Carbado has used the term *racial naturalization* in a legal context to identify which paths to citizenship provide the greatest chances at legal naturalization. In his exposition of this concept, he grapples with "why we might conceptualize racism as a naturalization process" and how racism is a "technology of racialization; indeed it is precisely through racism that our American racial identities come into being . . . socially situating and defining us *as Americans*."[55] Carbado's conception, that we are not "overdetermined by racism" but that "racism is already a part of America's social script, a script within which there are specific racial roles or identities for all of us," is helpful to keep in mind inasmuch as corporate America is steeped in this ideology, especially in terms of who is an expert about diversity.[56] In Asian American advertising this is largely accomplished through the work that ad executives do as they transform Census Bureau categories into socially meaningful representations. Signifying Asian American, a category encompassing over a dozen nations whose unifying language is English, is an exercise in biopolitical and spatial labor that realizes Asian Americans as consumers with a presence in geographically precise "designated market areas."

Still these specific racial roles or identities are open to remaking, and this sort of refashioning is precisely what advertising aims to undertake in its creative work and, to some extent, in agencies. Evidence of this contestation and shift can be found in the data I discuss that illustrate differences among ad agencies and between them and clients in interactional styles, notions of expertise, and the labor that produces capital via assemblages of ethnoracial diversity. Such conditions make the politics of the anti-, especially antiracism, so much harder to struggle against—a point that Barnor Hesse, David Goldberg, and others have noted about capital's ability to obscure racism and in some ways subsume it.[57] Throughout the book I point out how assemblages work to illustrate both racist and antiracist positions in this struggle and leave open possibilities for change. I present numerous ethnographically illustrated discussions about how corporate America prioritizes, conceives of, and expends capital to attempt to shape assemblages of ethnoracial diversity. The work that production does in making certain imagery seem normal and natural, how abstract concepts like the postracial are rendered in advertising, and how immigrants with particular social and cultural capital find their way into the upper echelons of corporate America connect the makers of ads with the representational work they do.

Advertising, Media, and Race

Anthropological approaches to media production and consumption have created a rich field of theoretical concepts and ethnographic particularities that dialectically link ideologies and actions of producers and the viewing practices of audiences. "Media worlds," as Faye Ginsburg, Lila Abu-Lughod, and Brian Larkin have conceptualized, underscore the dynamic possibilities of media production, among other things, in a variety of industries and locales.[58] Media worlds consist of contexts of consumption, in which audiences engage with various media in ways that affect their practices of identity making, community, and social affiliations.[59] Language ideologies, varieties, and uses, which I discuss further in chapter 2, are also central to media consumption, and may be reshaped in turn as certain mediated language circulates.[60] Studies of media consumption are certainly relevant to considerations of how audiences are imagined and how content is developed for them. Ethnographies of media production, such as Barry Dornfeld's study of public television production in the United States, Jeff Himpele's work on Bolivian television production, and Tejaswini Ganti's ethnography of the Bollywood film industry, chronicle how audiences are imagined in the quotidian rituals and practices of directors, actors, agents, and distributors.[61] These and other works underscore that ethnographically examining media production is an excellent complement to media consumption studies because it brings to light processes of development and contestation that are usually obscured in the final product.

A rich body of ethnographic studies of advertising has illustrated contests between agencies, clients, and consumers. Centered on questions of globalization in China, Japan, India, and Sri Lanka, these studies provide illustrative and varied evidence of how ad executives imagine audiences in these nations, and I draw on them throughout the book.[62] In the Western Hemisphere, Daniel Miller's analysis of advertising and globalization in Trinidad and Arlene Davila's work with Latinos in the United States and transnationally across the Americas provide the most relevant benchmarks for my study. Identifying and investigating the emergence and growth of Latinos in advertising, also called Hispanic advertising, Davila outlines the cornerstones of multicultural advertising. Her first study of advertising, *Latinos Inc.*, captured important dynamics of race and capitalism that I build on and extend. As these works illustrate, the advertising industry has a long history of creating problems that can be fixed only with a particular product or service.[63] And like other media, advertisements acquire a life of their own once created and put into circulation, especially when they are available for multiple viewings, comments, and discussions on YouTube and other Internet-based platforms. Anthropological approaches to commodities and consumption are also part of this broader discussion, as they are intimately linked to the development and production of brand identity that I focus on in this book.[64] This generative feedback loop includes the interactions of clients with the executives they commission to develop identities for their brands through ads, placement in media (usually a combination of broadcast, digital, and other platforms), and responses from consumers.

In an era when media has long been mobile, considering its impact in diasporas creates additional possibilities and opportunities for circulation and consumption. Diasporic media consumption, a topic I have explored in depth in another research context, is certainly important here.[65] Hamid Naficy's pathbreaking work on Iranians in Los Angeles, Louisa Schein's work among Hmong in Minneapolis, and my earlier work with South Asian American teenagers in Silicon Valley and New York City all show the generative possibilities for identity and community-making practices.[66] In discussing the imaginative potential of media in Asian diasporas, Purnima Mankekar and Louisa Schein draw attention to how media creates certain types of mobility. Mankekar asks how, even when people are not mobile themselves, media might be transportive and connective and engender options beyond the context of consumption.[67] This is a trope that Asian American advertising executives have employed in a number of ways by indexing homelands, suggesting possibilities of lives lived elsewhere, and using the affective force of longing for homeland and belonging. At the same time these ad executives also consider the simultaneity of media as a site of mobility and the experiential potential of goods and services to bring people together through shared media and communicative platforms. These ways of imagining Asian American consumers offer a response to Mankekar and Schein's question, quite relevant here, "How do these discontinuous histories inflect cultural productions by Asians themselves?"[68] As I discuss in chapter 1, money transfer companies, insurance, automobiles, and other products offer agentive possibilities for Asians in the United States to bring about change in Asia. They do so despite the wide-ranging national, ethnic, and linguistic heritages of their imagined audiences, by targeting ethnic groups either individually or as a collective, based on data and knowledge about economic and social trends.

In this sense, a point of exploration in this book is the way the migration experience is recast in terms of marketability and how Asian Americans' nostalgia and sentiment about the nations they have left are reflected in their lifestyle, success, and accomplishment as consumers. Mankekar and Schein complicate representations of Asian men and women in a wide range of American and transnational contexts. Their distinctly American focus, like mine, brings to the fore central questions of what makes something "Asian" in America. Is it the rendering of Asian identities and subjectivities, consumption of culture, use of language, or something else? Advertising is explicitly created with intended audiences in mind, and advertising's main purpose is to convey messages to consumers in ways that create identification with brands. Robert Stam and Ella Shohat remind us that media making is a social and intellectual project, but always open-ended and susceptible to alternative readings.[69] Advertisements, like documents, acquire a life of their own once created and put into circulation. Asian American advertising capitalizes on these imaginings and conceptualizes diaspora and nation, as well as the promise of movement and mobility, in its creative concepts, artwork, and advertising copy. I examine this dynamic keeping in mind Fred Myers's approach, which draws attention to the materiality of subjects and objects "in situations in which human beings attempt to secure or stabilize — or limit — the flow of culture, to turn culture into property form."[70] Myers describes Aboriginal painting as a material and social practice, and, with very different objectives, I consider advertising as a material, linguistic, and capitalist process with social impact and implications.

My ethnographic approach to advertising development and production allows me to examine not only representations such as advertisements but also linkages between these and the identities of the advertising executives involved in their creation. Deborah Poole identified how anthropologists' engagements with visual technologies were largely in "the affective register of suspicion," especially with regard to race.[71] Remarking largely on early visual anthropological work and its attention to the indigenous subject, Poole's point nonetheless resonates with my project of interrogating commercial media for reproducing certain types of racism through representational and discursive strategies. Such a critique is well established with regard to Asian Americans in a variety of media, including Hollywood, television, and advertising. For instance, regarding Asian Americans in the media, Kent Ono and Vincent Pham ask, "Why do we still see racist media in a post-race society?"[72] They draw attention to the ways historical representations have "residual effects" still in play, a contention that others who have looked at correlations between immigration policy and public representations have also made. In a related media context, Rana has noted that the work of racializing Islam largely occurs through social identifications—bodily comportment, dress, gender, and sexuality—and that these are depicted in media.[73]

An important body of critical work analyzing textual representations of race, as well as Asian Americans in media, underpins my observations and analyses. I have found helpful critical cultural studies and critical ethnic studies approaches, as suggested by Stam and Shohat and executed by Alsultany and others, who have argued that whether images are "good" or "bad" matters less than the ideological work they do. For instance, Alsultany illustrates how television dramas play an important role in postrace racism by including images that could be construed as good or bad.[74] Showing a Muslim as "good," for instance, does not signal the end of discrimination against American Muslims. Rather, good or bad image analysis can slip into moralism and draw attention away from the complexities of the ideological work a particular representation may do. In a different media context, Judith Farquhar notes how aware media consumers are about the reductionism of images, and ad executives credit their audiences with similarly discerning abilities.[75] They think long and hard about which kind of representation and message will accomplish their desired ends and how to make Asian Americans model consumers for certain brands. Moreover their claims are carefully calibrated to match what they believe will resonate best with their consumers.[76]

Textual analyses of advertising that consider racial representation, especially the prevalence of the model minority stereotype, have shown that this image continues to be relevant in American advertising in ways that can further the problematic dynamic established between Asian Americans and other minority groups in the original formulations of this stereotype.[77] What is intriguing about this current turn of racial representation is that it makes far more sense economically to depict upwardly mobile Asian Americans alongside, rather than in opposition to, Latinos and African Americans. Multicultural advertising relies on all three of these groups coexisting happily in consumer culture, and purchasing power trumps race as a measure of differentiation. In other words, good minorities are good consumers. In fact wealthy consumers of all races are valued. As I noted earlier, understanding media production is illustrative in its own right, and there is great value in understanding the process of producing something that ultimately stirs controversy, as the backstory may not be as straightforward as the end product would suggest. Foregrounding these emergent themes, *Advertising Diversity* offers a look at what commercial media production can tell us about the perpetuation of racism, the ways new immigrants create and negotiate race and ethnicity in corporate America, and the discursive and material ways these things are accomplished.

RESEARCH DESIGN AND ETHNOGRAPHIC FIELDWORK

In what is perhaps only partially a tongue-in-cheek branding statement, Ulf Hannerz has suggested that anthropology's tagline should be "Diversity Is Our Business" and that "a study of diversity remains the best antidote to unthinking ethnocentrism."[78] Yet diversity seems to be everyone's business these days. The March 2013 issue of the *Atlantic* magazine featured a cover story that garnered much buzz among anthropologists of advertising, both inside the academy and in the industry. It featured Red, one of several prominent firms that undertake ethnographic research for hire. The article, as well as other recent accounts, suggests that it is a good time to be an anthropologist in advertising. Anthropology is having a moment in the ad industry, especially the use of ethnography as a method to collect market research data. Melissa Fisher and Greg Downey argue that "the corporate enchantment with cultural anthropology's two iconic symbols — culture and ethnography — must be understood within more widespread developments in the New Economy," including business ethnography, and an "intensified interest in branding."[79] Anthropologists are routinely hired for account planning, branding, market research, and audience testing. Recent books exploring how anthropologists engage in consumer research and what anthropology can offer advertising have attempted to bridge the two fields.[80] Generally written for corporate clients, advertising industry executives, and marketing students, these works illustrate the impact that anthropologists have had on advertising, especially in showing the value of ethnographic research and how anthropological insights on culture and language can be effectively used to create need and aspiration.

As an anthropologist, I was certainly a known entity when I approached agencies, but doing academic ethnographic research did not earn me the same welcome and status as those who worked in agencies. Douglas Holmes and George Marcus offer the concept of "para-ethnography" as both a descriptor and a methodology for fieldwork encounters such as mine. Para-ethnography refers to overlap in interests and concerns between anthropologists and their subjects. If anthropologists and advertising executives are both invested in formations of culture, language, visual representation, media production, and audience reception, how do their objectives and agendas differ from each other? Marcus has written about the complicated nature of such fieldwork; even when the ethnographic search for the "native point of view" is welcome. He suggests that "counterparts" rather than "others" tend to "share broadly the same world of representation with us," and that similarities between anthropologists and "managers of capitalism" may be greater than what we once thought.[81] In such settings "anecdotal data" hold greater value in illustrating the interworkings of "cultures of expertise."[82] For Holmes and Marcus such data signal "breaches in technocratic knowledge" and offer ways of "realigning the relationship between ethnography and political economy."[83] Such an approach is helpful in thinking about advertising development and production as something other than completely negative and totalizing, as earlier accounts suggested.[84] Indeed my time in corporate America was full of stories, descriptions, recollections, and certainly anecdotes that could be interpreted as parables, cautionary tales, strategic plans, or simply lunchtime banter. There was much to be drawn from these "thin" moments that at the time seemed unconnected or unimportant, but they eventually allowed me to tell a "thicker" version of an overall process, to echo Holmes and Marcus's use of the anthropologist Clifford Geertz's terms.[85]

Using ethnographic observations, recorded conversations, and interviews I conducted, as well as analyses of other advertising and media representations, I present an inside look at the agendas and priorities of the corporate clients who commission this work, the ad executives who undertake it, the casting directors who find the bodies to populate the ads, and audience feedback about ads, in ways that update and raise new questions about the advertising process. Overall it was quite challenging to gain access to the American advertising industry, though being an anthropology professor probably helped. General marketing agencies were very hesitant to allow me to observe on an ongoing basis, but they did allow me to conduct interviews, observe on a limited basis, and attend industry events. I was permitted to shadow ad executives for a few days, interview people in various positions, and hear their thoughts on diversity, either when asked or as volunteered, at the New York offices of three large, multinational agencies: BBDO, Ogilvy, and Young and Rubicam. I was able to visit two of these agencies in 2008 and again in 2011. Additionally, through an Advertising Education Foundation Visiting Professor Program Fellowship, I spent two weeks at Euro RSCG in Chicago in July 2010. To locate Asian American agencies, I used the Asian American Advertising Federation's (3AF) website to arrange visits to eight agencies between 2008 and 2012:

in New York, Ad Asia, A Partnership, Admerasia, ASB Communications, and Kang & Lee; in Los Angeles, InterTrend and IW Group; and in San Francisco, Dae Advertising. In New York I also visited the umbrella organization Multicultural Marketing Resources, which creates a sourcebook for clients wishing to reach multicultural markets, as well as the Advertising Education Foundation and the Association of American Advertising Agencies. I additionally attended numerous industry events that these entities held during Ad Week and at other times of the year.

I conducted, audio-recorded, and selectively transcribed interviews with advertising executives at both general market and Asian American advertising agencies. The interview format was open-ended but tailored to the person's title and position in the agency. In general market agencies I asked ad executives to describe their work, recall details of accounts that went well and those that garnered controversy, and relate their thoughts on diversity in their work and in their agency. In two of these agencies I spent several days observing meetings and client calls. In some Asian American agencies I was granted greater access. The independently owned and operated agencies were, by and large, more responsive and open to speaking to me than those held by larger media conglomerates. In one, which I call Asian Ads, I spent several months, four of them continuous, observing the day-to-day activities of ad executives and following several accounts. I was present but silent for these recordings, and all names of advertising executives, clients, and brands have been changed. All recordings have been selectively transcribed, and numerous excerpts, along with contextual information I observed in situ or at a different point in time, have been included in this ethnography. I present transcripts using a simplified format, featuring line numbers in the left margin to call out specific utterances for analysis and limited notations (including those for overlap, pauses, quoted speech, and emphasis) that can be found in a transcription key in appendix 1.

Focusing primarily on my ethnographic research, I limit my textual analysis to ads whose production I did not observe but that executives discussed with me, as when an account executive or creative showed me his or her past work and imparted otherwise invisible details about the conception, copywriting, casting, shooting, and postproduction of the ad. Here I employ what Mankekar and Schein call "ethnotextual" analysis to offer historically contingent and contextually driven readings of these ads. My ongoing ethnographic involvement in these agencies contributes to my textual readings of these ads as a way to more fully understand them. Unable to collect actual audience feedback, I relied on what ad executives told me about how certain ads tested with focus groups, the broader public response to a campaign, notable comments posted on YouTube for certain ads, and how their client regarded the work.

I have taken several steps to comply with the stipulations of my Institutional Review Board agreement as well as the nondisclosure agreements (NDAs) I signed in agencies, to protect individuals who were candid about their opinions, and to avoid exposing sensitive information about clients that could indemnify agency executives. In chapter 1 I selectively use the real names of agencies and some individuals to trace the emergence of this industry, but I use pseudonyms for agencies and individuals throughout the remainder of the book. For those accounts that I observed in pitch, development, production, or postproduction stages, I have created pseudonyms for the agencies, clients, brands, advertising executives, and production people. For completed work that ad executives discussed in interviews with me and among themselves, I have left the brand name intact and included images and links when available, but I use pseudonyms for agencies and personnel. I have modified small identifying details to provide additional safeguards against violating any agency NDAs, such as which DMA the campaign targeted, a television station it was intended to air on, the outfits worn by certain characters, and so on. I have left the cultural and linguistic details intact, as they form the primary basis of my analysis. Since this is not a journalistic or industry report, I believe these small changes to hide the identities of individuals, agencies, clients, and brands ultimately allow for greater flexibility in discussing the details of what I observed.

As an anthropologist who finds the linguistic and the cultural equally fascinating and ultimately inseparable, I am drawn to the minutiae of what is said and not said in a single, routine creative meeting as much as to what has happened in advertising over the past century. As I completed this research in 2012, the ads I observed in production have already been completed and released. Still, the process of advertising development and production can be contentious, both within an agency and between agencies and clients. Observations of what ad executives say about their clients behind closed doors and how they speak among themselves when outside the public eye are wonderfully insightful but quite sensitive, in that this information could paint a negative picture of these executives and their views on their clients. That is certainly not my aim here. Most executives I met held their clients in very high esteem, bought and used their clients' products in their personal lives, and displayed brand loyalty in their offices and elsewhere. Of course there was joking and gossip about clients and other ad executives, but this seemed to me, as an outsider, to be akin to the type of talk that happens in all workplaces. The agencies I observed hadn't adopted the free-flowing, Ping-Pong-table work environment of Google, Yahoo, and other tech companies, but they had a more casual atmosphere than law and finance offices. Freedom of sexual orientation, bilingualism, shared workspaces, casual dress codes (unless there was a client meeting), and free tea, coffee, and soda created a relaxed, open work environment filled with social media updates, discussions about what was trending, and finding amusement and satisfaction in everyday work.

Even in agencies that were very open, there were limits to what I was allowed to observe. I was occasionally asked to turn off my recorder but was permitted to continue to take notes on my laptop. There were some meetings above my security grade and others that I was asked to leave midway. I was successful in meeting one client during an agency visit, but by and large I only heard voices of clients through a speakerphone and spoke to them at industry events. Occasionally things got tense in meetings, and people got angry, shouted, blamed, and gave orders. Such was the culture of nearly all of the agencies I visited, in that people raised their voice when they were angry. However, most days passed without such incidents, and overall my time was pleasant, if a bit strange. Visiting a workplace where I was not an employee never felt entirely normal. For the most part I brought my small laptop to meetings and stared at it when things were quiet, awkward, or tense. I brought my smartphone everywhere else so that I could productively use my thumbs when everyone else did. During my long stint of fieldwork at Asian Ads, I had the good fortune of being seated at a workstation next to the agency copywriter, who was very friendly and forthcoming. I was privy to his routine work of creating and translating general market slogans, generating content in English and Filipino, in which he was fluent. The office was composed primarily of Chinese Americans whose lunchtime chatter was in Cantonese or Mandarin, and I did not develop any mealtime rapport with them. I often ate lunch at the same time as the copywriter and chatted in English, or ate with the South Asian American ad executives who invited me to join in their "Hinglish" banter, and thus got to know them better.

There were few instances in which I was able to reciprocate the kind welcome Asian Ads and other agencies extended to me, including buying lunch, allowing people to run ideas by me as an Asian Indian and a Hindi speaker, and helping when asked. Regardless of being transparent about my nonexistent business and marketing background, I was occasionally put to work. I was once asked to do market research about automobile purchasing, but was not asked again once they saw my results. I was occasionally asked to help with pitch presentations, and in one instance had the pleasure of scanning through about a dozen Bollywood films to locate scenes and dialogue requested by an account executive. My most public contribution was during the 2011 3AF Marketing Summit (their annual meeting) in Las Vegas. One of the speakers on a panel about Asian American stereotypes in advertising canceled at the last minute, and I was asked to fill in. On stage with three creative directors and a member of an Asian American NGO, I was happy to make a modest contribution to what was already a very intelligent and politically progressive session—somewhat of a departure from the rest of the conference but certainly revealing of the multiple ways ad executives were thinking about Asian Americans. That panel, as well as sentiments expressed in interviews and observed in everyday conversations, reiterated 3AF's broader commitment to combating anti-Asian prejudice and to being less marginal in this industry and society at large.

COMING UP

The chapters that follow loosely mirror the stages of the advertising process but also serve as a broader framework in which I present the theory, history, and ethnography of Asian Americans and diversity in advertising. Like other agencies, ad agencies act on behalf of others, and in so doing may seem at the mercy of opinionated clients, the caprice of audiences, and the ire of consumer watchdog groups. Under such scrutiny it is no surprise that the ad would take on a life of its own. From the moment it becomes an object of agency attention, to the numerous stages of development and production through which it is vetted, the advertisement takes on an animate, material quality well before it is recognizable as a print ad, a "spot" or television commercial, an Internet sidebar, or a radio message. Executives talk about what the ad "requires," what the creative "calls for," the type of characters the script "dictates," and so on. With so many in charge but the ad itself calling the shots, it seemed only appropriate that the advertising development and production process serve as the organizational rubric of this book and the central current of every chapter. Advertising and marketing experts may find this quaint and somewhat dated, as this model is being eroded in different ways by an increased reliance on social media, guerrilla marketing, promotional events, direct marketing, and public relations that extend beyond the process of making ads for print, radio, television, and the Internet. Nonetheless accounts still begin with The Pitch—the compelling ideas and narratives that advertising executives perform to win a client's business—and unfold in a certain sequence. I focus primarily on Asian American advertising but do discuss general market advertising quite extensively in some areas, including general market treatment of minorities in chapter 1 and the conclusion, approaches to creative in chapter 2, and the politics of casting talent in chapter 4.

Once an agency has won an account, the paid work begins. Account planning is a stage that allows for gathering the relevant marketing data that informs the creative work, which is overseen and presented to the client through account services. Chapter 1 provides a historical discussion of representations of Asian Americans in select media from the late nineteenth century to the present. I explore key points when minorities became targets of advertising and how the Asian American advertising industry emerged. I discuss the ways this niche grew in the footsteps of Latino and African American advertising, how they together compose "multicultural" marketing, and the ways they create and delineate ethnic categories within the broader umbrella of Asian American. Chapter 2, "Creative," is an in-depth exploration of brand and message construction. How creatives develop "in-culture" concepts, write "in-language content," and make choices about language variety, regard humor and affect, and construct narratives for what many regard as fifteen- and thirty-second films are my points of focus. The work of *indexicality* and *iconicity*, terms that advertising executives used routinely, are also useful in signaling how meaning is conveyed through visual and linguistic elements. I attend to materiality in intertextuality and interdiscursivity to understand how brand identities are transformed from general market to Asian American audiences while still remaining consistent with the former. Intertextuality is especially useful in considering issues of translation and what executives I worked with called "transcreation," an agency term that refers to the creative process of crafting messages for select Asian audiences. As they construct brand identities, the prevalence of language ideologies that signal prestige and value can be found in details such as language variety, accent, and "back-translations" (English translations of in-language elements) and augur broader trends of language use in diasporas, including how certain language varieties are held up as standards while others fall out of fashion.

Chapter 3, "Account Services," foregrounds what Myers has called "inter-cultural spaces," in which meanings about creative work push up against questions of value, as mediated by individuals. Expertise is demonstrated through the process of enregisterment, that is, how multicultural advertising executives develop a specialized lexicon and use other linguistic features to create a vision of ethnic and racial difference on which they construct knowledge about difference. Performances of affect and stance are integral to how ad executives negotiate what *Asian American* means among themselves, to clients, and to others in this industry. Account executives, those who interface with clients and their own creative and production teams, manage conflict and create humor to make the category of Asian American meaningful among themselves and perform their expertise to clients and colleagues.

Once the client approves the creative, it moves into the production process. Chapter 4, "Production and Media," investigates contentious issues of representation through casting and how a changing media landscape is leading executives to rethink audiences. Digital platforms, guerrilla marketing, and neighborhood-specific promotions come to the fore as agencies attempt to track the efficacy of their work and reach broader audiences. Finally, audience testing may be employed to understand the broader reception of ads. While I did not conduct audience reception research, the conclusion does provide a useful space in which to examine the convergence of a number of theoretical and ethnographic issues. It considers contests of authenticity and expertise about whether multicultural or general marketing advertising is best positioned to reach minority audiences in the United States. Taken together the chapters illustrate contemporary versions of diversity, racism, whiteness, and racial naturalization in commercial media production as well as connections between the message and those in corporate America who produce it.

CHAPTER 1

Account Planning

Having won the account for continuing business with the Chinese American market and launching the client's brand into Korean and Asian Indian "segments," the real work of making U.S. Census categories such as "Asian Indian" and "Korean" into effective messaging was about to begin. Which in-language and in-culture insights would work best for each ethnic group being targeted, and could a single creative concept be modified to reach all three? The account director, Sheng Li, posed these questions to the broader team, encouraging them to keep the very different segments of Chinese, Korean, and Asian Indian in mind when generating the creative concept. During the pitch George, the client, had reminded them that he is "ethnic," identifying his Hispanic heritage, but added, "Eighty percent of our guys are white guys. I mean no disrespect, it is what it is." He told the team that creative executions made by the Hispanic agency he worked with were also questioned and critiqued, and he primed Asian Ads to be as clear as possible in their presentations. George emphasized how important this was given the recession, as his company was still assessing its budget for multicultural advertising. Sheng Li reminded his ad executives that this was a major creative opportunity for the agency and that they had to launch the brand as strongly as possible in each segment of the Asian American market. He added that it was a major opportunity to introduce a brand through targeted advertising to particular ethnic groups and that it afforded creative possibilities that they did not have when they worked with the broader category of Asian American. As they nodded and considered this possibility, he reminded them of a recent promotion they had done for a home improvement store client, in which each of the three multicultural agencies was asked to provide a list of appropriate appliances that matched the price point for their ethnic audiences. During the joint conference call, that client had bluntly stated, "Asians prefer high-end appliances like Samsung or Electrolux, while African American and Hispanic probably prefer Whirlpool." Momentarily stunned, Asian Ads executives protested, "But it's a giveaway! All segments want good things!" The client quickly offered a detailed explanation of how each ethnic segment was willing to pay a different amount of tax on these appliances, and concluded, "We don't want to give them something so expensive that they look at the tax they have to pay on it and won't want it anymore. Ultimately we want to give them the context for buying power." Emphasizing the buying power he and other Asian American ad executives believed their audiences to have, Sheng Li reminded the team to play up this attribute in their creative.

Assumptions like these about the upward mobility and high per capita income of Asian American consumers, as well as how particular brands might resonate with specific Asian ethnicities in the United States, were not only common but also largely generated by Asian American ad executives themselves. Regardless of whether this agency was working on a pan-Asian promotion like the one for appliances, or the brand launch for a specific Asian ethnic group that Sheng Li asked his team to work on, the agency had to use available data about these populations to create meaningful cultural and linguistic representations. Careful manipulation of U.S. Census data and market research has allowed Asian American advertising to grow and flourish over the past three decades. This process has likewise contributed to shaping racial meanings about the category of Asian American in media and in the advertising industry.

This chapter considers issues of biopolitics and racialization by examining transformations of the census category Asian American into its current iteration as cultural and linguistic representations in multicultural advertising. Asian Americans have had a small but noteworthy presence in the United States since the mid-nineteenth century, and media representations of them in each time period reflect political and social views about their economic and social status in the United States and are influenced by U.S. foreign relations, immigration laws, and regional economic landscapes. My discussion correlates major developments of the advertising industry with Asian immigration and public policy. Looking in particular at social representations relevant to advertising, I consider how advertising has naturalized meanings of race for Asian Americans during different periods and how it has done a great deal of work toward manufacturing and circulating representations that align with geopolitical events and economic trends.[1] I draw on numerous meticulous textual analyses of Asian Americans in nineteenth-, twentieth-, and twenty-first-century advertising to contextualize the current work of creating Asian American advertising. The second part of the chapter focuses on the rise and development of Asian American advertising and its connection to other multicultural advertising that targets specific ethnic and racial populations, especially African American and Latino consumers. I consider how Asian American ad executives engage with the very categories that shape their industry, especially Asian American, and the shifting collection of nationalities and ethnicities it contains. Through careful and selective rendering of the U.S. Census and other data, Asian American advertising has not only emerged but has faced economic downturns and found new ways to extend its reach and expertise.

CAPITAL, BIOPOLITICS, AND RACE

The category of Asian American has shifted and transformed in light of numerous economic and social forces since the late nineteenth century. The U.S. Census has been the most influential entity in defining the nationalities and ethnicities that fit into this category, as census-generated categories have been influenced by a variety of political and economic agendas. The broader cycle of knowledge production about the U.S. population in service of particular economic or state agendas can be understood according to what Kris Olds and Nigel Thrift have termed "cultural circuits of capital," which I discussed in the introduction. Considering how capitalism operates cyclically suggests a feedback system in which institutions impart knowledge and improve forms of conduct in capitalism. Such "discursive-cum-practical change," they argue, has an impact on work lives as well as culture and society in a broader sense.[2] I focus on the cultural circuits of capitalism to consider how advertising executives interpret and recast U.S. Census categories and data to suit their agendas of advertising development and production. Olds and Thrift identify how new knowledge keeps the cultural circuit of capital going,[3] and this is certainly the case with multicultural advertising, in which each decade brings new conceptions of ethnicity and race and increasingly sophisticated demands for expertise and strategy in advertising. In this sense cultural circuits of capitalism allow for dispersed knowledge to be collected from various sources, for skills to be codified, and for large amounts of data to be made manageable and sensible.[4]

Biopolitics is useful in understanding how ad executives use U.S. Census data to create particular assemblages that form the basis of ethnically targeted advertising. It also helps to illustrate how Asian American ad executives build on imagery such as the model minority stereotype to breathe cultural life and linguistic specificity into the characterization of particular Asian ethnic groups. How individuals are counted and classified according to racial and ethnic categories can be understood as a process of biomediation, through what Patricia Clough has described as the "biomediated body." Clough contends that racism occurs through the biomediated body "because it is a racism that is deployed each and every time a differentiation is made among and in populations, constituting additional bodies of data."[5] She extends Foucauldian conceptions of biopolitics, such that "the biomediated body allows the raced body to be apprehended as information." This contention is in keeping with the commonly held advertising belief I observed, that racial and ethnic difference is embodied and knowable in audiences, as well as in "talent," the actors or models in the ads. While I develop this point further in chapter 3, where I consider diversity as a qualisign embodied in ad executives of Asian descent, in this chapter I seek to understand the inception of this notion and briefly review the history of these biopolitical categories. Campbell and Sitze argue for the importance of biopolitics when attending to new formulations of racism that are no longer reducible to "biological essentialism" that suggests physical specificities based on race, or even "neo-racism" based on fixed "cultural differences."[6] Racial naturalization, a concept I presented in the introduction and develop further here, is not simply about inclusion in the United States through legal citizenship; it is also about how Asian American ad executives use their social networks to connect with a rising, trending Asia and leverage connections in ways that were not valued or even possible in previous generations.

Asia's rising global importance accounts for only part of why Asian American advertising has thrived. This advertising has also been influenced by the current status of race in American society and how society-wide racism is at times regarded as a thing of the past. In an era that the popular press has heralded and liberal academics have critiqued as "postracial," the importance of race is thought to be declining. This ideology has been further validated by the election of President Barack Obama and various right-wing policies and politics predicated on the denouncement of race-based systems of institutional preference.[7] Michael Omi has critiqued such claims of "colorblindness," articulating Asian American perspectives on a postracial United States.[8] This predicament stands in odd contrast to the ongoing counting and classifying done by the Census Bureau. It is also intriguing that in an era when race is being downplayed in the name of racial equality, multicultural advertising emphasizes race more than ever in the name of profitability. Indeed the postracial turn has been especially serendipitous for Asian American ad executives because it has made race safe for mainstream discussion. Ad executives emphasize that, *as a race*, Asian Americans are excellent consumers, and this is what makes them valued members of the U.S. economy. To put it bluntly, in order to make money, ad executives have to define, manipulate, and underscore the significance of race. To do so they must project the most attractive and appealing versions of race, those that let them play up favorable cultural and linguistic attributes compatible with brand identities, but downplay those that would threaten the status quo of an allegedly postracial America.

In a corporate world where race is largely avoided or ignored, neoliberal ideologies allow multicultural ad executives to market racial and ethnic difference through capitalism in ways that will benefit them financially. Neoliberal ideologies of race and ethnicity provide a fertile context for ad executives to produce the category of Asian American and further define the ethnic groups it contains. Under neoliberalism, meanings of race and ethnicity that are rooted in political economy are recoded simply as "differences" that can be considered equal. John and Jean Comaroff put it like this: "Here is the harsh underside of the culture of neoliberalism. It is a culture that . . . re-visions persons not as producers from a particular community, but as consumers in a planetary marketplace: persons as ensembles of identity that owe less to history or society than to organically conceived human qualities."[9] Asian, the shorthand for Asian American in multicultural advertising lexicon, is used as an aggregate category to emphasize the collective per capita income, spending power, and willingness to consume of a growing segment of the U.S. population. Asian American advertising executives construct "America" as well as "Asia" as points of contrast for how they envision their audiences. The term *Asian American*, first coined by Yuji Ichioka in 1968 at San Francisco State University during a third world strike, was intended to challenge racism, and its use still does in some institutional contexts, such as universities and NGOs.[10] Corporate America, however, has co-opted the term without these political agendas. How this census-derived racial category is invoked as a whole and how it is parsed into the shifting range of ethnicities and nationalities it encompasses speak to the biopolitics of counting and transforming ethnoracial difference into profit. The type of knowledge production that Asian American advertising executives currently undertake to make this category viable for advertising is done in conjunction with other institutional practices of state knowledge production and classification.

ASIAN IMMIGRATION AND AMERICAN ADVERTISING

The advertising industry, like Asian immigration to the United States, has undergone numerous shifts and transformations, especially in the latter half of the twentieth century. Prior to this time both existed on a far smaller scale. The postwar period, especially from the 1960s onward, was the most dramatic in terms of immigration as well as changes in advertising strategy and innovation in media platforms. While certainly not comprehensive, the sketch I offer here correlates demographic shifts and public policy affecting Asian Americans with commercial media development and circulation. Considered together they set the stage for the emergence of Asian American advertising in the 1980s.

Late Nineteenth and Early Twentieth Centuries

Prior to the early twentieth century, neither Asian immigration nor American advertising had a major presence, but minor events in both suggested larger changes to come. Most Asian immigrants came for physical labor such as agriculture and mining, and waves of immigration were small, were concentrated on the West Coast, and were curtailed a few decades after they began. The first Chinese immigrants arrived during the 1780s, but the discovery of gold in California in 1848 brought a large wave. Between 1851 and 1852 alone the number of Chinese in that state grew from 2,716 to 20,026. By the time the 1882 Chinese Exclusion Act was passed, over

300,000 Chinese were living in the continental United States. Several decades after the Chinese began to arrive, in 1830, Asian Indian immigration began, when Indian merchants, sailors, and indentured workers traveled on East India Company ships to North America. Most came to work in agricultural jobs in the Pacific Northwest, in Canada and the United States, especially Washington, Oregon, and California. Many hailed from colonial Punjab, a state that would be divided during the partition of India and Pakistan in 1947. Japanese and Korean immigrants arrived late in the nineteenth century. Japanese immigrants first began to arrive between 1885 and 1895 in the regions that would become Hawai'i and parts of the West Coast, on the heels of the 1882 Chinese Exclusion Act. The first wave of Japanese immigration peaked between 1886 and 1908, and the second from 1916 to 1920.[11] In 1882 the United States and Korea signed a treaty of amity and commerce, allowing Korean immigration to the United States, and many diplomats, merchants, political exiles, and students began visiting, but none reportedly settled. The first significant wave of Korean immigrants to the United States came in 1903, arriving in Hawai'i to work in the sugar plantations; they were introduced as strikebreakers as unrest grew among Japanese laborers.[12] Filipinos were among the earliest to arrive in the United States, when mariners under Spanish command landed in Morro Bay, California, in 1587.[13] The first significant influx of Filipino immigrants arrived only in the 1830s, and not on the West Coast. Hunters and trappers of Filipino origin permanently settled in the Louisiana region below New Orleans, which at the time was the busiest port after New York City.[14] No significant Vietnamese immigration was recorded during this period, although this population too would settle in Louisiana, among other regions.

During the mid- to late nineteenth century an established marketing industry did not exist, only what some historians of advertising call a "haphazard arrangement."[15] The beginning of the twentieth century, however, marked a period when "artists and designers joined copywriters on agency staffs and started asserting that the 'look' of an ad meant as much as its message."[16] Albert D. Lasker spearheaded the role of the account executive by helping to create and define this position. In every agency I visited, each account was assigned an account executive who acted as the coordinator of the entire development and production process and as the liaison with clients.[17] In fact early twentieth-century advertising history is often referred to as "The Age of Lasker." This age coincided with the Progressive Era and included an increased emphasis on visual presentation in ads, such as headlines, illustrations, and diverse typefaces. While this shift away from simply using plain language in layout had begun in the 1890s, a more overt emphasis on design could be seen during this time. Advertising became a more fit occupation for writers, and "eye appeal" emerged as a central way to capture an audience.[18] Moreover the role of packaging in selling a product also revolutionized the retail sector, giving way to chain stores and catalogues that were recognizable for their stylized products.[19] Further, the hard sell or "reason why" emerged as the dominant marketing strategy during this period. It is important to note that the 1906 Pure Food and Drugs Act was passed in response to a developing consumer movement critical of the moral implications and impact of such a "hard" approach to advertising.[20]

The increased emphasis on visual appeal in advertising could be seen sporadically in representations of African Americans, Asian Americans, Native Americans, and Latinos in early advertising, as they appeared quite infrequently. Asians were generally portrayed as curiosities for white consumers. An increasing circulation of Japanese manufactured goods in the United States starting in the 1860s spurred demand for what was perceived to be a uniquely Japanese aesthetic.[21] U.S. advertising images of Japanese Americans from the 1880s featured stylized visions of Japanese culture, especially tropes from Gilbert and Sullivan's *The Mikado* that created a new form of desire for the "Japoniste" among white middle-class American women.[22] Other Asians, primarily Chinese Americans, were occasionally featured in handbills posted in public spaces and increasingly in trade cards for regional businesses. Trade cards utilized advances in lithographic technology and are regarded as precursors of the modern business card.[23] Offering a gentler version of the Orient, trade cards featured a Japonisme that was a favorably regarded addition to stylish domesticity for a white middle class. Chinese tea merchants aiming to reach American consumers also utilized trade cards, in which the Orient was rendered as attractively as possible. This advent of lithography greatly increased the appeal and marketability of Chinese products, and overall these merchants catered to perceived American tastes by making the Chinese landscape "enchantingly picturesque" and the Chinese people "delightfully exotic."[24]

These trade cards furthered the circulation and consumption of an "Oriental aesthetic" in American public culture,[25] but this aesthetic was not always welcome, especially as tensions grew between white Americans and Asian immigrants in the mid- to late nineteenth century. Chinese Americans—the largest group and most involved in prospecting—were targeted for fines and exclusion earlier than other Asian immigrants. The threat to their livelihoods posed by Chinese miners led white miners to demand protection, culminating in the 1852 Foreign Miners Act. Passed by the California state legislature, it required every foreign miner who was ineligible for citizenship to pay a $3 fee, despite the fact that the Chinese had already been deemed ineligible for citizenship according to a 1790 federal law that reserved naturalized citizenship for "white persons" only. Further penalizing enterprising Chinese Americans was an 1870 San Francisco ordinance that taxed laundrymen for their delivery wagons, as the Chinese did not use horses for their deliveries. In 1882 all Chinese laborers were barred entry into the United States for ten years, although merchants, teachers, diplomats, students, and travelers were permitted entry with proper documentation. This ban was extended in 1892 and 1902 and made permanent in 1904. Further alienating those Chinese laborers already present, the 1892 Geary Act required them to register for a certificate of residence or risk arrest or deportation; the constitutionality of this law was upheld by the Supreme Court despite Chinese protest.

During these times blatant anti-Chinese hostility was depicted in trade cards, handbills, and other advertisements. Chinese laundrymen were characterized as rat-like, with disproportionately large front teeth and extra long switches of hair that resembled tails (fig. 1.1). The stereotype of the Oriental came to index a set of traits epitomized by "the sneaky, crafty, inscrutable Chinese."[26] Some images represented them usurping white Americans' jobs, while others highlighted innovations in clothes laundering that rendered these immigrants obsolete and called for their return to China (fig. 1.2). Noteworthy too was the distinctive register of speech prevalent in these ads, a variety that scholars have called "Yellow English." Exaggerated vowel sounds, dropped articles, nonstandard grammar, and halting intonation characterized captioned speech, often alongside white characters speaking standard English. As expected, white Americans remained the primary audience for this messaging.

Trade cards became an obsolete form of advertising just before the twentieth century, when magazine circulation rose and became a more viable medium for marketing and messaging.[27] The 1920s reflected what is often referred to as the "first boom" in advertising, led by J. Walter Thompson.[28] In 1927 the Federal Radio Commission was set up.[29] Changing notions of hygiene and cleanliness created market opportunities, and vice versa: as Stephen Fox observes, "Ads necessarily *reflected* the times, and as an independent force they helped *shape* the times. Ads and their general histori-

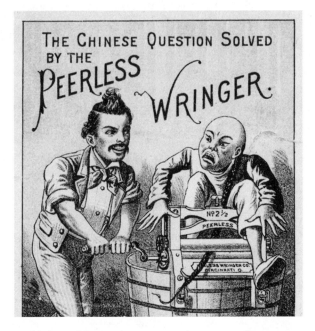

1.1 Trade card for Peerless Wringer, featuring a white man wringing a Chinese American man's exaggerated hair switch through the machine (ca. 1900s).

1.2 Trade card for Celluloid Collar and Cuff. "NO MORE WASHEE WASHEE, MELLICAN MAN WEAR CELLULOID COLLAR AND CUFF" (ca. 1890s).

cal context reinforced each other, forming a circle of cause and effect that doubled back and merged together."[30] Negative representations of Asian Americans were also rampant. Journalistic accounts of Asian Indians used the term *Hindoo* to refer to the predominantly Sikh population and found their turbans and beards objectionable on the grounds of hygiene. Like the Chinese, Japanese immigrants also experienced waves of discrimination and hostility. The 1907 Gentlemen's Agreement with Japan prohibited male workers from emigrating to Hawai'i or the mainland, but it did allow Japan to send family members of workers already living in the United States. California's first Alien Land Law in 1913 made it illegal for noncitizens to purchase land, a law challenged by Takao Ozawa, a Japanese immigrant whose case against the United States made its way to the Supreme Court.

This series of Asian exclusion acts, culminating in the 1924 Immigration Restriction Act, contributed to xenophobia against Asians in the United States. In a 1922 declaration the U.S. Supreme Court ruled that naturalized citizenship was limited to whites and African Americans, though children of Japanese immigrants would be considered citizens. Following this the 1924 law curtailed Japanese immigration for nearly three decades. Asian Indians were not able to naturalize their children, and most men (it was primarily men who immigrated) were unable to bring their wives or own land.[31] Already subject to the 1917 Immigration Act, also known as the Asiatic Barred Zone Act, which restricted immigration from Asia, they were denied citizenship on racial grounds through the 1923 *United States v. Bhagat Singh Thind* ruling, which declared that Asians were not included under the "statutory category as white persons" and consequently denied the right to naturalization. Previously naturalized Indians were also stripped of their citizenship. Likewise early twentieth-century legislation curtailed Korean immigration; by that time Korea was effectively ruled by Japan, so Korean workers were also banned under the 1907 Gentlemen's Agreement. After Korea was forcibly annexed by Japan in 1910, Korean immigration halted completely. For those already in the United States, California's 1913 Alien Land Law prohibited all Asian immigrants from owning land and limited their leases in California, and the 1924 U.S. Immigration Act instituted discriminatory quotas based on national origin.

Like the negative imagery of Chinese Americans in trade cards, "Yellow Peril" imagery characterized Asian Americans as dangerous invaders who required containment as well as licentious, amoral, and infantile individuals in need of patriarchal control. Motion pictures released in the interwar period routinely depicted Asian Americans as sinister, untrustworthy, or a threat to miscegenation with whites, and unlikable fictional characters such as the inscrutable Fu Manchu and the evil "dragon lady" were widely circulated. Such imagery occasionally found its way into advertisements, although there was virtually no Asian immigration during the interwar period. The few who did immigrate did so as a result of shifts in American imperialism in the Philippines, at the rate of fifty persons per year. Overall there was hostility and distrust of Asian Americans during this period, a marked contrast to the immigration from Asia after 1965, which media represented more positively. During the early interwar period, advertising overall was curtailed by the 1929 stock market crash. The Great Depression too had a significant impact, as it emphasized saving.[32] During the 1930s the "maturing of the radio" played a critical role in expanding advertising's audience—and advertising encouraged the growth of radio as well.[33]

World War II and the 1950s

Advertising shaped wartime efforts by reinforcing notions of patriotism based on emerging consumption patterns.[34] By the start of World War II the basic technology for TV was available, and the National Broadcasting Corporation (NBC) began regularly airing commercials in 1939.[35] At a time without new Asian immigration and some Asian immigrants marrying Mexican Americans, ethnic imagery in advertising and film focused on ethnically saturated areas like Chinatowns. Following the Japanese bombing of Pearl Harbor, California fired all state employees of Japanese ancestry without reason or due process in 1942, and Executive Order 9066 empowered the military to remove any persons from any area of the country where national security was at risk. Though not explicitly named, Japanese Americans were the primary targets, and tens of thousands from California, Washington, Oregon, and other regions, the majority of whom were U.S. citizens, were sent to internment camps scattered throughout the country. During the internment, Japanese soldiers were depicted as the enemy in patriotic advertisements for products such as Coca-Cola and in wartime propaganda. Besides the Japanese, other Asian groups had disappeared from the American public imagination, even though small changes were occurring in immigration patterns. For instance, in the midst of the Japanese internment, the United States passed the 1943 Immigration Act, also known as the Magnuson Act, which repealed all Chinese exclusion laws passed since 1882 to permit Chinese resident aliens to apply for naturalization and allowed 105 Chinese to immigrate annually.

The postwar period did not increase immigration beyond the wives of U.S. servicemen from the Philippines and, in the 1950s, Korea. The 1948 Education Exchange Act promoted the immigration of a new category of Filipinos who would settle in the United States and join the growing Filipino American population. The law also enabled foreign nurses to spend two years in the United States for study and professional experience—a "cultural insight," ad executives would call it, as the Filipino nurse remains relevant for contemporary Asian American advertising. Between 1946 and 1965 as many as half of all immigrants from the Philippines arriving in the United States were wives of U.S. servicemen. The 1946 Luce-Celler Act increased the Philippines' immigration quota from fifty to one hundred persons per year, although spouses of U.S. citizens were not included in this quota. In refugee cases from Japanese rule or as wives as American soldiers after the 1945 U.S. War Brides Act, a small number of Koreans were admitted as nonquota immigrants, until the 1952 Immigration Nationality Act repealed racial exclusion and relaxed national quota criteria. Before the United States entered Vietnam in the 1960s, fewer than a thousand Vietnamese lived in the United States. Between 1950 and 1959 only 290 Vietnamese became permanent residents; most were teachers and students, with a few involved in commercial business.

The 1950s marked a period of prosperity, when postwar America was flush with suburbanization and housing construction, cars, new patterns of consumption, and infrastructural growth and development. Advertising rose dramatically: "Breaking away from the long drought of Depression and wartime austerities, the gross total of advertising expenditures doubled in only five years from $2.9 billion in 1945 to $5.7 billion in 1950."[36] This postwar baby boom was characterized by increased spending; "keeping up with the Joneses" became a prominent concept, and credit enabled families to purchase goods and services previously unavailable to them.[37] Teenagers became a lucrative market for advertisers as a growing segment acquired more disposable income. More generally, however, white suburbanites remained the key market for advertising.[38] During this period negative images of Asian Americans in ads did not persist, as this population was more or less absent from public culture. The Korean War yielded some patriotic ads, but perhaps due to the popularity of Korean war brides, the advertising industry steered clear of the overtly negative imagery it had produced in World War II–era depictions of Japanese, and altogether ignored other U.S.-based Asian populations.

The 1960s through the 1990s

Referred to as the period of the "creative revolution," the 1960s was a vibrant time for advertising.[39] Historians of American advertising attribute this to leading figures such as Leo Burnett, David Ogilvy, and William Bernbach. About one hundred small, boutique-like operations sprang up, although the majority did not last for long.[40] Fans of the AMC television drama *Mad Men* will recognize this period as one in which creative burgeoned thanks to temperamental geniuses like Don Draper, and advertising's notions of audience were tested and reformulated. Viewers of the show will also be familiar with the overwhelmingly white, male-dominated character of ad agencies of this time (fig. 1.3). Other segments of the population wishing to enter this field did so via more marginal paths. For some the creative revolution also marked an "ethnic revolution," when advertisers began targeting Jewish and black audiences.[41] At that time multicultural advertising was generally handled in-house, by a specialized department that targeted "urban" consumers. Such targeted appeals certainly lend support to the notion that ethnicity and race have for some time now been considered areas of specialized knowledge. Yet outside of select cities, minority populations were not believed to have enough purchasing power to disrupt the general market conceptions of a white, English-speaking America. Gradually advertising began targeting other white ethnic groups, such as Italians, as well as women.[42] Juliann Sivulka points out that prior to this time, few clients had developed specialized campaigns aimed at African Americans, and even those that did primarily adapted campaigns from white media, "substituting non-white models and running the ads in African American oriented media such as *Ebony* (1945), *Tan* (1950), and *Jet* (1951)," a technique that continues to be used, referred to as "the copycat ad."[43] Stereotypical images of nonwhite minorities began coming under fire from civil rights groups, and ad executives were forced to rethink how they depicted particular groups (fig. 1.4).

This was also the era of America's largest wave of Asian immigration, which began after the 1965 Hart-Celler Act lifted national-origins quotas and solicited highly skilled migration. The numbers of immigrants who came under these specifications far eclipsed the flow of earlier Asian immigrants. In 1960 the number of Chinese Americans was nearly 100,000,

1.3 The AMC dramatic series *Mad Men* epitomizes the white, male-dominated 1960s advertising world (2009).

but that amount jumped to over 172,000 by just 1970, including Taiwanese. Likewise the 1960 Indian population was estimated to be 12,296,[44] but it grew rapidly to 51,000 in 1970, 206,087 in 1980, and 450,406 in 1990. The 1990 Immigration Act created a lottery for immigrants with high technology-based skills, advanced degrees, and exceptional professional talents, thereby drawing talent from India to tech-saturated regions of the United States, especially Silicon Valley. Prior to 1960 there were nearly 110,000 Japanese Americans in the United States, a number that grew to nearly 300,000 by 1990. The number of Filipinos grew from approximately 100,000 in 1960 to just under 1 million in 1990. The 1960 count of 11,171 Koreans had reached over half a million by 1990. As late as 1964 only 603 Vietnamese lived in the United States, but by the end of the Vietnam War in 1975, the population had risen to 20,000, consisting largely of spouses of American military personnel stationed in Vietnam.[45] Immediately after the war and in the decade following, however, tens of thousands of refugees entered the United States.

Until this time, the advertising industry was entirely dominated by white males, a trend that slowly began to shift during the 1960s. Women were slowly allowed to take entry-level jobs that were elevated slightly above secretarial work. In 1968, at the height of the civil rights movement, when most of the United States was fixated on questions of racial integration, the American advertising industry seemed to be blissfully unaware of

1.4 Print ad for Hoover featuring Chinese American laundrymen, one holding an iron, peering at a washing machine. The ad features Chinese characters, followed by "If you know a little Chinese, you might sense these aren't the kindest words you've seen" (ca. 1950s).

the importance of racial diversity in their ranks. This year, marked by the assassination of Dr. Martin Luther King and widespread civil rights riots, was the same one in which New York City's Human Rights Commission exposed the whiteness of Madison Avenue. Based on hearings and data collected in the top advertising agencies in New York City, the report offered damning evidence of the industry's attitudes toward race and recommendations for affirmative action throughout agency ranks, which were implemented at a glacial pace. Around this time, in 1966, as major Asian immigration was just beginning, the *New York Times* and *U.S. News & World Report* described Chinese and Japanese Americans as "model minorities." While the popular print media further developed this concept, the advertising industry continued to see the country in black-and-white terms, and mostly white at that.

In the 1970s and 1980s these racial dynamics continued to pervade the advertising industry, but other aspects of advertising changed considerably. In the difficult economic climate of the 1970s, advertising suspended hard-sell approaches, and copy style and management became softer and more emotionally evocative. Children emerged as a new target group for advertising, and overall, messaging took a less hard-edged tone. Asian Americans began to appear sporadically during this era, as characters in campaigns that also featured other ethnic and racial minorities, as well as occasionally in ads that offered a modern twist on the Chinese laundry, as in a memorable campaign for Calgon water softener (fig. 1.5). When the blonde American customer asks the owner of the Chinese laundry how he got her clothes so clean, he replies, "Ancient Chinese secret." But his wife emerges from the back of the store and disrupts this narrative by announcing loudly in American-accented English that they are out of Calgon. The punch line uttered by the white consumer, "Ancient Chinese secret, huh?," is a lighthearted nod to the image of the "inscrutable" Asian while confirming this laundry's use of an American product. Toward the end of the 1970s, however, the industry began to focus more on "image-building,"[46] and this transformed into an emphasis on "branding" in the 1980s. Corporate sponsorship of events ranging from sports to arts and education became a business in and of itself. Brands and advertising also went global, and corporate mergers and consolidations became more commonplace.[47] Historians of advertising refer to the 1980s as a period when advertising executives used more gimmicks and drew on sex appeal to market products.[48]

From the late 1980s into the 1990s selling became more complicated as advertisers faced an increasingly fragmented audience.[49] Consumer

1.5 Calgon water softener spot featuring Chinese American laundromat owners admitting that their "ancient Chinese secret" is actually this product (ca. 1970s).

awareness grew, markers of status came under criticism, and "green marketing" emerged as a concept.[50] During this time public opinion was generally positive regarding growing minority representations in advertising, but underrepresentation remained chronic. Before the 1980s Latinos were "even more underrepresented than blacks in advertising. They were virtually nonexistent."[51] During the 1980s martial arts stereotypes of Asian Americans abounded, as did ethnic humor based on mocking English spoken with a Chinese, Indian, or other Asian accent, not unlike the Yellow English depicted nearly a century earlier.[52] Asian Americans largely appeared as miscellaneous characters or foils for white characters in general market ads. Still, minorities were not the imagined audiences for these ads, which created both space and impetus for multicultural advertising to form more fully.

Multicultural advertising emerged as blacks, Latinos, and Asian Americans entered the advertising industry and founded agencies, and it developed in a more differentiated way than the in-house black and Jewish advertising of the 1960s. Multicultural ad executives harnessed the increased level of detail enumerated in each U.S. Census after the 1965 immigration wave to support their initiatives. Douglass Alligood, a veteran in this industry, told me that he was hired in Detroit by a general market agency in the early 1960s to develop marketing programs for black consumers.[53]

There he became the first black account executive in a large agency in 1963, and several years later at a major New York City agency. He left the agency business in 1971 to work on the client side. Maintaining his involvement in multicultural marketing, he returned to the large general market agency at which he previously worked and was appointed to the same division that had once focused on blacks and Jews, and asked to expand its program efforts to include Latinos, Asian Americans, LGBT, older Americans, and teens as well. The importance of diversity, as Mr. Alligood viewed it, was not inclusion or fairness: "Diversity is business. You can't ignore any population." Multicultural advertising thus grew and diversified during this period, while some general market agencies continued to keep minorities in their purview, even if they were not a priority.

Multicultural advertising seemed to be an especially welcoming place for minorities themselves to work because general market agencies remained steeped in whiteness, both in their personnel and in their overall corporate culture. In 2006 the New York City Human Rights Commission conducted a follow-up study to see how hiring practices and agency personnel had changed in the past forty or so years. Very little, it turned out. With top advertising agencies joining forces to forestall diversity hearings, numerous top executives skipping the hearings altogether, and one sarcastic industry editorial asking, "Will we be reading this same story in 2036?," the advertising industry seemed to be only marginally closer to accomplishing the type of racial and ethnic diversity reflected in recent U.S. Census data. Perhaps even more to the point, the 2006 Commission report, like the 1968 report, left the work of deciding what *minority* means to the advertising industry.

MULTICULTURAL ADVERTISING

Multicultural advertising is an umbrella term that primarily includes advertising targeted to African American, Asian American, and Latino consumers. Secondarily it includes advertising and marketing to Native Americans, Eastern Europeans, Middle Easterners, and North Africans in the United States, but these latter groups constitute a much smaller portion of multicultural advertising overall. With each U.S. Census since the 1960s, multicultural advertising executives have used data about the country's major demographic shifts to place increasing pressure on clients to reach new ethnic and racial groups. Multicultural advertising emerged in response to these shifts and today consists of small, sometimes independently owned agencies that present themselves to corporate clients as best able to reach specific minority audiences. Latino advertising agencies that emerged in the 1970s and grew steadily in the 1980s saw dynamic growth and legitimation. Arlene Davila's work chronicles the emergence of Latino marketing and the racial and ethnic formations it has engendered.[54] Ad executives at Latino agencies claimed that in-language and in-culture messaging would best reach their audiences. They also contended that they were uniquely qualified to make these highly specialized communications and that this work should not be left to general market agencies. The conceit of multicultural advertising is that it creates the potential for consumer identification and brand loyalty in more specific ways than general marketing advertising.

Latino advertising paved the way for Asian Americans to make similar claims regarding their importance and centrality to the American advertising landscape. Saul Gitlin, who when we spoke in 2011 was at Kang and Lee, one of the oldest and most successful Asian American ad agencies, described multicultural marketing and advertising as "a hand-engraved invitation" to minorities in the United States.[55] He explained to me that even though it exists in addition to mainstream media that minorities consume, featuring one's country, culture, and "Who I am!" is the real draw for minority consumers. Mr. Gitlin elaborated, "Minority groups in this country are used to not seeing themselves everywhere they look." Doing targeted promotions for major holidays such as Diwali and Lunar New Year, he suggested, creates new potential for brand identification and loyalty. For instance, in an ad for MassMutual (fig. I.4), the depiction of a young woman creating a *rangoli* (colored powder design) offers a ready motif through which to create audience identification around the Diwali holiday for Asian Indians. Likewise every year of the Chinese zodiac elicits ads featuring the animal of the year. The implicit claim is that general market advertising during earlier decades was so dominated by white actors and scenarios that minorities at best were unable to relate to the messages and at worst found them alienating. Such identification, Mr. Gitlin maintained, is far more relevant for Asian Americans than price or other product attributes.

African American advertising, as I noted earlier, has been a specialization in American advertising since the 1960s, but in recent decades some have questioned whether black audiences are most effectively reached through multicultural marketing. Some Asian American ad executives remarked that because African Americans are an English-speaking population, they are effectively reached by general market advertising.[56] Still African American advertising agencies remain a key part of multicultural advertising. In those multicultural campaigns I observed that created tailored versions of ads for all three minority segments, African American agencies were asked to tailor ads in-culture to their audiences, if not always in-language. This rise of Latino advertising and the continued emphasis on "urban markets" to reach African American consumers fit well with the structure of American media, which by the 1990s featured specialized channels, periodicals, and websites organized by ethnicity and race. Univision and Telemundo, BET (Black Entertainment Television), countless radio programs, and numerous periodicals all served as excellent venues in which to place ethnic advertising. Likewise, with satellite channels, periodicals, and websites aimed at various Asian ethnic groups in-language or in-culture, Asian American advertising began to burgeon and diversify during this period.

The Emergence of Asian American Advertising Agencies

"Telecommunications basically made Asian American advertising. It really did. If it wasn't for the [advertising] budgets of AT&T, Sprint, and MCI, Asian American advertising would have been really print-ad driven," Julia Huang, founder and CEO of InterTrend in Long Beach, California, explained to me.[57] Zan Ng, founder of the agency currently known as Admerasia and formerly LTT, offered this description in a 2008 *AdWeek* supplement about Asian American advertising: "When 'Ma Bell' was split up by the Department of Justice in the early 1980s, 85 percent of Asian Americans were immigrants with friends or family to call back home. To capture that business, AT&T, MCI and Sprint came into the market and a price war started. The campaigns began with the Chinese market, then expanded to Korean, Japanese, Vietnamese and South Asian Indian. That opened up opportunities for everyone else." Other agencies that started during this period include Kang and Lee in 1985 in New York City, Dae in 1990 in San Francisco, and InterTrend in 1981 in Los Angeles. Several Asian American agencies got their start by securing telecommunications accounts. Ms. Huang told me that around twenty years ago there were no agencies targeting Asian Americans, and at that time AT&T was expanding and invested in reaching this segment and retained Kang and Lee; MCI worked with Admerasia, and InterTrend covered Sprint. Jeff Lin, a senior executive at Admerasia, recalled that within three months of the agency opening, it won the MCI account, which enabled the agency to grow rapidly, from five or six people to over one hundred in three years.[58]

While there was not a lot of press about these agencies in the 1990s, coverage of this emerging sector of multicultural advertising highlighted the culturally and linguistically tailored expertise these agencies were able to offer. For instance, the *International Herald Tribune* published an article in 1995 noting translation gaffes in ad slogans in Asia and suggested that such mistakes of mainstream advertising paved the way for "a small group of advertising agencies run by, and targeted at, Asians" in the United States. Ms. Huang explained to me that in the early 1990s she did content analysis of the industry and found that advertising to Asian Americans in print and broadcast was "really almost embarrassing, you know, most ads were translated—of course not translated well—you know it was like an afterthought or just slapped together. It was as though, 'Oh, we **have to** do it, so we'll do it, but we don't care about this market." Similar to the copycat ads that were dubbed or replicated for black and Latino audiences, these ads for Asian American audiences seemed to fall short of building consumer identification.

The 1990s proved to be a time of growth and diversification for Asian American advertising agencies. When telecommunications began to decline in the late 1990s, financial institutions interested in reaching Asian American audiences turned to these agencies, as did automotive clients, the entertainment and hospitality industries, and others, perhaps because of the limitations of the copycat formula. Staying current for these agencies required finding the next category of business that would be a potentially good fit to advertise to Asian Americans. Vicky Wong of Ad Asia in New York remarked in *AdWeek*, "The newer success stories are among automotive, airlines, casinos, liquor, wireless and technology. All these came in the late '90s, driven mainly by the fact that after Asians set their roots and are financially established, they begin looking to lifestyle things." By this time several other agencies had emerged, including A Partnership in 1998 in New York, Admerasia in 1993, IW Group in Los Angeles, and other, smaller shops. Ad Asia was founded by Elliot Kang and Kevin Lee after they sold the highly successful Kang and Lee to their parent agency, Young and Rubicam, which is now held by the media conglomerate Omicon. Most other Asian American agencies, however, remain independently owned and operated. In 1998 these and other agencies formed the professional association Asian American Advertising Federation to increase their presence in multicultural advertising and attract clients and media part-ners. Such moves allowed them to demonstrate to corporations that they were a large, viable group for targeted marketing, from individual brands to branded experiences, such as casinos and other destinations (fig. 1.6).

In contrast to African Americans and Latinos, who constituted far larger audiences and, ad executives claimed, shared a common language, Asian Americans presented a far less manageable set of ethnic and lin-guistic differences. From the start Asian American agencies have had to demonstrate to clients that the myriad ethnic groups contained in the U.S. Census category Asian could be effectively managed and presented though in-language and in-culture copy. As several ad executives told me, Asian American agencies tried to target "all six major ethnic groups," or "seg-ments," as they called them, in order to retain enough agency business to remain viable. When I asked about other ethnicities not included in their scope of Chinese, Korean, Asian Indian, Vietnamese, Filipino, and Japa-nese, or why Japanese was not one of the groups targeted by several agen-cies, the answer was they were not "viable" targets for multicultural adver-tising. They were too small a group, there were not enough media sources in which to place ads, or there was simply too little data about them to do anything effective. The biopolitics of counting and enumeration in the census and other market research enabled ad executives to present some ethnic groups as large enough to make the prospect of advertising appeal-ing to clients, while smaller groups required different types of interven-tions. The concept of emerging markets, targeting some of these newer populations, has become a necessity for economic growth.

Creating and producing effective messaging directed at one of the pri-mary five or six Asian segments or an emerging ethnic group required in-language and in-culture expertise, and Asian American ad agencies staffed accordingly. To be hired by an Asian American ad agency, executives were expected to have work experience or educational qualifications in adver-tising and marketing, as well as fluency in Mandarin, Hindi, Korean, Taga-log, or Vietnamese. Additionally executives were expected to have cultural knowledge about one of the five major ethnic groups in the United States: Chinese, South Asian American, Vietnamese, Filipino, and Korean. Execu-tives indicated that first and foremost their interest was advertising and marketing broadly conceived, and Asian American communications were secondary. Some ad executives were themselves taken aback at this seg-mentation. Mr. Lin, who was born and raised in Taiwan, expected to simply be "American" when he moved to the United States but was stunned to

1.6 Foxwood Casino print ad featuring in-language copy and Chinese American talent promoting a "Dream Card" tailored to Chinese American consumers (2009).

learn firsthand how "segmented" the country could be and how relevant categories such as Hispanic, African American, and Asian American were in society, not just in advertising.[59] Yet the executives I spoke with realized the centrality of these rubrics in their industry's organization and went along with these differences as conceptualized by the Census Bureau. Within the category of Asian American, most ad executives agreed that Japanese Americans have become more acculturated in terms of culture and language, especially compared to the "intensity" of new immigrants, as Dae's creative director Sunny Teo put it.[60] Outside of specific regions of the West Coast, advertisers tended not to target them explicitly. If agencies did not have first- or second-generation immigrants on staff who were fluent and literate in the requisite language and culture, they hired freelancers who were.

Displaying pan–Asian American expertise was an initial selling point for Asian American agencies, and they used this strategy to grow. Agency names were one way to signal this orientation. A Partnership was founded by Jeannie Yuen, who was president and CEO when I spoke to account director Ed Chang.[61] He relayed that the agency's first name was Asianese Partnership, to convey to American clients, "We speak this language called Asianese, encompassing Chinese, Korean, Vietnamese, what have you." Finding the name to require more explanation than they had intended, they evolved into A Partnership, with an initial staff of five and a small client roster, including the U.S. Postal Service. They later acquired an automobile client, an insurance client, and a bank, among others, with a staff of thirty-five. Other agencies too used their names to index their pan-Asian scope and expertise. When I asked Zan Ng, CEO and co-owner of Admerasia, about the agency's name, he replied, "It's quite funny, actually."[62] Mr. Ng, who told me that he did not have a "formal education" in advertising and was a photographer before he entered this field, recalled that he had told his American-born Chinese wife about his idea to start an Asian American marketing agency. When he asked her what she would name the company, she replied, "Amerasia," which he misheard as "Admerasia." He recounted, "So, immediately I thought, 'What a great name! What a great idea!' because it brought together advertising and a pan-Asian image. It was not until after the company was off the ground that he discovered he had misheard her. "She thought it was a misspelling and told me that I spelled it wrong. I said, 'No, it was the perfect name for marketing and communications, **Ad**merasia.' We both laughed at the misunderstanding."

Having *Asia* in the name or something else indexing their areas of specialization was one approach agencies used to signal their expertise to clients.

Admerasia, like some of the other agencies I visited, hired family members and friends and built business networks through social networks. Like the close-knit world of Asian American fashion designers detailed in Thuy Linh Tu's work,[63] ad executives assisted interested friends and family living in Asia, in the United States, or elsewhere in the diaspora by helping them to find relevant positions in multicultural advertising. For instance, Tommy Ng, Admerasia's general manager, chose to work there "for two reasons. The first reason being that it's a family operation, and the second because me and them are related."[64] His uncle runs the company, and he started part time in accounting and eventually became the office manager. Even those who did not join Admerasia through family connections found something that appealed to their broader goals.

For some, Asian American advertising represented something valuable to aid the transition into American consumer culture and financial institutions, if not for themselves, then for their extended family. Sid Yi, who joined Admerasia from the "client side," meaning he used to work for a bank as the liaison to marketers like Admerasia, was impressed with how engaged and present people seemed at this agency.[65] He elaborated, "Our advantage is the people—having someone who's Korean or Vietnamese or Filipino, that really **live** their culture outside of work, is a big advantage for us. It's a key part of our strengths. . . . It's very easy for these guys to go back and talk to their aunts, their uncles, their parents, and get us some of the information that we may need that'll drive insights for our clients. So I think that's a big advantage for us, is to retain a very diverse company." Mr. Yi added that as a second-generation Chinese American, he does not regard himself as the primary target of Asian American advertising. Although he frequents Asian grocery stores and consumes Asian American media, he is influenced by general market advertising far more than multicultural advertising. He lamented, however, that the diversity he sees in mainstream advertising is "token. I mean you have your token spot where it's diverse, you have an Asian talent in there, but ultimately they don't do a good enough job in marketing **to me**. . . . I want to make sure that the Asian voice, no matter which generation you come from, is accurately represented." For Mr. Yi, in-language financial services and other messaging was less essential to him but did lighten his familial responsibility somewhat, in that it helped his in-language dependent elder relatives who relied on him to help manage their finances and field questions about mortgages, credit lines, and similar matters. He remarked that the in-language education and assistance these ads provide his family and friends made him loyal to these brands. Reaching second-generation consumers like Mr. Yi, however, remained a major concern. Rather than identifying with in-language or in-culture messaging, this group saw the broader benefits it offered for their extended family, thereby creating a different type of identification with second-generation Asian Americans.

The question of generation that Mr. Yi raised was one that most Asian American ad executives admitted was an unresolved, growing concern. Tommy Ng from Admerasia agreed that their primary audience was first-generation and 1.5-generation Asian immigrants, but second-generation immigrants were also of interest to them. Second-generation Asian Americans, as Mr. T. Ng, Mr. Yi, and others remarked, were also reached well by general market media. Conceptions of culture and selective uses of language, then, were the best line of appeal. Mr. T. Ng characterized them as "not just fluent in their homeland language, they're fluent in English also. And on top of that you have a constant influx of new immigrants, so our base will always be there." Reflecting that the growing 1.5- and second-generation, English-speaking segment cannot be ignored, and that general market executives are targeting that audience as well, he added, "We have to be culturally relevant, we have to know they're different. You can't just post up any ad, and yes they'll see it, but how well they'll receive it is different." Either way, the general market strategy of "put one Asian in there and we'll cover it all," as he described it, is certainly not an optimal approach.

As Asian American agencies strategize how to best conceive of and reach an expanding and diversifying Asian population in the United States, they are also competing with one another for business. Given how small Asian American advertising is compared to advertising overall, competition could be far more hostile between agencies were it not for the "do not compete" clauses that most advertising agencies are required to follow. Such agreements prohibit agencies from accepting more than one client per product category, meaning they are limited to representing one automobile maker, one bank, one insurance company, one soft drink, and so on. In Asian American advertising this arrangement has enabled agencies to compete but also remain on amicable terms with one another. Max Niu, a producer at Dae, remarked that "Asian American agencies are friendly, not as competitive and cutthroat as general market agencies."[66] He added that the stakes were lower for clients to reach multicultural audiences, and Asian American audiences in particular, so this kept rivalries somewhat contained as well. Mr. T. Ng likewise suggested that there were enough clients in each goods and services category for larger agencies to secure a client, but nonetheless emphasized that they did vie for "the eyeballs. We're competing for the same audience, but there's enough clients for us to share." Most agencies have twenty to seventy people on staff, and several saw growth as a long-term goal. Sunny Teo, creative director at Dae, remarked that expanding his twenty-person office to perhaps fifty would be an ideal way to increase the range and scope of projects they could undertake.[67]

Regardless of size, Asian American advertising agencies strive to appear unified as an entity in multicultural advertising and create a visible presence to clients and general market agencies in order to be recognized in the industry. To bolster legitimacy, Mr. Z. Ng explained, he cofounded the Asian American Advertising Federation because he and colleagues from other agencies decided they needed an industry organization to represent them. Established with a handful of agencies, the 3AF has since grown to include media companies, public relations firms, and even corporate clients invested in advertising to Asian Americans. Mr. Chang, a 3AF board member, told me that most agencies understand that they need industry collaboration to be successful and that this may be helpful in terms of understanding "the community."[68] Once clients decide to advertise to Asian American audiences, however, the usual competition kicks in, and "as the market expresses interest there's a section process of agencies, obviously this is competitive." As the opening vignette to this chapter suggests, the pitch materials and presentations that each agency develops to secure the leading brands in each category are highly competitive.

Another strategy to legitimate multicultural advertising is to make data about these groups readily available to clients and media outlets that may be interested in reaching them. Lisa Skriloff, founder and CEO of Multicultural Marketing Resources, a public relations and marketing firm in New York City, explained that her firm acts as a conduit for clients who wish to reach multicultural audiences.[69] The firm primarily works with ad agencies, research companies, and public relations companies, as well as corporations, and also acts as a liaison between marketers and journalists. Their scope extends past multicultural advertising to include niche groups such as "women business owners, the gay/lesbian market, people with disabilities, and any niche community that has discretionary or disposal income that corporations would want to target." All these efforts to create and maintain legitimacy helped to make the smallest group in multicultural advertising seem as large and established as Latino and African American advertising. Intra-agency efforts to construct and project a recognizable, accessible Asian American agency culture also contributed substantially to this mission.

Asian American Agency Culture

In the Asian American advertising agencies I visited, the overall office culture was relaxed and open; several agencies were run by women, and many workplaces welcomed gay and lesbian executives and staff. Depending on the agency, there seemed to be tolerance for a range of personal needs and choices, ranging from lactation rooms for nursing mothers to bringing pet dogs and rabbits to work. I came to understand that this was part of their broader philosophical approach about how they viewed their role in advertising and the public sphere. Like the Latino agencies that Davila found to credit themselves with "erasing stereotypes" about Latinos, many Asian American advertising executives saw their mission, in some part at least, as educational. Increasing public understanding about Asian American ethnicities, languages, and cultures was as much a part of office culture as it was in their work. Especially with other Asian Americans (including me), they were welcoming and assumed a shared outlook with regard to valuing education. Agencies occasionally tried to partner with business schools and universities to promote their perspectives about Asian American diversity and align their creative approaches with emerging marketing data, and kept an eye out for potential interns and new hires. Some of these agencies, especially those that were independently owned and operated, were flexible about hiring new talent from Asia on visas that require sponsorship for permanent residency and citizenship. According to one veteran ad executive, each Asian American agency is known for a particular strength and skill set, be it strategy, public relations, or meeting business objectives. Most, however, fancied themselves to be good at everything and did not shy away from any type of business opportunity.

In all agencies, individuals mentored one another according to their skills and experience. In a professional development meeting with upper-level account executives, one agency vice president declared, "I will help any Asian who wants my help." Adding that this was how Asian Ads built itself, he declared the agency founder to be a great mentor who wanted to make those around him better than him. "It is our job to build our team," the vice president said to his talented group of ad executives in charge of day-to-day account work. One account executive described her small agency like this: "This is still a family-owned agency. It's not under big corporate. So we are very innovative and if there are any ideas, it's really easy to push forward and make them happen. So for example, another agency located in New York, Kang and Lee, belongs to Young and Rubicam, the Omnicom network. Their approach is very different from us, they are very corporate-like."[70] Suggesting that other agencies require ad ideas to pass through layers of approval, she contrasted her agency's upper-level management process: "You just go from this desk to that desk and make the idea happen. That's the main difference." Such flexibility and mentoring appeared to be critical to remaining innovative and open to new business opportunities.

Ad executives told me about other advantages and disadvantages of being at small, niche agencies. Some described their agency as a place of shared ethnicity in language and culture, and in race, in that it was a predominantly Asian American space in an otherwise white corporate America. The culture of pan-Asian hospitality, from welcoming guests to treating other Asians as friends or even family, also prevailed. In one firm the agency-wide weekly meeting was referred to as "the Family Meeting." Even I was welcomed as a friend more than as a researcher, I believe because of my Indian American heritage. People spoke Mandarin, Korean, Hindi, and other languages to their coethnics, permeated agency space with pungent food smells, and celebrated minor and major Asian holidays. Of course they also spoke English, ate odorless sandwiches, and had an annual Christmas party, but the former set of activities set these agencies apart from much of corporate America, and certainly from the general market ad agencies I visited. In these small agencies everyone knew each other and knew about all of the agency's current accounts.

Ad executives were often expected to perform many roles on an ongoing basis. Mr. Lin described his early days at Admerasia like this: "Everyone did everything. And that is sort of like what we're doing now, except that we're adding people and we are growing, but we want to blend roles for what everyone does." One graphic designer, born in Singapore and educated in design at Parsons, explained how her art background led her to Asian American advertising.[71] She was hired to do digital art for the company, as well as "a lot of tasks for which I am not trained," she laughed. Most staff seemed willing to work on whatever part of the advertising process was necessary, especially when their agency needed to weather an economic slump or when it found new opportunities during flush times. Some advertising executives considered being in a small agency exciting because of the creative opportunities it offered. An ad executive at a West Coast agency told me that her agency head "always encourages us by saying you can do whatever you want, on a smaller scale. I don't think I'd have the luxury to do that in a big agency."[72]

In the leadership meetings I attended at these small agencies, managers reminded account executives that everyone on their team needed to perform multiple roles in the development and production process. Differing in approach from general market agencies, where ad executives rarely step out of their designated roles of account planning, creative, and production, Asian American agencies sometimes had only creative and production departments and contracted services from freelancers and editors as needed. This meant that the vital account planning and the requisite research to develop a strategic plan for the creative were either provided by the client or left to the account team. "We don't have an account planning department," Sheng Li reminded his account executives at one Asian Ads meeting, "so everyone has to play a part in generating insights for ads." From what I observed, this included everyone offering his or her social capital to do account planning. This could include consulting family and friends about in-culture insights, providing assistance with in-language copy as a native or heritage speaker, leveraging professional and social contacts for business, and finding good contract labor, such as regional networks of professional photographers, graphic designers, copywriters, and directors, and production companies, as well as the same in Asia. Using regional and international social networks in some cases offered higher degrees of production quality and control, often at a reduced cost.

Asian American agencies intentionally strove to make their payroll as heterogeneous as possible to demonstrate their wide multicultural expertise. Ad executives varied across nationality, religion, generational status, gender, sexuality, and even race. There were some non–Asian Americans working in these agencies, usually white men whose fluency in a major Asian language and knowledge of the culture through their time living in China, India, or other countries made them very appealing, especially for capturing the nuance of translations. Ad executives who had come to the United States to pursue an academic degree found their lack of contacts and visa status barriers to entry in general market advertising, while Asian American agencies often valued these individuals for their skill set. For instance, Mr. Lin explained the difficulty of entering general market advertising; despite his work experience at a Taiwanese agency as well as a master's degree from NYU, no agency would give him a job due to his student

F-1 visa. He recalled, "The Asian agency said, 'Okay, you got the job. Come to work tomorrow.'" At that time, LLT, the firm that hired him, was one of the main pioneers of Asian American advertising, and no one in the early days had an advertising background; they were journalists or graphic artists. He was immediately impressed by two of the founders, Jenny Tong and Joseph Liu, and described Liu as a mentor, big brother, and teacher, who had offered him the job on the spot. In Mr. Lin's case, an Asian American agency not only welcomed him when general market agencies did not but also mentored him and sponsored his permanent residency—a process that made him even more loyal. Mr. Lin proclaimed his love of the advertising industry—the creativity, the challenge, the potential media impact. He found these elements in Asian American advertising and had no desire to enter general market advertising.

Others found working at Asian American agencies appealing because of their ability to use their heritage culture and language in their everyday work. For instance, one account executive grew up in Taiwan and found her way to Asian American advertising after design school; she was drawn to an Asian American agency because there "your background is actually your strength." She enjoyed performing a number of different roles as an account executive, such as giving input on planning, creative, and production based on her language and culture skills. Other ad executives liked this environment but preferred to freelance at different agencies to build their skills across creative and production. One freelancer, for instance, worked for three years on a large insurance company campaign and learned a great deal from generating the creative at an agency in New York City, shooting the ads in India and Africa, and working with the postproduction team in Malaysia. Prior to that she worked on a radio ad for an agency based in San Francisco; the productions studio was in Santa Monica, she was in New York, and the singer for the jingle and the voice-over actor were in Mumbai. She was able to direct each take remotely via Skype. She emphasized how commonplace this development and production model has become, and that even though the sound quality was not as good as it would have been in the Mumbai studio, it was still amazingly efficient and allowed her to connect with individuals she may not have met at a larger agency.

While many in multicultural advertising were first-generation immigrants, others were drawn to this type of advertising work as second- or 1.5-generation Asian Americans who had immigrated during their childhood or teen years. One of the few second-generation ad executives I met at an East Coast agency worked as a media buyer. This was his first job after graduating from college in New York and majoring in multicultural marketing.[73] He grew up in the United States but speaks Vietnamese, which he called a "requirement" when he sought work at Admerasia but admitted that over time it had become a less important criterion. Enjoying the agency's atmosphere and accounts, he said that he had no visa concerns and simply enjoyed working at an Asian American ad agency and appreciated the work environment and colleagues. Vivian Li, a senior executive at Admerasia, similarly admits that she could work anywhere in the ad industry. She was raised in Manhattan's Chinatown and attended New York University, but her love of her in-language and in-culture work keeps her from entering general market advertising. As a Cantonese speaker who could understand a good deal of Mandarin, she opted for the Asian American market over the mainstream market, explaining, "Because I love the language!"[74] She suggested that there are greater challenges in Asian American advertising than in the general market: "You work three times as hard!" Ms. Li confirmed that "there are so many more steps than in mainstream advertising, and this is a challenge." Yet the additional work seems to be worthwhile, especially in New York agencies, where Madison Avenue general market advertising poses numerous barriers to entry and advancement for some Asian Americans.

A somewhat different dynamic prevailed in California-based agencies, where Asian Americans have long been part of public culture. These agencies employed more 1.5-, second-, and even third-generation Asian Americans. I met one director of digital marketing who had emigrated from Vietnam as a teenager and grew up in Los Angeles, where Asian Americans are a major presence.[75] Her work in Asian American advertising brought together her intimate knowledge of Asia and of the greater Los Angeles area. Another producer I spoke with explained that he is of Chinese and American parentage; he learned Mandarin from his mother and took a few years of coursework in the language while in college.[76] Having gone to Taiwan every summer with his parents, he could still speak the language. Beginning in advertising as a graphic designer with a degree from UC Berkeley, he worked for a number of smaller Asian American media production companies before directing commercials. He was drawn to working in an Asian American advertising agency through friends telling him about the great work environment and thought that his language skills made him marketable. Max Niu, born in California and based in San Francisco, previously worked at a Korean American ad agency where his Korean heritage and language skills were in constant use; he used his UC Santa Cruz art degree to start as a graphic artist and moved on from there. All these ad executives chose Asian American agencies because they are drawn to the work through their love of Asian languages, cultures, and work environments and value contributing to Asian American art and design through advertising.

The trajectories of West Coast executives like Max and others suggest that those who work in multicultural advertising took many different paths into this profession, including from the general market and the client side. Stan Toyama, who identified as a third-generation Asian American and is half Japanese and half Okinawan, went to language school for seven years but never heard Japanese being spoken at home because his parents did not want him to hear or use the language in order to better assimilate.[77] Unlike many of his first- or even second-generation colleagues, he did not feel as confident in his language skills, but he believed that his cultural knowledge was sound. Having recently moved to Asian American advertising from a general market agency, he mentioned that people in the general market called him "the least 'Asian' Asian we know" and that he is learning a lot from the first-generation immigrants with whom he now works. Finding a different path into Asian American advertising, Jane Nakagawa's father was born in the United States but raised in Japan, foreshadowing the bicultural context of the family he would raise.[78] Ms. Nakagawa used to work on the client side with a car company but decided that she would find it rewarding to work at a company that focused on the "Asian community." She has a graduate degree in architecture and was a studio art major at Smith College, a background that helped her work with designers and engineers. She found the work engaging, as the agency was small enough for productive interaction between people of different ethnic backgrounds as well as skill sets.

While Asian American agencies were generally positive and collaborative spaces of shared work and creativity, there were certainly disadvantages as well. One of the main detractors seemed to be financial. As Zan Ng at Admerasia explained it, without a media holding company that could act as a financial underwriter and offer "unlimited funding," independently owned agencies have to be more cautious about growth and risk. General manager Mr. T. Ng explained, "It affects our decision making, definitely, because we do not have deep pockets upstairs. One of our competitors can just say, 'We need money!' and then their holding company can send their payroll or whatever. We don't have that, we don't have that cash on hand, so that definitely affects our decisions on some things. We cannot be as risky on certain decisions and we can't take as many chances." Although being acquired by a holding company is something several agencies, including Admerasia, have considered, most prefer to remain independent. Even prior to the 2008 recession, as telecommunications declined, it was difficult for some agencies to sustain larger scale productions. "We are kind of stuck, unless we convince other industries to come in and advertise to us," explained one account executive. One way they do so is to present Asian Americans as a potentially lucrative group and their agencies as able to address demographic trends.

CREATING ASIAN AMERICAN ADVERTISING FROM CENSUS DATA

The project of advertising in the United States, as elsewhere, links population segmentation to social recognition in the public sphere. Daniel Miller has illustrated that for advertising executives in Trinidad, identifying social differences in the population thought to be intrinsic lent authenticity to their marketing appeals while also legitimating those differences.[79] In the United States, where multicultural marketers make analogous identifications about race and ethnicity being intrinsic categories of difference in the population, and where the Census Bureau and research foundations also segment the population according to these differences, multicultural advertising adds additional layers of legitimacy to these categorizations while also fueling their everyday presence in media and other realms of the public sphere. Ms. Skriloff from Multicultural Marketing Resources remarked, "Differentiation goes by census years, and in the 1980s Census, everybody was aware of the Hispanic market and African American market and were focusing on them for several decades. The 1990 and certainly the 2000 Census really showed a lot of statistics about the Asian American market and the different segments, including multiracial individuals." She later added that this latter trend has increased in light of the 2010 Census, as has an overall interest in reaching minorities.

Asian American ad executives worked to shape ethnoracial assemblages by molding the Census Bureau category of Asian American to their financial goals of increasing business and expanding their agencies. As they attempted to gauge the efficacy of certain in-language and in-culture strategies with their audiences and aimed to better understand how audiences might relate to the broader category of Asian American, they also sought to infuse these demographic terms with cultural meanings. This was perhaps more challenging for the category of Asian American than it had been for other categories, such as African Americans or Latinos. Mr. Lin at Admerasia remarked that he did not initially see the same levels of pride and soli-darity among Asian Americans that he perceived among these other groups, and that the intrinsic lack of unity in this category made it more difficult to present to clients. Making this category seem united, then, remains an important part of selling Asian American advertising to clients. Similarly analyzing how multicultural advertising and marketing executives created Latino from the category Hispanic and the different ethnicities, nationali-ties, and varieties of Spanish it encompasses, Davila illustrates that con-sumer culture rarely has a ready-made market. Rather the role of multicul-tural advertising is to produce desire among certain segments and suggest reasons why niche audiences would buy a product.[80] As Davila illustrates, advertising executives could effectively accomplish this only when they made the category of Latino appear united and ready for consumption.

Many Asian American advertising executives I spoke with explained that clients often targeted the larger, more lucrative Latino market first, and even characterized this approach as "automatic" and "obvious." Espe-cially because it was newer and smaller, it was difficult for Asian American advertising to have the same kind of "power and leverage," as Ms. Huang put it. Asian American ad executives found their work cut out for them and took on the challenge of being a lower priority in the hierarchy of ad-vertising spending in which the general market was at the top, followed by the Latino, African American, and finally Asian American markets. Their strategy was not to compete with the Latino market but to find a place for themselves alongside it. Ms. Huang remarked, "It would be a crime for any brand to not have a Hispanic American strategy, almost idiotic, even if it is not language-centric. Asian Americans, again, it's very differ-ent." When clients had limited budgets for multicultural marketing and a proportionately larger amount allocated for Latino advertising, ad execu-tives remarked that their clients were inclined to skip the Asian American market altogether. To deter clients from doing so, Asian American ad ex-ecutives concentrated their efforts on those goods and services that have been shown to be well-suited for their audiences, such as, in past decades, telecommunications. Currently industries such as banking, insurance, fi-nancial services, automobiles, fast food, liquor, and casinos have become dedicated clients. Identifying and targeting clients in relevant industries remains a primary focus for Asian American agencies. Also important has been the promotion of Asian American advertising through write-ups in major trade periodicals such as *Advertising Age* and *AdWeek* and in digital media. These can include special issues and materials such as fact sheets, research articles, media stories, and roundtables with prominent Asian American ad executives to promote their advertising work, such as the one cited earlier in this chapter. These media-based marketing strategies signal to the broader advertising industry and to clients that Asian American advertising is a legitimate part of the advertising world.

First and foremost, however, Asian American ad executives are concerned with defining the category of Asian American from the vast U.S. Census and American Community Survey (ACS) data that are released on an ongoing basis. Since the 1960s, census classifications have been somewhat arbitrary in their use of categories to count those who identify as Asian, alone or in combination, and Asian American ad executives make these inconsistencies work for them. A crucial part of this process is to decide which ethnic groups to focus on, based on their size and other metrics such as purchasing power and assessments about their level of assimilation. For instance, the Japanese American population numbers approximately 750,000 and, as I mentioned earlier, is thought to be "too assimilated" to be effectively reached through multicultural advertising outside of California and Hawai'i. By contrast, there are 3.3 million Chinese in the United States, and adding Taiwanese bumps this count to 3.5 million, making them the largest group. Vietnamese immigration grew substantially in the aftermath of the Vietnam War; there are currently 1.6 million Vietnamese Americans, even though earlier counts grouped them with Cambodians as "Other Asians," which makes them a potentially attractive group for multicultural advertising. Koreans remain among the fastest growing ethnic groups in the United States, experiencing a 27 percent increase in growth from 2000 to 2007, compared to the country's overall growth rate of 7 percent.[81] The current Filipino population is just over 2.5 million, and Asian Indians, which refers only to India, not other South Asian nations such as Pakistan and Bangladesh, number 2.9 million. Ad executives use these and other statistics to make these last five groups the most viable to target through multicultural advertising.

This may seem straightforward, but considering how many census-based reformulations this category has undergone based on U.S. relations with Asian nations suggests just how much flexibility there is in this endeavor. For instance, China and Taiwan were originally grouped into a single category but were subsequently separated, due perhaps to rocky U.S.-Sino relations in the late 1970s. Countries counted as Southeast Asian have included Vietnam, Cambodia, and Laos, but not the Philippines, which many consider to be in Southeast Asia, while the 2011 ACS update puts Vietnamese in a category separate from "Other Asian, specified," "Other Asian, unspecified," and "Two or more Asian." Other reference sources, such as the Historical Statistics of the United States Millennial Edition Online, lump Vietnamese with "Other Asia," a category that has served as a catchall for smaller Asian and some Middle Eastern nations such as Palestine, a holdover from earlier decades when terms such as *Near East* and *Far East* indexed orientation from Western Europe and the United States. In the Historical Statistics of the United States Millennial Edition Online, at least until 1990, India had its own category for international migration data, whereas Palestine, Pakistan, and Nepal were lumped within "Other Asia." In the 2011 ACS update to the U.S. Census, Palestine was no longer included in this grouping, and South Asia included Bangladesh, Bhutan, Nepal, Pakistan, and Sri Lanka.

These different ways of categorizing, grouping, and counting are processes on which Asian American advertising executives pride themselves as experts. They assure clients of, and explained to me, their coveted ability to create order out of conflicting data and using this skill as the basis for effective advertising strategies. For instance, while most of the advertising industry still used the Census Bureau category Asian Indian, some marketers deployed geopolitics and census inconsistencies to make bigger claims. Sunil Hali, CEO of Cinemaya Media, explained to me that their publications and marketing efforts address "People of Indian Origin" from the subcontinent as well as those whose migration paths are via the Gulf, the West Indies, and other regions.[82] Neeta Bhasin, president and CEO of ASB Communications, took a similar tack.[83] She identified categorical shifts in the Asian Indian category in the 1990 and 2000 Censuses that she has found useful for drawing in clients. When the population growth of Asian Indians, Pakistanis, Bangladeshis, Sri Lankans, and other groups reached 106 percent in the 1990 Census, she began getting invitations to multicultural marketing events to "educate this American corporate world that we are the third largest ethnic group here in the U.S." She contested the claim that Chinese Americans were the largest Asian ethnic group: "Not anymore! Before partition in 1947, India was one country. The language, the food, the culture, the tradition of India, Pakistan, Bangladesh, and Sri Lanka are the same. There is no difference between us. We are close to five million people now." This is in keeping with other sources that have included Bangladeshis, Bhutanese, Indians, Maldivians, Nepalese, Pakistanis, and Sri Lankans in a "pan–South Asian American" identity and allows marketers like Ms. Bhasin to make broader claims to clients about the reach of their work.[84] Before she employed this approach, her clients were less interested in reaching South Asians because "they didn't know anything about Indians, or South Asians. They knew India as a poor country and had the wrong impression."

Asian American ad executives thus shape the category of Asian American to reach clients for marketing and commercial representation by manipulating the subgroupings it contains. They select not only numerical statistics but also cultural and linguistic trends about ethnic groups and link them to ideologies that further positive representations of Asians in America. This primarily happens by choosing which languages, ethnic heritages, religions, and other aspects of language and culture will be primarily used to depict each ethnic group. For instance, Filipinos and Asian Indians are thought to be the most fluent in English. Many Filipino Americans are bilingual in Tagalog or another Filipino dialect and English. Asian Indians are multilingual, but most speak the two languages of the Indian government, Hindi and English, Hindi being the official language.[85] Generally they also speak their state language as well as their ethnic group's language. Additionally Asian Indians predominantly observe Hinduism or Islam, as well as Sikhism, Jainism, Buddhism, Christianity, and Zoroastrianism. In the Asian Indian creative work I observed, English and Hindi were the main languages, and characters were either Hindu or depicted without any identifying religious markers. Such choices were necessarily reductive, as Christianity is most often depicted in Filipino ads, despite the presence of Muslims, Buddhists, and Taoists among Filipino Americans.

Although Chinese, Vietnamese, and Korean ads all required in-language copy, there are still myriad cultural and linguistic choices to be made about how best to tailor each to reach the most speakers and religions. According to the 2010 Census, Chinese Americans are officially the largest of all Asian groups in the United States, and after Spanish, Chinese is the most widely spoken non-English language in U.S. households. The major Chinese languages spoken are Mandarin and Cantonese, as well as regional dialects such as Taishanese, once the dominant language of American Chinatowns. In the advertising work I observed, Mandarin was often simply called Chinese, and the variety used in copy was simplified Mandarin, which is increasingly taught in Chinese schools today. Although Chinese Buddhism and Christianity are the largest recognized religions among Chinese Americans, many favor a mixture of Buddhism, Confucianism, Taoism, and folk traditions known as "popular religion."[86] Perhaps for this reason religion was rarely depicted in the creative work I observed. Vietnamese is still widely used in speech and print among first-generation Vietnamese, although low Vietnamese-language proficiency among younger generations causes concern among older Vietnamese Americans regarding the community's ability to sustain its "goc Viet" or roots.[87] Vietnamese are largely Protestant, although Catholicism and two native religions, Cao-Dai and Hoa-hao, have added to Vietnam's religious diversity. Domestic religious practices in Vietnamese American homes center on folk-religious creation and maintenance of altars to ancestral elders and religious figures. Both North and South Koreans speak Korean, as do first- and 1.5-generation Korean immigrants. A growing number of second-generation Korean Americans are predominantly English speaking, but some are learning Korean.[88] While Koreans practice a variety of religions, Christianity and Buddhism are the two major religions practiced by Korean Americans. Church plays a major role in the Korean American community, and Korean American churches, which are overwhelmingly Protestant, serve as both a place of worship and a site of socialization. For groups for whom church has played a major role in diaspora, it is accordingly recruited in marketing strategies and as a backdrop for ads.

Ad executives selected and chose languages and religions to highlight, as well as those to avoid, to carefully control how they depicted ethnicity and race. They steered clear of intraethnic tensions, fissures, or anything that could be perceived negatively. The language varieties they came to regard as standard, how they depicted certain religions as the norm, and other choices they made were carefully aligned with U.S. geopolitics. Asian American advertising, like most advertising worldwide, shied away from political and social issues anticipated to illicit unpleasant responses. This is evident in their treatment of minority religions after the events of September 11, 2001. Owing to militarized conflict abroad and the War on Terror at home, Muslims of Pakistani, Bangladeshi, Filipino, Southeast Asian, Indo-Caribbean, and Indo-Fijian heritage have experienced far greater scrutiny, often leading to detention and deportation. One representational strategy I observed resulting from this was neutralization of Muslim religious imagery of any kind. Even when individuals had Muslim names, they were given secular identities. Indeed ethnic Muslim costumes usually appeared only in creative that featured festivals and weddings, such as one ad for Nationwide insurance (fig. 1.7). The absence of a *bindi* (a mark Hindu women apply on the forehead) coupled with other ethnic markers makes this ad distinctively Muslim for those knowledgeable about wedding costumes. This careful selective approach ultimately shapes the mass-

1.7 Print ad for Nationwide South Asian, one of the few that features Muslim in-culture elements (2009).

mediated category of Asian American in advertisements. It is also note-worthy that while ad executives can downplay Muslim imagery in Asian Indian and other Asian American advertisements, they seek it out in other venues. As the Arab American population in the United States has become more visible it has become more attractive to advertisers and marketers. Especially as the Middle East has become its own Census Bureau category and Palestine is no longer included in "Asian, Other," since the 2003 Gulf War, Asian American agencies have made the case that similarities among Pakistan, Afghanistan, and other regions of the Middle East mean they warrant specialized advertising. The ongoing, microlevel work of this vet-ting contributes to the selection of certain ethnicities, languages, and so-cial attributes over others, resulting in imagery that is far more narrow and selective than the actual Asian population in the United States.

Elsewhere I have used the term *racial naturalization* to discuss the ways multicultural advertising is helping to transform Asian Americans from model minorities to model consumers, and how their perceived impor-tance as consumers has begun to erode their status as "forever foreigners," a concept Mia Tuan has introduced.[89] Tuan, Claire Jean Kim, and others contend that the model minority stereotype has thrived because it keeps Asian Americans from being considered an economic or social threat to the state; instead they are regarded as perpetual outsiders, with no legiti-mate place in the body politic.[90] Advertising and corporate America are arenas in which this narrative is being replaced by a new one, wherein this category is being applied in unexpected ways, and expertise about Asian Americans, as well as connections to Asia as a global power, are actively valued and sought. This advertising work has naturalized Asian Americans into an elite consumer corps that can be relied upon to keep the American economy afloat during tough economic times, thus naturalizing their once foreign status.

Prioritizing and shaping cultural and linguistic differences into orderly ethnic groups is one way that Asian American ad executives make cen-sus data work for them; another is to actually map them onto physical landscapes of the United States. Areas of geographic concentration of each ethnic group, while specified by the Census Bureau, take on specific com-munity formations in certain cities and suburbs, and understanding how ethnic groups map onto the physical space of the United States is another skill that Asian American ad executives showcase as part of their exper-tise. This was evident in the creative work of advertising, by indexing re-gional differences and immigration histories specific to certain locations;

through media placement, by placing ads in regional broadcast and cable media based on audience concentration; and by "out of home" and "place-based advertising," including billboards, in-store displays, and a variety of sponsorship opportunities that allow for brands to become part of ethnic community heritage celebrations. Part of being able to reach small ethnic populations is demonstrating an understanding of their spatial dispersion and pockets of concentration. These ad executives knew, for instance, that Vietnamese populations are concentrated primarily in California, Texas, and Washington state, with other notable communities in Louisiana and regions of the Midwest, while the Filipino population is concentrated in California, Hawai'i, and Illinois. They also knew—and could inform clients—that given Filipino Americans' English proficiency relative to most other Asian American groups, they do not tend to form traditional cultural and linguistic "towns" with the prolificacy of other Asian groups and thus tend to settle in more ethnically diverse areas. There remain, however, concentrated populations based on professional and familial chain migration patterns; Chicago and New Jersey, for instance, have Filipino American populations that emerged from the 1970s settlement of medical workers and their families. Sites such as Stockton, California's "Little Manila" and LA's "Historic Filipino Town" are officially recognized for their regional significance; Asian American ad executives can point to such places to display their insider knowledge to clients.

Ad executives emphasize the importance of the highly specific knowledge of designated market areas (DMAs), suggesting that clients would simply not be able to effectively target Asian Americans without their expertise. DMAs are significant because, as the executives told their clients, they enable the placement of advertising in those regions where it will reach the largest audiences. According to the 2010 Census, over 70 percent of all Japanese Americans living on the West Coast are regionally concentrated in Hawai'i and California.[91] Focusing on DMAs allows ad executives to access and expand their social networks with local businesses and media to do more effective marketing and public relations. Being able to sponsor events and distribute promotional materials in these densely populated DMAs is considered vital for grassroots marketing. Asian American advertising executives know, for instance, that Los Angeles has one of the most active concentrations of churchgoing Koreans, so they tie in promotions with those communities. Such an approach was very successful in a 2010 advertising and public relations campaign for State Farm that harnessed the popularity of churches and singing among Los Angeles Koreans. Like-

1.8 Nissan Korean American spot featuring in-language copy and voice-over, with a Korean American father and young daughter. The ad features a large, modernist home in a nonurban setting (2012).

wise San Gabriel County, a suburb of Los Angeles, has the largest concentration of Chinese anywhere in the United States, followed by Flushing in Queens, New York, and the Richmond district in San Francisco; these areas were regularly targeted for public relations events and grassroots marketing efforts. DMAs are also useful because clients can tailor retail and promotional offerings to broader demographic shifts in the United States. For instance, because the majority of Chinese Americans today live in suburbs,[92] this demographic trend has spurred the need for different kinds of creative that move beyond Chinatowns and depict affluent suburban lifestyles (fig. 1.8). Asian Indians are similarly dispersed in the suburbs, but several of these regions have visible ethnic neighborhood and retail centers in California, New York, and New Jersey. These can be found in high-density areas of Silicon Valley, including Sunnyvale, Milpitas, Fremont, and San Jose; Jackson Heights in Queens, New York; and several towns in New Jersey, especially Edison. Ad executives use this knowledge to create robust opportunities for marketing, especially during flush economic times.

THE CURRENT ERA: 2008 AND ONWARD

Ebbs and flows in the advertising industry have affected the growth of Asian American agencies, the most dramatic of which can be seen in the impact of the 2008 financial crisis on U.S. advertising more broadly, according to Standard and Poor's *Net Advantage Reports*.[93] Prior to this time the United States was the "bread and butter" of the ad industry, although "ad spending in several international markets was growing at a significantly faster pace."[94] While American advertising agencies and conglomerates had operated in Asia for decades, in the years leading up to 2008 their expansion sharply increased, especially in China, Vietnam, and Indonesia, among the top ten countries at the time with the strongest ad spending growth prospects. Indeed by 2007 U.S.-based marketing groups had already begun taking advantage of a 2003 Chinese government policy that allowed foreign firms to hold a majority stake in Chinese companies. Especially after China lifted all restrictions on foreign ownership in advertising in 2006, this market flourished.[95] In August 2007 an S&P advertising industry survey reported a slowdown in U.S. advertising momentum that was not wholly attributed to cost-cutting measures or the economic slump. The rise of smartphones further encouraged consumer movement away from traditional print and television platforms and provided new opportunities to reach consumers with promotions and advertising.[96] Digital media had a significant impact on the newspaper ad industry, especially real estate classifieds during the housing decline and subprime mortgage crisis. Newspapers had begun to explore "strategic alternatives" in order to counter or offset this decline. During this time, however, magazine circulation and advertising revenue continued to grow due to their targetable audiences. As the Internet continued to garner a larger share of ad spending, so too did alternative forms of advertising and marketing. Indeed the 2000s were a decade of emerging media platforms, and American advertising underwent major changes with the Internet, digitally based advertising, mobile devices, and the like.

In 2008 consolidation among ad agencies also remained a trend, which continued into 2009, when I conducted the majority of my fieldwork. Industry reports from the time acknowledged those to be "tough economic times for businesses and consumers,"[97] with weak consumer spending overall, but especially in automotive and financial services. Although the recession officially ended in June 2009 according to the Business Cycle Dating Committee of the National Bureau of Economic Research, consumer spending remained cautious "as unemployment levels remained elevated and consumer confidence remained weak."[98] During this period Asian American agencies struggled to stay afloat; some contracted their personnel and others expanded their expertise to stay relevant. The state of the overall advertising industry and the Asian American market in particular were topics of ongoing internal discussion at Asian Ads during this time. Successes, such as market launches into previously untapped segments of the Asian American market, were celebrated as unqualified victories. Agency-wide meetings I attended in 2009 featured ongoing encouragement from higher-ups, such as "You guys have done great during the recession, and 2010 will be a very aggressive year for [Asian Ads'] growth. People will be spending again." Ad executives at several multicultural firms remarked that major insurance, automotive, and banking clients "who used to spend millions in the Asian American market, retracted," as Mr. Gitlin explained it.

Some of this shrinkage was due to the economy, but some was due to personnel changes, in which supporters of multicultural marketing were replaced by those with different priorities. Some clients that agencies had worked with prior to the recession were forced to cut their budget for multicultural advertising, despite the "real progress" that they saw from various measures, including Polk data collected from automobile sales. Asian American advertising and marketing for auto makers that accepted government bailout money disappeared from marketing priorities. Ms. Skriloff confirmed that multicultural advertising is often scrutinized when budget cuts happen. This is one of the reasons seasoned executives do not classify their work as "initiatives," which can seem like extras, but rather integrate them into overall marketing strategies in ways that make them harder to cut. Mr. Chang described the process as cyclical and explained that in his experience when the market is slow, Asian American advertising in general "takes a hit because it can be viewed as a lower priority" than Latino and other multicultural markets. The 2008 collapse of the American economy that affected countless corporate entities and their advertising budgets meant shrinking budgets for multicultural advertising, as well as a rise in aggregate approaches in which African American, Latino, and Asian American marketers were asked to collaborate to reach multicultural audiences. One strategy under such budget constraints was to make a spot that was adaptable and would appeal to both general markets and multicultural audiences, an approach that seemed to be favored in automobile ads.[99]

Coming out of the recession, Asian American ad executives presented Asian American consumers as "recession-proof," a descriptor that some ad executives leveraged more cautiously than others at first, until it started to sound like a well-proven fact. Such biopolitical moves, in which certain economic findings were linked to seemingly innate qualities in this racial group, underscores how Asian American ad executives managed this category in careful and deliberate ways. Even in a difficult economy, Mr. Chang elaborated, marketers are still looking for opportunities where they can find them, especially because they consider Asian Americans to be less affected by the economic downturn and they are able to "make a good case" based on research data that a product is a great fit for this niche audience. After the crash Asian American ad executives continued to tout the viability of this group by claiming they have the highest per capita income and education levels of any racial group. To balance out this viewpoint, which is not inaccurate but nonetheless skewed, I consider their claim in light of other economic and social research that has suggested a more varied range of economic positions. For instance, in response to the Pew Research Center's glowing 2012 report "The Rise of Asian Americans," the National Coalition for Asian Pacific American Community Development produced its own report (released June 2013) based on U.S. Census data, ACS updates to the census, and information pulled from the National Bureau of Economic Research. Key findings include that Asian American and Pacific Islanders (AAPIs) are one of the fastest growing poverty populations in the wake of the 2008 recession. From 2007 to 2011 the number of AAPI poor increased by 38 percent, whereas the number in the general population grew by 27 percent. The only other racial or ethnic group with a larger increase was Hispanic, at 42 percent.[100] There is other evidence to suggest that Asian Americans have the highest average income and education levels of any racial group, but they also have a higher poverty rate than non-Hispanic whites. A 2013 National Public Radio segment entitled "Asian-Americans: Smart, High Incomes and . . . Poor?" invited Algernon Austin of the Economic Policy Institute and Rosalind Chou, a Georgia State University sociology professor and coauthor of *The Myth of the Model Minority*, to weigh in on these issues.[101] A central point raised was that geography matters for cost of living; because Asian Americans are concentrated in some of the highest cost-of-living cities, their poverty rate is increased.[102] Such data offer important counterpoints to marketing claims of Asian American upward mobility and are important for the provisioning of vital social services for these and other struggling Americans.

The U.S. Census data that ad executives showcased predictably touted a different biopolitical narrative about this racial group and the ethnicities it contains. Asian American economic resilience, even triumph, through the recession has been vital for multicultural advertising recovery. As Ms. Skriloff put it, "The census is big and the results coming out have had a huge impact, so there is more interest than ever. The multicultural agencies feel vindicated and the people who haven't are now thinking about it."[103] Knowing "how to pull data" to foreground certain favorable attributes of Asian American consumers is an important skill. For instance, deciding whether to represent "Asian Alone" or "Asian Alone or in Combination," the latter of which would yield higher numbers in most categories, allowed marketers to show larger changes in advertising return on investment. Agencies reconfigured ethnic categories as needed and expanded their areas of expertise to keep clients interested. For instance, Ms. Bhasin, who focuses on Asian Indian and other South Asian populations, remarked that she had wanted to enter Chinese and Filipino markets for a while but did not feel pushed to do so until the economic downturn. During the 2008 recession, when small agencies were hit hard with budget cuts, she reached out to one of her larger clients for support, and they offered her additional ethnic market segments, including U.S.-based populations from "Asia, Africa, and Eastern Europe." She thus extended her expertise to portions of East Asia, North Africa, the Middle East, and Eastern Europe, broadening her opportunities considerably. Ms. Bhasin told me in 2011, when she expected the upward trend to continue, "We were really just looking for a way to survive in tough times."[104] In September 2013 her agency staged the public relations event "Diwali Times Square," with merchants, vendors, and performances taking over a sizable portion of this congested New York City locale (fig. 1.9). Considering that the long-standing South Street Seaport Diwali Festival was to be held as planned that year farther downtown, this venue for corporate promotion increased the visibility of brands as well as of South Asian Americans more broadly.

Overall in 2010 the advertising and publishing industries continued to experience contraction, but digital media was offering new opportunities for advertisers, as well as more serious threats to newspaper publishing. At this time the Federal Trade Commission was considering providing support to news organizations, in the form of regulatory measures, subsidies, or special tax treatments. By 2011 newspapers such as the *New York Times* had shifted to paid online models, while newspaper publishers more broadly benefited as advertisers boosted spending in an effort to protect market share and drive sales growth. I discuss these shifts at length in chapter 4 and consider how these new media have allowed for different spatial and temporal possibilities and a sense of urgency to rethink message for this new era. Noteworthy here is how multicultural ad agencies highlighted relevant aspects of 2010 Census data to reclaim advertising business at a

1.9 Diwali celebrated and promoted in Times Square, New York City. Photo by author (2013).

moment when general market executives reasserted their ability to best reach America's growing minority population. Some marketers call this "the new mainstream," and in the conclusion I discuss how general market agencies have been asserting their own set of terminologies about ethno-racial difference to substantiate their claim that they are better positioned than multicultural advertising agencies to reach minorities.

TOWARD CREATIVE

Asian Americans have appeared in the American public imagination largely during moments of conflict: with the alleged threats to American jobs posed in the early twentieth century; during militarized conflicts with Japan, Korea, and Vietnam; and most recently in the War on Terror and troubled relations with Pakistan and other Asian nation-states suspected of anti-American activity. The damage and hostility wrought by these conflicts are massive and never to be underestimated; yet in American advertising, these struggles have been made to appear distant threats or those that can be managed with a certain product or service. Both of these renderings contribute to overall meanings of race and ethnicity. Recent representations of Asian Americans in media have been favorable, especially compared to other minority groups. Latinos, for instance, are often negatively rendered in the media as an ongoing threat to the U.S. border, partaking in state education and services as illegal immigrants, and not contributing productively to nation-building projects or neoliberal economies.[105] By contrast, Asian Americans are more positively presented in public media reports as good citizens who are affluent or at least upwardly mobile, but who are nonetheless unassimilated, and in advertising worlds thought to be culturally and linguistically isolated.[106] In popular media they are recognized as model minorities but nonetheless treated as outsiders, leading some scholars to question whether this gentler, more socially acceptable model minority stereotype is not simply the yellow peril ideology in disguise. Jane Iwamura calls some Asian American stereotypes "virtual orientalism" and identifies modern counterparts to racist figures of the past, such as the "inscrutable Oriental, evil Fu Manchus, Yellow Peril, heathen Chinee, and Dragon Ladies."[107] These representations continue to obscure Asian Americans as a varied and complex group.

The persistence of yellow peril as a media discourse has been demonstrated in an excellent body of scholarship that identifies the ongoing xenophobia, yellowface, and fear and suspicion of Asian Americans.[108] General market ad executives can inadvertently or intentionally use stereotypical or racist imagery of Asian Americans in their ads, through casting and other means. It was apparent to me that many who work in Asian American advertising are acutely aware of these mass-mediated stereotypes of Asian Americans and the role advertising has played in perpetuating them.[109] Some advertising executives, however, considered their work a way to empower Asian Americans. The critical race and media theorists Robert Stam and Ella Shohat assert that the act of critique is necessary for dismantling domination and that identifying media stereotypes is essential to not reproducing them. During the 2011 3AF annual meeting, Asian Marketing Summit 2011: A Deep Dive into the Emerging Priority Segment, one of the many panels in this packed two-day conference was dedicated to "stereotypes versus insights in Asian American advertising" and featured the creative department heads of two major Asian American ad agencies, other creatives, and the head of an NGO focused on Asian American history and culture. The panel underscored the heightened degree of reflexivity in Asian American advertising and the social and historical awareness with which these ad executives approached their creative work and interactions with clients, as well as considered the reach of their media outlets. As I turn to this creative work, I consider the politics of what appears to be a positive representational shift.

As I look more closely at how Asian American history as well as current biopolitics and geopolitics shape ethnoracial assemblages, I find it useful to keep in mind that visual culture need not always reflect history or current events. Christopher Pinney has written, "The visual is also shown to be a zone in which new narratives are established that may be quite disjunct from the familiar stories of a nonvisual history." He identifies "disjunctures between images and their historical location."[110] This is an intriguing proposition, as it leads us to think about the generative possibilities of multicultural advertising. Such creative work, as my discussion of advertising and media has illustrated, is part of the anthropology of the contemporary. Hiro Miyazaki and Annalise Riles have strategized about how aesthetics plays a role in working through new ways of seeing and doing work. They quote Michael Fisher: "Traditional concepts and ways of doing things no longer work, . . . life is outrunning the pedagogies in which we have been trained." They contend that "it is not so much the failure of knowledge *per se* that is interesting, but rather the way this failure precipitates the 'assemblage' of old and new knowledge practices in expected and unexpected manners."[111] Advertising is being pushed to transform in a digital age, as is how we conceive of ethnicity and race through traditional metrics like the U.S. Census. My use of the concept of assemblage is to show the work of producing diversity for advertising and to reveal how biopolitical knowledge production is attempted and accomplished for commercial ends. Assemblages are inchoate and fleeting enough to capture the tension between biopolitical measures such as the U.S. Census, client demands for brand profit and growth, and advertising executives' desire to create evocative creative that inspires consumers to welcome advertising into the perceivable time and space of their lived existence.

Account planning here, as in the advertising industry, emphasizes the details that make creative work relevant and meaningful. The unique histories of each Asian ethnic group in the United States and how they have been variably counted and accounted for in the U.S. Census and other measures come to bear on how Asian Americans view themselves and their creative work. Like others in advertising, creatives are most concerned with cutting-edge approaches in advertising, focusing on branded messaging for broadcast media, digital media, and grassroots marketing. With the 2008 recession only beginning to fade from view, Asian American ad executives are cautious but also aware of the data-crunching opportunities presented in the 2010 U.S. Census and other surveys. With extensive background research and strategy developed through account planning in place, creative becomes an opportunity to bring linguistic and visual strategies to bear on brand identities and their adaptation, or "transcreation," for Asian American audiences. Balancing both, ad executives approach the delicate work of creating brands by linguistic, visual, and material means.

CHAPTER 2

Creative

We have to get into the Chinese consumer mind-set," creative director An Rong had earlier told his team. "Most of the Chinese families, they think about their life journey at every step of their life. It's like the circle of life. So they are looking for something complete, to fulfill their lives, to fulfill their dreams. The circle, the round, has a good meaning in the Chinese family." Team members were studying the creative brief that contained the strategy and insights of account planning for the insurance company campaign they were developing. In this campaign each of the ads for the three targeted ethnic segments would feature themes of education, life goals, and financial planning that conveyed the promise of a sound future with Allied Country. Creatives Jun Yi and Esther joined copywriter Andrew in a booth-like seating area in the front of the loft-style office, near elevators whose sounds punctuated their sentences. Cycling through ideas ranging from sport to art to family events, the creatives challenged one other about whether each concept conveyed enough "cultural insight." Midway through their conversation An Rong walked by with a mug of tea to check on his team's progress. Approving the use of the Allied Country logo to establish continuity across different Asian segments, he remarked on its potential to "build brand recognition in the community." Embodying the role of the intended consumer, Esther uttered the phrase "I choose Allied Country" as she mused over various concepts. Andrew suggested headline options that could work for each segment, assessing which ones held promise and which appeared to "overpromise," or make claims that could raise flags for the client's legal department. Later that week, when the team presented their creative on the phone, George the client responded favorably but nonetheless requested further glosses on the concept and copy. He politely explained, "I wanted to try to clarify, and I'm trying to adjust my thought processes. I'm looking at this and I'm trying to consume the concept in my English-speaking brain." In response to the uneasy laughter this comment drew, George added, "I like what you have to say. Maybe because I'm this English-thinking person who is not thinking about this from a cultural perspective." George's comments reiterated the importance of not only creating great in-language and in-culture creative but also making these translations and concepts as legible as possible to clients.

Constructing brand identity and messages for Asian American advertisements is a complex process, in which ad executives bring together linguistic and visual elements, including aspects of culture and language that are intended to resonate with audiences and convey the distinctive and affective dimensions of brand within the legal boundaries of what an ad can actually promise. The process of generating concepts and copy, what ad executives call *creative* (a term that is also used to describe the ad executives who do this work, e.g., the *Mad Men* character Don Draper), is premised on certain ideas about ethnoracial diversity, specifically how ideas about culture and language are linked with Asian ethnicities and the broader category of Asian American. At the same time creative also imagines consumers interacting with branded products and services in ways that reveal the assumptions about audiences that ad executives use as a basis for aspirational imagery. A mainstay of Asian American creative work is the generation and deployment of in-culture and in-language elements that are intended to set it apart from general market advertisements in ways that signal it as multicultural but also stay true to general market brand identity.

I focus on advertising development and production throughout this book, but especially here, to consider the semiotic aspects of racialization. I am particularly interested in how language and materiality interact in the construction of brand for Asian Americans, and how diversity acts as a qualisign because it is materialized through different visual and linguistic elements that index ethnicity. I also examine how certain language varieties become commodified in advertising, how they become resignified with visuals to take on new meanings, and the ways new norms and uses may be intentionally or inadvertently created with profitability in mind.[1] I present numerous examples drawn from different advertising accounts to illustrate the process of generating assemblages of ethnoracial diversity and how they are shaped and vetted by different constituencies and according to various agendas. Form and content of advertising creative are both important in this process, and I focus on the kind of storytelling and narrative production ad executives see themselves doing as they construct brand by connecting language, culture, and qualisigns of diversity. Assemblages of diversity, comprising lexical and visual indexes and icons intended to create brand identity, inform broader processes of racial naturalization.

BRANDS, DIVERSITY, AND CULTURE

Branding and consumer culture are integral parts of the work of the new economy, and advertising does a great deal of work in generating connections between goods and services and consumers. In chapter 1 I discussed how constructing and managing brand image became a mainstay of the advertising process in the 1980s; this trend has continued and diversified in the subsequent decades. Most large corporations have become deeply invested in how their products and services and the company itself are publicly represented. Individuals who act as brand managers are to maintain consistency and positive associations with brand identity, and do so through extensive interactions with the ad agencies they commission, through public relations, by hiring brand ambassadors, and by attempting to regulate the impact of consumer activity through brand consumption. Often brand ambassadors are stars from Asian countries, such as K-Pop (Korean pop music) sensation Hyuna (fig. 2.1), or the ubiquitous Psy, whose "Gangnam Style" led to his adaptation of the song for a "Wonderful Pistachios" general market Super Bowl spot. Highlighting the importance of connecting with the consumer, Robert Foster has argued, "The agency's explicit concern with the affective dimensions of the person-product relationship has now become the central preoccupation of brand managers."[2] There are indeed numerous players and parts in motion that all influence brand, and my focus in this chapter is on one aspect of this process: how brand identities are tailored for Asian American audiences in ways that are

2.1 Toyota Corolla print ad for Korean American consumers featuring K-Pop star Hyuna as a "brand ambassador" (2013).

consistent with general market advertising but that also convey tangible aspects of ethnically marked culture and language. I use the term *creative affect* in this chapter and elsewhere to refer to how ad executives use visual, verbal, and aural elements in their creative work. I differentiate this from *intercultural affect*, which I discuss in the next chapter, which refers to ad executives' stances in interactions with clients to gain and maintain their business.

Ad executives create brand identities for multicultural advertising in a process they call *transcreation*, a term I heard used in several Asian American ad agencies, glossed in a variety of ways. The term is a combination of *translation* and *creative* or *brand creation* and was never meant to be simply one or the other. A straightforward translation would likely miss the mark in terms of conveying relevant cultural insights, while creating brand identity anew would potentially cause disjuncture with the brand's identity in the general market. Thus transcreation is a way to tailor brand identities with in-culture and in-language signs to create identification for Asian American consumers. In practice this means that through transcreation ethnic differences are made identifiable and embodied in certain visual and linguistic elements, including actors, models, accent, creative affect, and voice. In looking at the process of transcreation, I am interested in the linguistic materiality of creative, the dynamic interplay of linguistic and material elements of signification.

Through advertising development and production indexical meanings can become iconic; that is, visuals combine with language such as advertising copy to project ethnic and racial culture. Charles Sanders Peirce's terms *indexical icon* and *qualisign* are useful for analyzing different aspects of this process.[3] According to Peirce, an index is a sign that stands for something based on its relationship and contiguity to it, and the relationship is established largely through either natural or cultural knowledge and shared context. "Smoke indexes fire" is a classic example, suggesting that the appearance of smoke indicates that something at that time, in that place, is burning. Icons, also signs, conjure a likeness between form and meaning. Indexical icons, according to Peirce, rely on spatially contingent elements that still bear likeness to the broader whole that they represent and contain a representation of the totality of which they are a part. Indexical icons are evident in some modes of signification ad executives use to represent ethnoracial diversity and help do the work of transcreation through in-culture and in-language signs. My discussion of transcreated brand identities as indexical icons draws attention to how conceptions of culture are incorporated into the work of creating brands for Asian American audiences. Through indexical relationships, in-culture and in-language elements stand for certain characteristics. Ad executives select indexical icons to do certain types of work, while the semiotics of cultural and linguistic translation complicate this process; considered together these processes reveal the ideological underpinnings of how ad executives represent diversity in ads as well as how linguistic materiality is operationalized in advertising.

Multicultural advertising's explicit use of cultural and linguistic elements allows it to create brand identities that act as indexical icons for diversity. Diversity, as I discussed in the introduction, is a concept that is difficult to pin down and tends to be defined differently by general market and multicultural market advertising. I use the concept of the qualisign—a sign that embodies a social or cultural quality—to draw attention to specific visual and linguistic elements that are intended to convey diversity in multicultural advertising. Nancy Munn developed Peirce's concept of the qualisign to consider how culturally valued qualities act as signs. Munn writes that qualisigns are icons in that "they exhibit something other than themselves *in* themselves."[4] These qualities cannot act as signs until they are embodied in some kind of materiality. Webb Keane has written extensively about this aspect of qualisigns and how qualities are conveyed as meaning through material forms, as well as how qualisigns are bundled to signify meaning.[5] If we consider how diversity is embodied in qualisigns, it is not surprising that the specific visual and linguistic materialities indexing diversity in an ad would vary between multicultural and general market advertising. In multicultural advertising, ethnicity and race index specific things: a language, a culture, a way of being part of a distinct ethnic or racial group in the United States. By contrast, in general market advertising diversity is indexed by anything that falls outside of a white middle-class norm, including the casting of nonwhite talent—actors, models, and real consumers. Indeed, as I discuss in chapter 4, ethnic ambiguity is a selling point for general market advertising because it allows advertising executives to signify diversity in the United States without having to include qualisigns that index specific linguistic or cultural difference. For general market executives the business of making ads diverse is essential for profit and growth, but specificity may not be the most effective approach, as it is for multicultural advertising. In the latter, representing Asian Americans and individual Asian ethnic groups can be done in a number of ways, but the specifics of language and culture make ambiguity difficult. Getting diversity right through transcreation means a potential boost in brand identity, while the consequences of getting ethnic and racial representations wrong can be disastrous.

In multicultural advertising, creative is about constructing assemblages of ethnoracial diversity. This involves creating consumer identification for Asian Americans and conveying creative affect in ways that draw in consumers to identify with brands in culturally and linguistically specific ways. I use the concept of assemblage to bring together a range of semiotic elements of brand identity, including indexical icons and qualisigns, with the cultural and linguistic labor of generating creative, as well as the intercultural affective labor of negotiating this work with clients. Assemblage allows me to integrate these material and linguistic elements as contributing to the overall qualities and meanings that transcreated brand identities are intended to convey. Anthropologists have argued that assemblages are difficult to study ethnographically precisely because of their ephemeral, emergent, evanescent, decentered, and heterogeneous qualities.[6] My efforts to bring language into the assemblage while considering materiality, in ways that are not overdetermining, help to overcome these challenges. Assemblages of diversity include the creative work of the ads themselves as part of a broader *process of assembling* diversity in the new economy. That is, they operate within the dynamics of racialized capitalism that govern the work of multicultural advertising in corporate America and the range of semiotic meanings that ads can convey to clients, to ad executives, and to audiences at different points in time. The creative process captures rare glimpses of how actual assembling happens, from the selection of cultural and linguistic signs, their shared indexical values, and other meanings they come to represent as they circulate.

Creative Strategy and Brand

The most important goal of advertising, whether niche or general market, is constructing brands to increase the sale of products and services. Much that has been written about brands in recent decades emphasizes their multifaceted role in consumer lives and their potential for social transformation, intended or inadvertent.[7] Mandy, a general market account executive, explained that the goal of the creative process is to "bring some kind of elevated brand presence through our work."[8] Many executives named exemplary brands that they believe succeed in capturing consumer loyalty. Drawing a comparison to a theme park account she was working on in 2008, Mandy remarked, "When you say 'Disney,' you have an emotional, visceral feeling. . . . They've invested in that brand for decades and decades and decades. . . . When you say [theme park], it's a very flat experience, and it's not an experience or a feeling that we've crafted and put into the marketplace." Brands that are able to elicit an intense emotional connection with the consumer, what Robert Foster calls "lovemarks," seem to be an ideal that advertising executives strive for, but first and foremost they try to please their clients.[9] Ad executives described clients as being either "product-oriented" or "brand-oriented" and approached creative accordingly. Using automobile makers to illustrate this difference to me, Alice, an Asian American ad executive, identified Nissan as very product-oriented, in that the specific models are showcased in ads, while Subaru is brand-oriented: "owning a Subaru" is far more powerful than the features of a specific model.[10] These considerations become significant when advertising executives are asked to launch a brand to a specific Asian American segment or to create a seasonal campaign tailored to their client's needs. In either case most creative was guided by a document called the "creative brief," which outlines a set of communications objectives based on market research. This research is conducted either by the client's marketing department or by the agency's account planning department, or both, and serves as an important basis of creative work. At more than one creative meeting I heard managers remind their creatives that advertising is less about art and more about executing the objectives outlined in the creative brief. As one creative director put it, "A lot of times, creatives get caught up in the artistry rather than the strategy. So setting them up to serve the client and establishing a framework for thinking is important."[11] While creative briefs take different forms, most offer key insights about the brand, the intended consumer, and the desired outcome of advertising. The following is drawn from a creative brief that was shared with me at a Los Angeles agency and is very similar to others I read. It indicates that a well-executed creative message should communicate:

1. The target: Who am I? What am I like? What am I into?
2. The current target perception: What do I believe about the category, brand, or product before seeing the communication?
3. Insight: What consumer understanding will inspire brand growth?
4. Evidence: Why should consumers believe the message?
5. Desired target perception: What should I think, feel, believe, or do after seeing the creative?
6. Tone: What do we want this communication to feel like?

Noteworthy here are the deictic shifts between the first-person and third-person pronouns that occur across these objectives. The first two objectives use *I* to place the creative in the place of the consumer; objectives 3 and 4 shift to *the consumer*, only to return to *I* to imagine the desired target perception. Objective 6, creative affect, uses *we* as a way to signal a shared emotional experience that ad executives and consumers could have with the brand. This suggests that creatives should ideally see the brand through the consumers' eyes while also maintaining an analytic distance so as to keep broader strategic objectives in mind. Such toggling is intended to remind creatives to generate the type of emotional connection that would appeal to them as intended consumers while also attending to market research and other relevant strategies.

The first-person perspective of objectives 1 and 2 of the creative brief often led to creatives spending a great deal of time fleshing out imagined consumers based along these lines. Sometimes this was best addressed in an ideal consumer character, developed for pitch and marketing purposes.

2.2 Character sketch for a client pitch (2009).

These consumer sketches, which I have discussed elsewhere in detail, allow clients to see how a particular population might interact with their brand.[12] In these sketches characters come to life; they are given a name, age, job, family, hobbies, place of residence, and other relevant demographic information (fig. 2.2). In presentations they are further personified through the ways ad executives give voice to them; for example, by introducing them as one would a person: "Meet Sally!" or "This is Mohammad!" Such voicings are common devices to flesh out for clients the contours of how an intended consumer might interact with a certain brand. They are thus useful to the creatives who do the work but also effective for illustrating to clients how target populations might engage with their brand. Many account executives I spoke with in both multicultural and general market advertising believed personal sketches are an especially effective tool for pitches in which data alone were insufficient to convey a broader experience. A key difference is that Asian American advertising executives used sketches, as well as other creative materials, to highlight specific ethnic cultural and linguistic signs that would index diversity, while general market executives emphasized the inclusion of nonwhite talent to do this work.

General Market Approaches to Branding and Diversity

General market ad executives I spoke with described their ideal creative as first and foremost being "normal." Multicultural advertising terms like *in-culture* and *in-language* were not used, because for them *culture* referred to something other than the white mainstream, and *language* referred to languages other than American English. General market ad executives used a different frame and were invested in how to make ads as normal as possible and avoid anything that would be construed as "fake." In a lengthy conversation I had with Greg, an account executive at a major general market agency, he emphasized his concern about "trying to make commercials that don't look like commercials. We're always trying to make things feel realer, because everybody is going to watch your commercials, **forever**."[13] Referring to the eternal life of advertisements on the Internet, especially YouTube, he emphasized the need for great care when making creative. The example that he and other general market ad executives repeatedly offered as undesirable was a United Colors of Benetton approach (fig. 2.3). This ubiquitous campaign from the 1980s and 1990s that assembled gaunt models of different races rang false to his colleagues and him; they considered it "bullshit." Greg remarked, "More and more people want [ads] to be real.... If you have five models, and they're all different colors, and they're beautiful-looking people, and they're all shiny, happy, you see through it right away. You can almost see the meeting where somebody said, 'We need to have one of these guys, one of these guys.'" Such a viewpoint underscores how "normal" should look, and how certain constellations of race and ethnicity do not fit this bill.

Often the mere inclusion of nonwhite talent acts as a qualisign of diversity. This approach to representing diversity, a strategy that was especially important for casting, was central to general market approaches to creative. Yet meeting the requirement of diversity simply through racial and ethnic quotas was off-putting to ad executives. Greg put himself in the position of a cynical consumer: "[We] don't want someone to be watching it and just going, 'Oh somebody must have said they needed a black guy.'" Instead he advocated for a much less curated look, even though this took just as much effort. He described what this could look like: "This is just a natural setting, and these are just the people who happen to be there on a particular day, and so that's kind of what we shoot for." Significant here is the careful meditation that goes into making something casual and natural rather than overtly inclusive. General market agencies thus strove to ad-

2.3 Print ad for United Colors of Benetton featuring an explicitly multiracial cast typical of this brand (1990s).

dress diversity but had far more flexibility about what it could look like and were held to less specific standards than Asian American executives about which visual and linguistic elements would index culture.

Asian American Market Approaches to Branding and Diversity

Creatives in Asian American advertising, by contrast, were subject to scrutiny about the "culture question." They often had to make apparent the need for multicultural advertising through the specificity of their creative and justify their work to their clients, as in the opening vignette. This involved drawing explicit attention to identifiable in-culture and in-language elements intended to resonate with Asian American audiences — often the same elements that made their work different from the general market campaign. The question often arose of why clients would choose to spend additional capital to hire multicultural agencies and buy additional media to make Asian American advertising if the ads would not be significantly different from their general market campaigns. In Asian American advertising, brand is culturally and linguistically constructed in executives' talk about their creative work and how they objectify culture as something conveyed by ethnically identifiable actors and marked cultural signs. Ex-

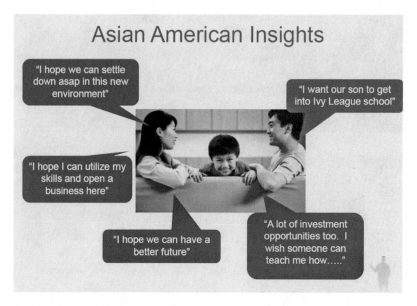

2.4 Slide from a client presentation for an ad featuring in-culture insights voiced by Asian American consumers (2009).

amining the specifics of in-culture and in-language transcreation further exemplifies how indexical icons are selectively used alongside what ad executives call "cultural insights" to produce creative that clients can recognize as "diverse."

"Where is the culture?" is a question I heard routinely on conference calls with clients during creative presentations, as well as preemptively in internal creative meetings. Providing tangible evidence of "Asian insights," "Asianness," "cultural insights," and simply "the cultural" meant explaining to clients the relevance of indexical icons about an Asian ethnic group and including icons that would appeal to their concerns about culture (fig. 2.4). "The culture" could take many forms, such as showcasing major Asian ethnic holidays, like Lunar New Year, Diwali, and Eid; characters of the Chinese zodiac; and Independence Day celebrations. Susan, CEO of an Asian American ad agency, referred to this as "graphic Asianness."[14] Admitting that she was exaggerating for the sake of illustration, she painted this picture: "[If a] character in this ad is drinking coffee, can you make him drink tea? There's always that security blanket of wanting to see an iconic Asian American thing to make **everyone**, including the advertising agency, feel comfortable that we're doing something Asian American. It can't be Asian

American if there's no Asian American icon."[15] Susan's frustration seemed to stem from the notion that creative has to contain signs that clients will recognize as icons of Asian America, such as tea, dragons, the color red, cricket, and Bollywood. But such icons may differ from those signs Asian American ad executives consider ideal. Indexical icons are more akin to cultural insights that Asian American ad executives generate to signify more nuanced attributes of Asian ethnicities.

IN-CULTURE TRANSCREATION

Asian American ad executives engage in a process they call transcreation, which requires a metalevel understanding of both general market brand identity and cultural and linguistic signs that will resonate with Asian American consumers. Transcreation calls for an intimate understanding of what *mainstream* means and how seemingly objective terms like *normal* are code for "white" and "English" as opposed to "Asian" and "non-English." It also requires intricate knowledge of how cultural and linguistic signs should be used to create brand identification for Asian American audiences. Elsewhere I have termed this process *metaproduction* to draw attention to the metalevel at which multicultural ad executives interpret general market brand identities for Asian American consumers.[16] In some ways this is a contradictory process that reveals the tense position Asian American advertising occupies in relation to the general market. If Asian American consumers really are so different from those in the general market, will Asian American ad executives even understand them? But if they are not really that different, then is multicultural advertising even necessary? In some ways Asian American ad executives presented themselves to clients and peers in the ad industry as cultural and linguistic translators for a group that was already fluent in American consumer culture. By positioning themselves as experts on this population, they offered the promise of furthering brand identities in ways that would not be possible through general market advertising alone.

Indexical Icons of Culture

Transcreation is accomplished in multiple creative and interpersonal processes and is premised largely on cultural insights that can be communicated visually and linguistically. Asian American ad executives I spoke with recognized the paradoxical nature of objectifying culture for advertising using a limited set of icons, primarily to please clients. In the white American imagination, Asians in the United States seem to be an extension of what has become iconic about Asia in U.S. popular culture. Motifs such as Bollywood, cricket, Kung Fu, yoga, and Confucian wisdom all came up in conversations as themes that have excited clients. These qualisigns certainly index diversity, but they may do so in ways that seem too simplistic and obvious for Asian American ad executives. Susan's striking comment about Asian iconicity was on par with what I heard from other niche executives. Creative director Ron called the use of overt cultural markers without any critical twists "Chinking it up," which his agency tries to avoid because their consumers live in the United States and know about general market advertising. This could include traditional Asian music or the unnatural inclusion of Asian food. "They don't need the pandering," he stated authoritatively, indicating that reliance on such common icons could backfire with Asian American audiences. When I asked Morris, a creative in a Los Angeles–based Asian American ad agency, for his thoughts on the topic of cultural insights, he politely smiled and replied, "Yeah, I think we're past that part?"[17] Likewise critiquing what he saw as a superficial approach, account executive Sunil, who frequently drew on his advertising experience in Mumbai, where he reached the "general market" of Indians, remarked, "Not everything is about language and culture."[18] He criticized the approach of using overt Asian imagery to "retrofit general market campaigns" for specific Asian American audiences.

Yet Sunil, like others, admitted how hard it was to convince clients that more subtle creative would resonate with Asian American consumers because it lacks iconicity altogether. Creative that bore no resemblance to Asian Americans ran the risk of not being an effective qualisign of diversity. He knew he would have to answer to his clients about this, and I heard Sunil ask his creatives on numerous occasions, "Where is the cultural?" Others also conceded that their approach included what I identify as icons alongside indexical icons to please clients. When I asked Morris to elaborate on what he regarded as cultural insights, he somewhat reluctantly admitted, "Yeah, like, we have to include a dragon, or like, green tea or *boba* (tapioca or 'bubble' tea), but we don't want to go that route. . . . We have to really go deeper into what [our viewers] are thinking and the insights behind how they perceive the world around them." About this account director Steve remarked, "We stereotype ourselves sometimes in the ads that we produce. You know, not **everyone** is a fan of the color red, or Bollywood, or cricket. I mean **a lot** of our clients want to do cricket ads because certainly there's an appeal, but you gotta do it in a way that's balanced." The ideal approach seemed to involve selecting aspects of immigration histories and displaying a cultural understanding about demographic patterns, rather than using more obvious icons of Asian culture. Effectively identifying a "consumer insight" was potentially a way to sidestep the need for these icons, such as dragons or tea consumption. Alice suggested, "If you are able to correctly identify a consumer insight, then you don't get comments like 'Where's the Asian insight?' because you've already told them what the Asian insight is." If ad executives generated indexical icons of Asian Americans that captured something meaningful about the *experience* of living, working, and consuming in the United States, this would trump the need to pepper ads with icons that the average Asian American consumer might find clichéd and therefore ineffective. Some cultural insights took the form of stories common to the post-1965 Asian immigrant experience. For instance, moving from an Asian country, establishing a home and family, and creating a comfortable life is a common immigrant story that plays itself out in a distinctive way for well-educated, post-1965 immigrants. Steve explained that the challenge for his creatives was to generate stories relevant to this aspect of the Asian American experience. For instance, ad executives believed that the American Dream of homeownership and life security to promote financial service companies would be an apt theme for Asian Americans, who are considered upwardly mobile people who plan for their fiscal future. Through this approach to their creative work, ad executives' versions of indexical icons could perhaps, over time, become more mainstream icons of Asian American culture.

Thus Asian American creative often boiled down to the question of what "culture" should look like. Ron, a creative director who joined an Asian American agency after decades in general market, told me that he had to be brought up to speed on the "cultural touchstones" for each ethnic group, but that these did not dictate his work. Alice, an LA-based account executive, similarly remarked that events like the Moon Festival have to be represented in a culturally specific way, but other products, like cars and theme parks, are things that everyone uses: "The ads for non-Asian-specific things don't need to be so Asian, not that much different. So the challenge is going to the client and saying that they have certain skills in advertising to the Asian market but the ads don't look that different at the end." These ad executives believed that being "modern" allowed them to get ahead in the long term and position themselves as legitimate competitors in the advertising world. This essentially meant being considered an "advertising agency" rather than an "Asian American advertising agency" and producing high-quality creative that would appeal to Asian American as well as general market audiences. Alice explained, "In advertising, you really want to be ahead of the curve." She offered the thoughtful illustration of using an iconic object such as chopsticks in original ways, as she had observed in a recent visit to Japan: "We have to be able to use the imagery that we're very used to seeing, chopsticks and even moon cakes and even dragons. But we rearrange it so that the creative is super, super modern. I think the next wave." Identifying effective indexical icons is one creative strategy to create audience identification; another is to feature Asian American talent and tailor the ad to resonate with Asian American leisure preferences. In one execution that involved a hip-hop and modern dance face-off in a large, sunny LA loft, the client was so enthused that she immediately saw the potential to run the ad in southern California and regions of the western and southwestern United States. In this instance messaging featuring Asian American actors and some in-culture elements nicely represented the "American" in Asian American.

Yet the in-culture element had to extend beyond casting Asian American talent, and in more subtle creative, in-culture elements had to be emphasized to the client. Ensuring that a "cultural touch" is not "old-fashioned" is something Joyce, a New York–based account executive, conveys to her clients. "So if you let [clients] know that that's what people want, that's what people are looking for, they're pretty receptive to the idea that tradition can also be fancy in a way." In a creative session I observed at one Asian American agency, ad executives discussed how to be "edgier" and "less Asian" in an iconic sense. They contemplated the tonality of a campaign for television by focusing on clever, hip conceits that might feature Godzilla and video game avatars. While these conceits could be risky vis-à-vis the "Where is the culture?" query, such an approach offered the potential to more subtly situate Asian Americans in the American consumer landscape while also catering to them as consumers. Along these lines, some creatives I spoke with found it difficult to sell their subtler creative. Midori, a creative, told me, "Some clients are pretty stubborn and they can't let go of what they believe in, so we have to ease it in to really make them believe what we are trying to say."[19] Doing this type of brokering between their imagined audiences and a white corporate America is "one of the hardest things that we have to do." These multicultural creative approaches suggest that the transition from iconic in-culture to indexically iconic creative was at its very early stages.

One of the reasons clients worked with multicultural agencies is that they feared general market agencies did not have the cultural and linguistic expertise to execute details properly. Even multicultural agencies that routinely did in-culture ads were quite careful about the cultural insights they presented. I learned this firsthand when I was revisiting an Asian American ad agency where I had already met most of the executives. On the schedule of interviews I had requested was an item called "Strategic meeting with Dr. Shankar." When I asked the friendly and helpful account executive who had put together my schedule what that meant, he cheerfully told me, "[It's] all about you!" And he was right, as it turned out to be a focus group in which I was the sole participant. A collection of account executives and creatives trawled for cultural insights about Asian Indian consumers and solicited my feedback on ads already made. I was asked to offer my perspective on tonality: Did I prefer that insurance ads be funny or poignant? Did I most relate to the Geico Gecko, Flo from Progressive, or Allstate's Mayhem or Andrew Haysbert ads? Showing me ads they had made, they asked if I was able to find the errors in certain cultural representations that they had been told they got wrong. For instance, did it make me angry that they forgot to put a *bindi* on a woman wearing a sari? Did the bearded man at the Hindu wedding look too Pakistani? Was their use of Bollywood too North Indian?[20] This showed me that doing in-culture creative was a highly subjective process that was open to both praise and criticism based on accuracy. When done right, these signs could act as indexical icons for Asian American audiences, while they also act as qualisigns of diversity for clients. A bindi, for instance, was a tangible sign that ad executives could indicate as important but would do the additional work of creating identification among certain Asian Indian consumers.

Getting this balance right was important because, as much as ad executives were concerned with accuracy, they were also interested in the quality of their work. Nearly all the Asian American creatives I met shared the ideals of general market creatives who wanted to make ads that were original, nuanced, and memorable. In-culture concepts for Asian American audiences varied according to ethnic group. Broader ideas that were thought to resonate across these ethnic groups were filial piety, education, respect for elders, and an active connection with a real or imagined homeland. Cultural insights could also be informed by experience. Creative director Joey noted the relevance of Asian Americans saving for future generations so that children may achieve a greater degree of success than their parents, calling this "decision making based on heritage and tradition."[21] He added, "You have to have lived through it or have been a part of it to understand it. Each ethnic group has a different way of going about their decision-making process. Even among these differences there are some universal similarities." Within the broader category of Asian American, these commonalities had to be fine-tuned. An Rong, another creative director, explained that to target Chinese American consumers one had to understand their "mind-set." Acknowledging the great variance among this group, he nonetheless contended, "I think they share some common ground or universal truth, and we inspire them to take interest." Getting indexical icons right is very important in multicultural advertising.

Transcreating Culture

For advertising executives, representing culturally specific norms is effective only if they are correctly nuanced. Jayshree, a creative and copywriter, used market research to divide South Asian Americans into class-based segments that would be the basis for developing creative concepts and writing appropriate copy for a pitch for Send Cash, a money-transfer company. To properly define the three segments—blue collar, white collar, and businessman—she interviewed people and conducted her own research. This was one of the few campaigns that moved beyond Asian Indian to include Pakistani, Bangladeshi, and Sri Lankan sketches as well. When I told her I did not know how to answer her question about whether her classifications were correct, she agreed that it was complicated to choose representative types because there are so many options. As a creative, it was largely up to her and others with specific in-culture knowledge to make decisions about how to represent culture. In another ad for this campaign, two creatives sought to generate a concept based on similar class distinctions among Filipino Americans. As Andrew, a Filipino American, and Jun Yi, a Chinese American, sat discussing scenarios and camera angles during a creative brainstorming session, they began to debate the class-based implications of the Filipino practice of pinning money on a bride. Unfamiliar with this custom, Jun Yi hesitantly remarked, "It's kind of funny?" "If you say so," Andrew countered. Jun Yi suggested that it might not happen in all social classes: "I think it's mostly below middle class. So middle-class people, I think they find it tacky." Andrew concurred that this may not be as relevant for higher social classes, confirming that getting this cultural insight correct would require attention to class, not just ethnicity.

Gender is another area that ad executives often considered overtly or in ways that seemed to rely on certain norms. The notion of the patriarch seemed to prevail in Asian American advertising, and male characters were preferred in those ads where financial decisions were involved, not unlike general market creative. Such a choice suggested a fairly traditional notion of men as the primary household earners and decision makers. In ads for cars, especially minivans, women tended to be the principal characters. Some creatives seemed to have a strong point of view about which gender would convey the attributes they wished to project as part of a brand's identity, often resulting in differences of opinion. In a print ad that could have featured either a girl baby or a boy baby (although both babies who were photographed for the ad wore white T-shirts and their sex was not easy to distinguish), An Rong thought the boy baby would be more appropriate, even though most of his colleagues chose the girl. He offered this rationale: "Besides me, everybody felt very confident with the girl because she is so cute. I thought the boy baby could [better] sell this product. He looks smart. As a parent, you want to give him the full potential to grow and have a bright future. That girl is just cute, you want to hold her, but she doesn't have the selling power." As we spoke further, I learned that everyone else in the office had laughed at his assessment and asked, "How can you tell that the boy is smarter?" He countered, "Some babies look sweet, some look mature, some look smart. And that's my personal judgment." For the most part gender was dictated either by market research about the brand or product in question, the creative, or the available talent. In many cases, however, the specific discussions about gender and the significance of certain choices suggested that Asian American ad executives imagined their audience to be far more patriarchal and steeped in hierarchies of gender than was reflected in their own agency culture. Individuals of all sexual orientations were welcome in agencies, but I observed only heterosexual couples in creative.

Minute creative details pertaining to gender and class were critical, as they constituted the grist of in-culture creative that would ideally become well-received qualisigns. Much of this was handled in production during casting, art direction, and filming, but the placeholders or mock-ups that creatives make to show to clients have to convey in-culture details as accurately as possible. In a new campaign for Send Cash, many small adjustments were made in executing the broader conceit of connecting Asian

Americans to their home countries through money transfer. In an internal creative review meeting, Jun Yi pored over every visual detail in order to get the smallest elements right. The notes he and creative director An Rong gave Jayshree included the following: "Can you make your IT guy look less corporate? Get rid of his suit and tie, and put some servers in the background." In another sketch, to be set in a fabric store, Jun Yi and An Rong quizzed Jayshree about whether the owner of a small fabric store in India would be lower class or middle class. Should the saris be folded on shelves, in stacked fabric bolts, or hanging from circular racks? Jun Yi preferred hangers, but Jayshree convinced him that the stores with blankets on the floor and folded piles of saris were more authentic and would have a bigger selection. This worked well on all fronts, as the folded version looked cleaner visually. Other matters, such as whether the store should be carpeted, whether it had air-conditioning or an open storefront, track lighting or lamps, men wearing shirts and pants or *salwaar kameez*, were all debated extensively. Similarly detailed questions were asked about an ad featuring a family in a Diwali scene to balance out the male-centered ads in the South Asian segment.

The ads for the Filipino and Chinese segments for the Send Cash campaign were likewise scrutinized for in-culture accuracy. For the first, a female nurse was a central character, drawing on an archetype while also keeping true to the types of geopolitical and historical events that would make a Filipino nurse a very apt choice. Other lifestyle markers—about marriage, children, homeownership, living with extended family, and similar matters—came up periodically and were carefully considered. Debating the applicability of copy Andrew had written for a mock-up of a Chinese ad featuring a couple, "Sharing a wonderful life together," the team questioned whether this would imply marriage. Andrew conceded that it could simply suggest that the couple lived together and that this could be perceived negatively. He countered, "How about 'Love at first sight'?" An Rong agreed that would be fine, but quickly added, "But after that you should get married, right?" That An Rong was himself an unmarried gay man underscored his commitment to having the creative reflect the mainstream ideologies and beliefs of the intended audience. He had certainly professed other beliefs and hopes in casual conversation, but as far as ads were concerned, heterosexual and married prevailed as the norm. Attempts to establish norms in-culture were open to discussion, but only to an extent.

As these creative concepts illustrate, details such as class, gender, reli-

2.5 Hand-drawn rough creative sketch for initial creative brainstorming session, segmenting targeted Asian Indian consumer base into categories of "IT," "Taxi Driver," and "Business Man" (2009).

gion, leisure preferences, and dietary trends were complicated and elaborated within each Asian group and became even more confounding when variances across the Asian American category were considered. For this reason Asian American ad executives often generated "character sketches" or "reels" to personify and visually convey cultural information to clients in friendly, easily digestible ways. For example, Jayshree used the class-based categories I described earlier to design sketches so that the agency's prospective client could better understand these differences. Often the most challenging part of doing creative was to convince clients of an idea or a concept; for multicultural advertising, being able to represent this visually was a tried and true strategy. For instance, creatives often used stock photos from Internet sites as placeholders for creative concepts that they could execute with original artwork should they get client approval. Presenting these visuals to a client could begin to diversify the familiar visions of white consumers with friendly, ethnically marked minorities. Jayshree admitted that even finding images for this type of work was difficult because "there are many more pictures of Caucasians." When faced with this issue, she resorted to using an image of a white person in a particular pose or setting and "made them Asian" by using the graphic design program

Photoshop. She remarked casually, "There are plenty of pictures of Indian heads on the web, so I change the skin color of the body to match the face."

The assumption here was that clients needed a more user-friendly way of digesting unfamiliar cultural information and that visual representations would work far better than a simple fact sheet or print presentation. This was the approach taken in a pitch for the company Send Cash. Account executive Sunil assembled a team that included account director Sheng Li, account executive Maya, creative Jayshree, and me to explain that we were to collaborate to create what he called a "brand print." Sunil defined this as an "audiovisual format for presenting a consumer insight that focuses on people." The execution was essentially like a movie trailer, and this one would feature a montage of Bollywood clips. According to Sunil, Bollywood would be an accessible motif for this client. Explaining that he successfully used this technique in the large multinational agency he had worked for in Mumbai, he underscored that the intent of this type of pitch tool should be "above all, fun!" When Jayshree could not quite grasp the larger point of this approach, Sunil broke it down like this: "The consumer sketch is great, but it's nothing new that they don't know, right? We want to make it lighter, we want [our clients] to have smiles on their faces." He recounted a recent print ad by a Mumbai colleague that featured the title song from the popular Bollywood film *Main Hu Na*. Before he could elaborate, Maya and Jayshree spontaneously burst into song and did the work of illustrating just how fun a brand print could be. Indeed, they were being asked to create an entertaining, feel-good brand experience for the client and impress them in the process. Consumer sketches and brand prints contained qualisigns of diversity, such as Hindi songs, bindis, ethnic clothes, and the talent themselves, all of which would help transcreate this brand for Asian American audiences while also acting as visible signs of diversity to the client. By personifying indexical information through iconic figures, the brand print moved beyond simple icons such as dragons and gave the client a more nuanced sense of an ideal Asian American consumer. Moreover such marketing tools transformed what would otherwise be a tremendous amount of detail into a friendly, accessible visual with a limited amount of vital details. By sketching out the lifestyles, priorities, and consumption patterns of these consumers with the use of attractive actors, the team made Asian Americans a normalized yet appealing consumer population. Such activities do the important work of making in-culture indexical icons tangible and accessible to clients, while still emphasizing their difference from general market signs of diversity.

Ad executives innovated to generate in-culture creative that was relevant to a brand but seemed new and different from past campaigns and executions. For many agencies the Chinese zodiac of annual symbols offered a good basis for creative. As they prepared for 2010, the Year of the Tiger, creative abounded in images of tigers. Suggestions were even made to "Sinocize" relevant figures in American popular culture, such as Kellogg's Tony the Tiger, for an Asian-themed promotion. In other accounts innovation was more carefully monitored and limited by a company's or product's "brand bible." Such a set of constraints protected a brand's image and ensured consistency across executions. While the tone of a brand's identity could shift according to campaign—from playful to poignant to serious—other elements were kept consistent so that brand recognition was accomplished despite creative innovations. Even in executions that clients loved, details about color choice for a background, font, and other details were critically examined. For example, in one Asian Ads print ad presentation for a home improvement store, the client voiced concern to the account team over the speakerphone: "I'm wondering about the color choice for the background, about the pinkish. I want to make sure, it is a bit off in terms of the [store name] brand." The account executive explained that it looked red on her computer and offered to change it to beige. The client reminded the team about the permitted colors listed in the brand bible and suggested, "The concept is good, let's try a couple of different colors for the background and go from there, okay?" Even though this color modification was done as part of their in-culture transcreation, it nonetheless had to comply with the brand's general market identity as specified in the brand bible.

While all transcreation requires creative concepts and copy, some clients gave their Asian American agencies more latitude than others. Some clients, such as one major home improvement chain, usually wanted ethnic versions of their general market ads. Others, like financial services clients, were much more open to original creative. Either way, generating a number of possibilities for the account team and eventually client to consider was standard in most agencies. At most agencies the creatives met first before presenting their concepts to the rest of the account team. In a few, collaboration occurred with executives from all departments, so that creatives could "visualize the execution," as Morris explained to me, and others could ensure that it supported "the branding message behind the campaign." Morris added, "So I want to make sure it all makes sense and it also makes sense to the Asian audience." This team approach was especially important in smaller agencies that did not have large budgets and were limited in how much creative they could develop. These ad executives had to be selective about how to address the creative strategy, given that they sometimes made only one print ad or spot for a given campaign rather than an entire series of ads.

The process of doing transcreation was in some ways like creative brainstorming in general market advertising, where ad executives sat in a room with a creative brief, discussed the objectives and format of the communication, and generated ideas, often with the product in the room. For instance, in one creative brainstorming session for a mango-flavored drink, creatives jokingly asked the account executive, "How come you didn't bring any smoothies for us?" The account executive quickly diverted attention away from the lack of smoothies by praising the recent good work her team had done and how this had resulted in increased investment by the client in the form of longer commercials. Going from the fifteen- to thirty-second spot was a significant move, and the team had to consider how to adapt their approach to this longer format. They then considered how to create an "umbrella concept" that could be tailored to different segments of the Asian American market. One of the team's first tasks was to resolve the language issue if they went for a pan-Asian creative strategy. Generally pan–Asian American ads were reserved for public service announcements that were intended to reach a broad audience, such as the San Francisco Hep B Free campaign (fig. I.5). One creative reminded the others that pan-Asian potential for the ad meant that they "cannot have the principals speak because of the language issue, as the client has asked for the ad in English, Taglish, Cantonese, Mandarin, and Korean." In this case a voice-over would be added in each language. Other concerns included ideas about consumer mind-set and which regions of the United States they would focus on to target certain Asian American communities.

Many creatives approached their creative brainstorming sessions by sketching their concepts, as I saw Asian Ads creative Esther do on multiple occasions. She outlined to me how she responds to a creative brief: "When you get that creative brief from your client, you make some sketches that address it." She added, "**You** should try it." Later that afternoon she gave me a copy of a creative brief she had just received from her creative director and suggested I get busy sketching. The next day, before the creative brainstorming session, I showed her my amateurish scribbles. Glancing admiringly at hers in the meeting, I was grateful that Esther kindly did not share my failings with the team. It did help me experience firsthand how challenging creative work was, especially moving from a rather dry brief to a lifelike concept. At the meeting creatives each came with their concepts, some sketched, some explained verbally, others conveyed with a combination of visual, verbal, and embodiments. In a conversation with me later Esther explained, "Usually we create a few different possibilities. Ninety percent of the time [clients] follow the recommendation. Ten percent of the time they say, 'We think this other one is even better than your recommendation, so we want to go with that.' We always say yes to that."

Creatives can approach the process of creating messaging for brand in dialogic ways, voicing the role of the consumer interacting with the ad. At an internal creative review for an ad for the insurance and financial services company Allied Country, which I observed and audio-recorded, creative director An Rong framed the conversation with the guiding question "How do we create a strong brand?" Although they had already had several preliminary meetings and conversations, the presentation to others outside the creative team was reframed in terms of broader goals and objectives, and the creative presented was discussed and assessed as such. The following excerpt from this meeting took place after creatives Andrew and Jun Yi presented two concepts for an ad campaign, each with several executions. After their presentation, creative Esther and office manager Paul were asked to judge, and each focused on why they liked the creative concept, which made clever use of the client's logo. In this portion of the conversation they comment on two creative executions for this campaign, one of a bride-to-be showing an engagement ring and another of a baby leaning toward a pacifier.

Excerpt 2.1. *They are very common in Chinese culture*

1 ESTHER: (to Paul) Go first. ((laughter))
2 PAUL: Why don't you go first.
3 ESTHER: I prefer the first one, because of the logo approach. I like
4   it, and it's very good for branding. The engagement, and the
5   other one is the second phase—the baby. And visually, I think
6   Allied Country will have some promise with you. And the baby,
7   Allied Country will help you to get on in your life from now on.
8 AN RONG: By the way, why we picked these two—getting married
9   and having a kid—is because they are two major important

10   stages of your life. That's why we picked these two. They are
11   very common in Chinese culture.
12   ESTHER: And also, the marriage and the baby, they are once-in-
13   a-lifetime experiences. The engagement is a once-in-your-life
14   experience. So I choose [Allied Country].
15   PAUL: Mm hmmm.
16   ESTHER: And the baby—I . . . the parents always gave the baby the
17   best things, so Allied Country.
18   PAUL: Mm hmmm. I prefer the first one, the logo approach. I like
19   it, it is very good for branding.

In this internal creative review, branding was the primary goal, and in-culture indexical icons about what would be important to Chinese American consumers—namely starting a new family and life in the United States—depicted key moments. An Rong identified certain milestones as "very common in Chinese culture" (lines 10–11). Although brides and babies are not unique to Chinese culture, once they were represented in-culture and appropriate talent was found, Asian Ads was confident that their consumers would connect well with this brand through this messaging. To ensure this, Esther interacted with the concepts, embodying the role of the consumer experiencing the message and affirming brand identification in lines 14 and 17. The use of the logo was a central way to promote brand recognition (lines 18–19), and the overall work of communicating in-culture was accomplished through indexical icons. In this example the visual and copy worked together to create brand identity. The same flexibility and constraints came to bear on choices of language made for in-language copy.

IN-LANGUAGE TRANSCREATION

In-language transcreation was a far more visible and definitive process than in-culture transcreation, primarily because copy is always carefully vetted in advertising. In addition to going through numerous iterations and checks among creatives and between creatives and clients, text was also subject to extensive legal vetting. This is because the Federal Communications Commission and consumer watchdog groups like Ad Busters monitor advertising to ensure that they do not overpromise or make false claims that may dupe consumers. Advertising executives and clients were mainly concerned with generating copy that either introduced a brand to an ethnic community through multicultural advertising or furthered a brand identity through ongoing messaging. Numerous criteria for assessing suitable copy were considered, including how to pair it with visuals, how to select the language varieties and lexical elements that would best suit the brand in question, and how to make choices about accent and humor. All of these require metalevel knowledge about language use and how it correlates with cultural meanings. For instance, language varieties should be paired with the ethnically correct image. To do this type of metaproduction effectively, advertising executives considered how these elements could be structured into narratives that effectively conveyed an ad's message in ways that attended to poetics and acoustic patterns of sound. Indeed they were concerned not only with the content but also with the form of language in ads.

Here I examine the linguistic materiality of brand construction to address the form of language, as well as how it conveys message when paired with visuals. Linguistic materiality pertains to the shape of sounds such as accents and the pairing of visual elements with text in a print ad, such as a tagline, or with spoken discourse. Brands may appear ethereal to consumers, but not to advertising executives steeped in the linguistic materiality of creating them. Fred Myers has written extensively about the materiality of subjects and objects, especially with regard to "situations in which human beings attempt to secure or stabilize—or limit—the flow of culture, to turn culture into property form."[22] Myers made this assertion with regard to Aboriginal painting as a material and social practice, but questions about ownership of culture, language, and heritage central to his investigation are very relevant to my thinking about advertising as a material, linguistic, and capitalist process with social impact and implications. Advertising executives were very assertive about the proprietary nature of their cultural insights and valued their transcreation as their intellectual property, regardless of its being work for hire.

Looking at processes of development and production allows for a consideration of materiality that includes how certain aspects of language and culture are objectified and presented not just for their referential meanings but also for their sensual qualities that are also intended to create consumer identification. Ad executives' emphasis on sound, the poetics of discourse, the way music and talk fill space and animate a product or a service all speak to the materiality of language and sound and underscore the centrality of linguistic materiality to brand construction. At its core, Myers contends, materiality is a "theory of quality of objectness" that is less about "matter" and more about how it "is constituted through ideological frameworks" and thus formulated and understood through conflicting understandings about subjects and objects.[23] With regard to ownership there is far less at stake in advertising than in Aboriginal art, as ads are commissioned, paid work; nonetheless in multicultural advertising, culture and especially language are subject to different ideologies and uses, and these can vary and conflict between clients and advertising executives. Such tensions are especially evident in debates about grammar, register, accent, and deictics (pronouns such as *I, you, them*; location markers such as *here, there, up*; and temporal markers such as *now, later, tomorrow*) and are exposed by looking at the process of transcreation. In-language transcreation especially, in which linguistic elements are translated and created anew for an ethnic audience, is subject to a great deal of scrutiny that reveals the value of different language ideologies.[24] Processes of intertextuality and interdiscursivity come to bear on how meanings subjectively shift and transform when extracted from one context of use and reinserted into another. I have looked at this process with regard to how elements from general market campaigns are remade for multicultural consumers in ways that create new genres, as well as how brand translation allows for connections of time and place through linguistic materiality.[25] Here intertextuality is especially helpful in considering several aspects of language, including form, narrative, and translation. Indeed, the peculiar Asian American advertising product of English back-translations (English translations of in-language copy) exposes the gaps in brand transcreation in ways that bring to light central assumptions about Asian Americans, qualisigns of diversity, and ethnoracial assemblages of language and culture.

Visual Form, Language Choice, and Narrative Structure

The best creative, seasoned ad executives told me, is about good storytelling. The overall structure of storytelling, or narrative, is important for commercials and for campaigns that have several ads that are to be recognized as parts of a whole campaign. Conveying a coherent narrative in a pitch, or in the span of a fifteen- or thirty-second ad, is no small feat. One account executive remarked that narratives are very important devices that allow them "to find that 'catalyst moment' where story meets brand." Some creatives even likened TV spots to films, a significant shift from earlier periods when advertising was more factual in approach and touted the merits of a product, its ability to outdo its competitors, and its proposed relevance to intended consumers. The narratives ad executives created to describe and illustrate their creative exhibited characteristics described by Mikhail Bakhtin in his analyses of narrative in the novel.[26] Heteroglossic narrative, containing multiple voices and language varieties, is rooted in words as well as in the material world and indexes social values and beliefs broader than any single image within it. Expressing and even acting out narratives allowed ad executives to experience how consumers would interact with brand. In the following creative brainstorming session, Andrew and Jayshree break from discussing creative ideas to argue about the process of constructing message and make metaproductive assessments about narrative structure in the creative process.

Excerpt 2.2. *Containing the beauty of that story*

1 ANDREW: Having a structure is easy. It's easy to come up with
2   better headlines if you have, like, a form to go by or something.
3   They say that the narrower the creative brief, the easier it is to
4   come up with headlines. You know, with no structure it's like,
5   everything is all over the place, we can come up with so many
6   things that may not be one strategy.
7 JAYSHREE: But the thing is, each ad has a very powerful story,
8   right? If the structure is limiting it and containing the beauty
9   of that story, then that structure does not work. You know what
10   I mean?

In this exchange Andrew and Jayshree butt heads about how to structure the creative process to keep it on message. Building a narrative structure from the creative brief enabled Andrew to channel creative ideas into something coherent (line 2). Challenging this approach, Jayshree countered that the structure could limit the beauty of storytelling that she aimed to undertake (lines 8–9). The discussion was subsequently settled by creative director An Rong, who declared, "You should open your thoughts first, then worry about the approach, then narrow." Seemingly agreeing with Jayshree, he added, "Don't narrow and then try to fit it in." All three views of creative rely on the existence of a narrative form or structure for ideas and a belief that structure can productively direct or unproductively constrain the creative process. The projection of a structure, one that has to be viewed similarly by all participants even though it has no materiality apart from the words that give it form, underscores the linguistic materiality of this process in shaping the creative. Copy has to fit the broader thematic concerns of the creative, but these parts can be effectively conjoined only if they are woven together in a coherent story.

Narratives that do not cohere expose themselves to failure, in terms of both projecting the brand as well as being recognized as effective transcreation. Internal pitch meetings provide a glimpse into the metaproductive value of narratives and how failure to convey message effectively amounts to a failure to do great creative. Alex, the vice president of marketing for Asian Ads, attended an internal creative presentation for a pitch and found a number of shortcomings in the creative. He stood up, began to pace around the conference room, and addressed the account team in general, and the creatives in particular, in an elevated voice:

> I'm not sold on it because it's taking you guys so long to tell me what it means! I mean, I figured it out by myself. And if I'm looking at it from the client's perspective, they have to get it **right now**, you understand? I mean, a lot of these are good ideas [but] I'm really just trying to look for your big idea, and proof of that big idea through your ideas, your concepts. When we tell a story it's gotta be a consistent story, so I just don't see the connection. How, in this ad, can you change perception by changing the story? This requires **big ideas** and tying it in with content!

Alex reiterated the urgency of message, that it should be conveyed clearly and immediately through creative, and if it is not, it is open to failure. If the clients are unable to understand what is being conveyed about their own product, the message is unlikely to be clear to intended consumers. Alex demanded "big ideas" that "change perception by changing the story," reminding the team that telling a story is the first step to changing perceptions about a brand through advertising. Glancing around the room of glum faces before staring at a point on the wall, he lapsed into this teachable moment:

> As great as we thought we were as storytellers, when we did a pitch, [the client] actually came back and told us that our storytelling was fragmented, and I think that helped us to really tie back into a good storytelling mode where you say something in the beginning and then everything that you say after that is a proof point back to that main thing. So that's the advice that I would give you, is when you're saying something, tie it back to the original main concept and then it'll flow a lot better and the storytelling won't be fragmented.

Alex's point was that in-culture and in-language elements alone do not make for excellent transcreation. Rather the real work of conveying brand is done through cogent as well as culturally relevant storytelling that is properly transcreated. Alex ended the meeting in frustration, but the team won this account because they were ultimately able to generate a compelling narrative and convey message coherently.

When done well, the potential of a well-developed narrative seems unlimited. Good storytelling can convey an elaborate tale, the best ones of which excite creatives with what they hope will be a contagious enthusiasm. During the internal creative review for the money-transfer company Send Cash, Andrew and Jun Yi started to talk about a spot that they had storyboarded. In the midst of describing the ideas, Andrew suddenly grabbed the table, ready to stand, and proposed a different approach.

Excerpt 2.3. Should we reenact it?

1 ANDREW: Should we reenact it?

2 JUN YI: Yes yes yes yes!

3 AN RONG: Yes! ((applause))

4 ANDREW: You see, I'm walking, right? I'm walking into the

5   bridal store to go and pick up the gift for my sister, okay? So

6   I'm picking up a nice gift ((mimes picking something off an

7   imaginary shelf and holds it in his hands)). So I'm thinking

8   of what to give to my sister. So I look at the trumpet, mini

9   trumpet ((stares into the distance)). And then I, I sort of think

10   about, "What can I send her, what can I get her to make her

11   wedding special?" So the next scene is the church wedding.

12   Because if there's anything Filipinos like, it's weddings. They

13   love weddings, the more lavish the better. And they like to

14   have the prestigious church setting for weddings. And families

15   gather at weddings. So we're looking at the bride and groom

16   and they're saying their "I do"s and everything and they're

17   walking ((points to a corner)). Right as they leave the church,

18   in one pew on the left side, one guy stands up with a flute. This

19   is a surprise, okay? And then on the right side, another guy

20   blows a trumpet. And then, so they're looking and people are

21   really surprised by the music playing and they're on the balcony

22   and there's a symphony of people playing the violin okay=

23 JUN YI: =Violins and trumpets? ((laughter))

24 ANDREW: Okay, so they're playing their wedding music also. And
25   then with the symphony there. And then the favorite singer
26   of the sister appears, singing their love song. So the people are
27   clapping and they're happy about, you know, what happened,
28   what transpired. And then we go back now to the scene of me
29   in the bridal store holding the trumpet. Now you get the idea
30   that the sender is already imagining what's going to happen.

Acting out the entire narrative, replete with camera angles and cuts, Andrew and Jun Yi created with words what they had envisioned in a highly specific way. The narrative reenactment began with Andrew standing up and actually walking (lines 4–5). Imagining himself as the consumer, he entered the bridal store to buy a gift for his sister. He picked up the trumpet, held it, and engaged in a process of contemplation that was about to take an in-culture turn (lines 8–9). He elaborated on the broader tastes and preferences of Filipinos, saying what *they* like (lines 12–13) as he aligned himself with them. In a deictic switch in line 15, Andrew extracted himself as the protagonist and became part of the audience viewing the ad by saying, "We're looking at the bride." Then he described the extradiagetic wedding scene that he envisioned, made even more wonderful by his gift of a wedding band (lines 17–22). As Andrew got swept up in his narrative, Jun Yi cut him down a bit with a friendly barb, suggesting that violins and trumpets are overkill (line 23), but Andrew was too taken with his tale to stop. He did pause to reorient himself in the narrative by remarking that the symphony was outdone by "the favorite singer of *the* sister" (line 26) rather than "*my* sister," consistent with the earlier deictic switch. As the room settled down after the laughter at Jun Yi's joke, Andrew closed by reinserting himself into the ad through one more deictic switch, to "the scene of *me* holding the trumpet" (lines 28–29). Orienting himself spatially in the diaspora, as part of the "here" that imagines what impact a money transfer could have "there," Andrew imagined himself as both the consumer and part of an audience looking at the Philippines from a distance. This storytelling, perhaps more elaborate than the time frame many ads would allow for, offers a structure to meaningfully convey in-culture and in-language transcreation while also furthering the brand.

In addition to offering an effective and compelling narrative, the creative affect evident in Andrew's narrative, as well as in others that ad executives created, was an integral part of transcreation. Asian American ad executives often referred to this as "tone" or "tonality," and it was considered an important part of conveying the broader mood, emotion, and temperament of an ad. Tonality was accomplished through in-culture and in-language elements in combination, and Asian American ad executives contended that tonality for their audiences nearly always differed from tonality in general market ads. Some clients required that tonality for multicultural campaigns match the general market campaign, and Asian American agencies were expected to generate in-culture and in-language creative accordingly. Although humor, sarcasm, and irony are difficult to transcreate, creative still had to effectively communicate aspects of general market tonality while maintaining brand identity. Ad executives often speculated about the shared affective norms for a particular ethnic group, noting that great variance was possible. Oliver and Jody, copywriters at an Asian American ad agency, shared their thoughts with me about the range of ways tonality could be accomplished. Jody suggested that music was very important to establishing tone, and because Asian musical genres convey a different mood and emotion from "Caucasian" music, as she called it, it could create in-culture tonality. Oliver added, "The raw emotion might not come across, so that has to be done in transcreation. We really have to discuss 'What is the meaning behind the words, what's the emotion behind the words?' The big issue is that what might have a certain emotion in one culture or language doesn't carry through in another culture or language." In addition to the constraints of brand identity and the necessity to stay consistent with the general market campaign and message, it was essential to get these elements right.

Humor can be the trickiest tonal dimension to transcreate from a general market campaign, especially sarcasm and double entendre. Creative director Joey cautioned, "We know we have to use humor carefully because it can be so sensitive. If we do use humor we usually have to have several consultants to make sure it will work and not be offensive." He added that, budget permitting, they test certain executions on focus groups. Oliver likewise elaborated, "For a lot of Chinese, sarcasm really doesn't come through. So an English speaker who's infusing sarcasm, it won't come across the same way to a Chinese speaker. It's not funny because a lot of it has to do with the local area and what's funny within a culture." Even when the humor works, it may not be compatible with the tonality of a brand's general market identity when it is transcreated. In some instances the general market creative concept overall is simply irreconcilable with the cultural and linguistic ideologies of an certain ethnic group, even if the ad resonates very well with general market audiences. Account executive Henry, a colleague of Oliver and Jody's, told me about an ad that tested very well in terms of being entertaining for young South Asian American audiences but tested "really poorly in terms of being in-line with the [name] brand." Noting that clients dislike such misalignments, he commented that the tonality was simply too different from the brand's overall identity and that ultimately their execution "did not feel natural. Because we were trying to be comical, incorporate those cultural cues, it was not accepted in the same way."

Because of concerns about irony and edginess backfiring in Asian American advertising, ad executives tended to regard these approaches as too risky for the brands they represented. Even though they were quite relaxed about joking and humor as part of agency culture, they rarely felt confident in featuring edgy comedy in their creative. Nonetheless Asian consumers were thought to "have a sense of humor," to "have a fun time," and otherwise not take things too literally, and these are things that transcreation is intended to convey, when appropriate. Such a characterization stands in sharp contrast to widely held stereotypes of Asian American model minorities who are thought to be humorless, studious, obedient rule-followers. Some ads featured humor based on generational difference between family members, amusing happenings while running errands, or comical misunderstandings between characters. Some went further to make light of aging, deception, and even adultery, all themes featured in spots for a 2007 campaign for Nationwide Insurance aimed at the Asian Indian segment. For the most part, however, ad executives believed the potential to offend outweighed the value added through humor. In most transcreations ad executives sidestepped humor and deployed other in-culture and in-language elements to create consumer identification.

Advertising executives expected that the in-language copy they wrote, be it in an Asian language or in a variety of Asian English, would work dynamically with the visuals to convey message. In a creative meeting brainstorming for the Send Cash company, copywriter Jayshree presented her copy, or "lines," as she called them, expecting her fellow creatives to consider how they would interact with other visual elements in the ad. In this part of the conversation, she is sharpening concepts that she generated for the Asian Indian segment.

Excerpt 2.4. Tagline

1   JAYSHREE: Yeah, I have lines to share, but I have only done them
2   for the South Asian IT guy. And I think this campaign requires
3   a baseline tagline, which translates the concept of "Send Cash,
4   transfer life." So that tagline will be the overarching connection
5   as well, for everything. I haven't gotten to that yet.
6   ALL: ((laughter))
7   JAYSHREE: I have some things but it's not there yet, but that said,
8   that is the way I look at it. I think each line has to powerfully
9   translate the visual. So based on that, that is the premise by
10   which I have done these lines.

What Jayshree calls "the baseline tagline" (line 3) is intended to bring
together the other copy and convey meaning along with the visual, that
one might not be able to do as effectively without the other. While this
seems in some ways readily apparent, her statements in other ways are
an important reminder of how central materiality is to doing advertising
creative. This interaction between visual and verbal, and the ability of one
to "powerfully translate" (lines 8–9) the other, is a version of what Roland
Barthes called "anchor and relay" and emphasizes the dialogic process of
meaning creation in the space of a print ad.[27] Like Jayshree, other creatives
qualified their ideas by noting the reliance of verbal elements on visual, or
vice versa. For example, in the creative meeting discussed at the start of
this chapter, Esther attempted to assuage her director's puzzled look after
her presentation by explaining that perhaps he could not grasp the concept as she was verbalizing it because "it is simply missing the visual, it is
ambiguous." To use Barthes's terms, the relay of her copy was missing the
anchor of the visuals, and so she failed to convey the message. For creative
to be effective, words alone were not enough to convey the intended brand
message. Even radio ads usually involved highly stylized voicings and other
musical elements in order to invite listener identification.[28] Agreeing with
Jayshree in the earlier excerpt, copywriter Andrew added that layout is indeed important, even when the headline captures the mind-set of the intended consumer. Such pairing is also effective in television commercials.
In addition to the spoken discourse or voice-over that conveys information while also creating a desired creative affective tone for the ad, subtitles can be used to further this effect. In a spot for Nissan that is otherwise entirely in Mandarin, three hip, young Asian American youth in the

Altima 2.5 S的2014年環保署現估油耗值為高速公路38哩／加侖。
實際里程數因駕駛操作而異。僅供比較之用。

2.6 Nissan Altima spot for Chinese Americans featuring texting-style English "OMG" in voice-over (2013).

backseat of the car voice the English texting abbreviation "OMG" while the subtitle appears beneath them, signaling the mixing of visual and linguistic as well as English and Chinese elements to create a message that will appeal across generations (fig. 2.6). These heteroglossic approaches create messages in ways that underscore the importance of linguistic materiality in creating brands. In this instance linguistic materiality is the outcome of the relationship between anchor and relay.

In-language copy does a great deal of semiotic work in making any ad appear in-culture and authentic. Indexical icons are evident in the materiality of a printed page, in the spatially and temporally calibrated television spot, or in the carefully stylized radio voice. Oliver, a copywriter in an Asian American agency, assured me that transcreation is "completely different than translation. . . . When we talk about transcreation what you're basically talking about is getting the essence and soul of the language." He explained that in a translation words do not always carry the emotional aspect or meaning; if something is translated directly, "the viewer might not get the feel of what we're saying." Oliver and other copywriters noted that some American slang does not have similar meaning for Asian American audiences, and transcreating this text requires a revision of both meaning and form. Likewise Joey, a creative director, explained that his agency certainly looks to the general market ads for campaigns they develop, but that theirs can be quite different. He explained that if done well, a transcreated ad makes viewers believe that it was explicitly written for them and applies directly to their lives. In his view, about 95 percent of the consumers they target are immigrants who are "constantly in conflict with their new and old cultures." Other creative directors I spoke with did not seem to share this view explicitly, but certainly emphasized that brands that can connect consumers to their homeland through a heritage language would create far more affinity than brands that take a "cookie-cutter" approach, as Joey called it. The indexical value of in-language copy is manifold. Latino ad executives, for instance, imagine that their audiences would be "symbolically touched" by the inclusion of in-language copy,[29] and Asian American ad executives seemed to believe this to some extent as well. Yet, given that each ethnic group operates under different language ideologies about language varieties and English, decisions about in-language copy were tailored to each Asian ethnic group.

Register and lexical choices are important for in-language copy, especially when word choice is intended to create identification with particular types of consumers. In ads for Asian Indian audiences, where English tends to be used alongside Hindi or another language, word choice was very important. In an insurance company brand launch for Asian Indian consumers, Sunil the account executive was concerned that the creative his team generated might not strike the correct tone in the brand's target audiences. Especially because the brand was not widely recognized in this community, the goal of this messaging was not only to reach well-educated, upwardly mobile Asian Indian consumers but also to do so in ways that would lure them away from other insurance companies that had already reached Asian Indians through multicultural advertising for several years. In the following example of in-language transcreation, Jayshree justified her creative choices to Sunil, who had alternative ideas about which words would work best. Jayshree's copy, "*papa-beta* moments," translated into "father-son moments," using the North Indian English word *papa* for "father" and *beta* for "son" in Hindi and some other North Indian languages. Sunil's use of *suriksha*, or safety in *shudh* Hindi—a "pure" variety of Hindi based predominantly on Sanskrit-derived words—pulled the message and tone in a decidedly different direction. An ideological struggle ensued over the value of using the common, everyday idiom of Hindi/Urdu (indicated below in *italics*) over the formal, prestigious variety of *shudh* Hindi (indicated below in **bold italics**). During the twelve-minute conference call excerpted here, Sunil and Jayshree reviewed the copy she had sent for this print ad.

Excerpt 2.5. **Papa-beta** *moments*

1   JAYSHREE: Yeah, the reason why I didn't use, you know, like
2   **suriksha** would be a more **Hindi** word, whereas I tried to stay
3   away from that, that's why I kind of went away from it, like
4   *papa-beta* moments are kind of not Hindi-centric, you know?
5   SUNIL: But then tell me one thing, I mean this is what I've seen
6   and I'll say **suriksha** was a very cool example. But when you say
7   "*papa-beta* moments," it's a literal translation of "father and son
8   moments."
9   JAYSHREE: Yeah, yeah.
10 SUNIL: So what are you trying to imply in that? How is Allied
11   Country coming into your picture here? I just want to know
12   what you are thinking.
13 JAYSHREE: Yeah, I don't think the exercise is to build Allied
14   Country intuition. You already have the communication and
15   you inject a cultural nuance into it, where the new ad should be
16   emotional or product-oriented, or what's my criteria? So here
17   the cultural nuance has been injected for the emotional target.
18 SUNIL: Which is just a translation of [*papa-beta*
19 JAYSHREE: [Yeah you are making it into
20   a *papa-beta* moment, but instead of having the culture in the
21   U.S., the culture is more the product's effect.

In this exchange differences in opinion about intended audience and the
work the copy should do come to the fore. The use of *papa-beta* indexes a
far more colloquial tone, one in which bonds of father and son are conjured in a pleasant, if somewhat vague way, as Sunil's question in lines
10–11 suggests. By contrast, *suriksha* is a decidedly formal term, belonging
to the *shudh* or pure Hindi register. While an official diglossia (differentiation between formal and informal varieties of a language) does not exist
between these varieties, *suriksha* is a term used for formal announcements
during transportation, for government and institutionally issued safety
notices, and in other authoritative communication and therefore conjures
a far more serious and important tone for the ad. In lines 19–21 Jayshree
tried to index a different affective state by suggesting, "The culture is more
the product's effect," meaning that using this product will bring the type
of warmth and closeness associated with affectionate fathers and young
sons who share memorable moments. As the account executive, it was
Sunil's job to assure his client that the creative his team generated would

effectively launch this brand to Asian Indian audiences. He reminded Jayshree that when Allied Country conducted research about brand awareness among this community, it was "almost nil, people had never heard of it. So all these, these are basically branding ads with an effort to bring up the brand, and, you know, imply that how Allied Country can help us help you, from a cultural perspective as well." Diplomatically countering that if the brand was already established, "*papa-beta* could have been really good," Sunil reiterated that building this brand with "very limited media dollars" required a different tack.

Trying a different approach, Jayshree then asked about using the copy from the general market campaign to do some of the branding work, and perhaps tailoring it in-culture. She drew attention to the evocative message her copy could convey when combined with these visuals.

Excerpt 2.6. So if we transcreate it

1 JAYSHREE: Okay, so basically, like, their general market slogan,
2   "We will be there for you," would that be translatable in a
3   cultural way?
4 SUNIL: Yeah yeah yeah. See, in terms of the subhead, we don't have
5   to only pick out particular words. When you say, "We will be
6   there for you," that is under Allied Country anyway. Right?
7 JAYSHREE: Uh-huh.
8 SUNIL: So if you say there's a possibility to translate "We will be
9   there for you," we can definitely give it a shot as well=
10 JAYSHREE: =okay=
11 SUNIL: =not translate as such, it's in a more transcreating it.
12 JAYSHREE: Okay.
13 JUN YI: Hold on, is the, is George okay with that? So if we
14   transcreate it=
15 ANDREW: =it's not [really
16 SUNIL: [No, "We will be there for you" is not the
17   tagline. "[Allied Country] helps you get there" is the [tagline
18 ANDREW: [Yeah yeah
19   [that's it
20 JUN YI: [Okay, okay. Okay, thanks, sorry, most people can
21   understand, when we transcreate it in your language,
22   remember they mostly speak English, [right?
23 SUNIL: [Absolutely. This

24	interpretation, maybe because it's only the copy and not
25	the layout, it's literally basically saying *papa-beta*. *Papa-beta*
26	moments is like, you know it's just a translation, I don't sense
27	any emotion attached to it. It's basically a translation of "father
28	and son moments," right?

Here Jayshree made a final case for what she considered to be an emotionally evocative relationship: the father-son bond. Highlighted as a hallmark of happy childhood and a stock dynamic in countless Bollywood films, the phrase is intended to index the type of warm interpersonal connection that *suriksha* never could. According to Jayshree, the tagline beneath the visual would effectively convey the brand and work well with her copy, especially if translated in-language (lines 1–3). Sunil, however, disagreed by asserting that it required at least a transcreation (line 11), and corrected her by pointing out that the tagline is not "We will be there for you" but rather "Allied Country helps you get there" (lines 16–17). With the incorrect tagline paired with a message that was not strong enough for a launch, Sunil declared that "*papa-beta* moments" was simply too direct a translation to do the branding work he envisioned (lines 25–28).

Moreover the transcreation here, as Jun Yi and Andrew interject in lines 13–15, was to be selective, based on what the client had specified (lines 18–22). Also important were decisions regarding what to do about the slogan and copy from the general market ad. Transcreating some copy in-language was permitted, but the taglines were to remain in English. Even though "helps you get there" might not have glossed meaningfully in Indian English, the term *suriksha* combined with the in-culture visuals certainly could. While English-speaking Asian Indians would likely know the English word *safety*, seeing *suriksha* instead could conjure a more formal sense of authority and capability. The next day Jayshree submitted the copy *Shaadi ke baad, parivar ki **suriksha*** (After marriage, security for your family). Sunil thanked her and said he would check it for gender agreement and applicability. Even he seemed unconvinced about the utility of using one line of Hindi, but he nonetheless agreed that these in-language elements made for a powerful transcreation. As the national language, Hindi conveyed the right message for this financial services company, especially the formal register chosen. This in-language transcreation was paired with in-culture elements of a North Indian Hindu bride in full wedding regalia, about to have a *mangal sutra* (wedding necklace) tied around her neck. Even though Hindi is the national language of India, it is not widely spoken in parts of South India. Thus the metaproductive choice of pairing this variety of Hindi with a North Indian bride underscores the importance of getting small details of transcreation correct.

As this example illustrates, deciding which copy to transcreate in-language, how to choose between relevant Asian language varieties, and how to use Asian varieties of English was not straightforward. Filipinos and South Asians, for instance, are reputed to be highly proficient in English and therefore best reached in English, while Chinese, Korean, and Vietnamese are thought to favor in-language television and periodicals, so in-language transcreation worked best for them. Susan, the CEO of an Asian American agency, told me, "Ethnic marketing has always piggy-backed on language. Now, it's not necessarily language-centric anymore, especially in the second generation." Even the use of English, however, requires careful selection. Choosing a relevant variety of Indian English or Filipino English would allow for a more relevant transcreation than simply retaining English from the general market ad. Discussions about norms of use, common lexical terms, and idiomatic expressions were thus always a part of transcreation, even for ads that were partly or fully in English. Having some in-language copy seemed preferable, perhaps as an obvious qualisign of diversity for clients and audiences. In a print ad presentation to a client for a Filipino ad, ad executives emphasized the value of translating just one word from the Christmas-themed general market ad "Joy, Love, Cheer" into Tagalog, making it "Taglish." Along with modified visuals, this transcreation would ensure continuity with the general market message while assuring Filipino audiences and their client that the ad had been tailor-made for them.

In other ads transcreation poses a challenge due to the specific gloss of an English word that has no satisfactory equivalent in another language. One ad executive reflected that in some campaigns it had been quite helpful to have some words in English alongside in-language copy. She remarked, "We struggle sometimes to translate something that's very refined in English [into] Chinese. We argue that 'this word should stay in English!'" Especially when paired with visual modifications, even those as small as changing the color of the ad or digitally adding Asian-looking actors, small linguistic tweaks can result in a significant semiotic shift. The simplicity of clear, strong messaging remains an important part of projecting brand identity, whether copy is in-language or in English.

Some elements are rarely translated, such as brand names and very successful brand slogans. For instance, on a call with an automobile client, account executive Alan politely explained that the client's Japanese auto brand was already so well recognized among Chinese Americans that it was not necessary to translate this Japanese name for Asian American audiences. Even if a brand name was translated in their home country, doing so here would not build the kind of brand identity desired for Chinese Americans. Especially since the name was not a phonetic challenge for this audience, Alan clarified for his clients the agency's broader position: "We try to communicate overall to Asian Americans, but do not tailor the name in-language. We do not want to create a different term, so that when they go to the dealer and communicate the car name in-language, the dealer may not understand what it is." Emphasizing how important it is that Chinese Americans who view their ads and look at the in-language website can go to a brick-and-mortar location and find the exact same product, he convinced the client that keeping these elements in English was very important for brand consistency and avoiding miscommunication. In this instance the client agreed that less in-language transcreation would be more appropriate, and the agency compensated in other ways that involved visuals and voice-over in-language.

Even though in-language copy acted as a qualisign of diversity, at times clients seemed to prefer using English, especially when their market research indicated English was more effective. Using in-language words and phrases for the sake of indexing diversity could, in these cases, work against the efficacy of the ad, especially where the use of two languages was considered "too informal." As Sunil remarked after his lengthy disagreement with Jayshree featured in excerpts 2.5 and 2.6, "If the Hindi doesn't help, why use it?" Other in-culture markers, such as using Asian Indian faces or changing small details, such as using an Asian Indian child and a stuffed elephant in place of a white child and a teddy bear, also did the work of transcreation, making in-language copy less vital. Clients were particularly concerned about getting this right, and in many instances they expected ad executives to comply with their market research findings rather than their own ideas about norms of use among Asian American speakers. In one creative review phone call account executive Rufus and client Vanessa debated whether or not in-language copy should be included in the print ad that Sunil and Jayshree had developed.

Excerpt 2.7. If we were standing on our research?

1 RUFUS: The headline, right? We're going for the combination of
2 Hindi and English, right?
3 VANESSA: Um, well, let me **ask** you about that, because we heard in
4 focus groups
5 RUFUS: [Right
6 VANESSA: **not** to do that, so I was really surprised to **see** it.
7 RUFUS: In the focus group, they were using Hindi for the headline.
8 VANESSA: Mm-hmm.
9 RUFUS: And all of those people said, "You know what, they really
10 should not be doing it." But after getting back we said, "You
11 know what? How can we still instill the whole cultural nuance
12 into all this? While not making Hindi the hero? Let's devise it
13 to be on a separate part of the ad. So it's not in your face, but at
14 the same time you get the whole Hindi feeling." So the headline
15 would still be in English and the subhead in Hindi, then it's a
16 combination of Hindi and English both.
17 VANESSA: ((sigh)) Oh . . . I don't **know.**
18 RUFUS: ((laughter))
19 VANESSA: I don't really know, because you know why?
20 JUN YI: Why?
21 VANESSA: I was looking at this strategy document yesterday, going
22 through all of that.
23 RUFUS: Right.
24 VANESSA: You know, if we were standing on our research?
25 RUFUS: Right, so what would you do then?
26 VANESSA: We shouldn't be **doing** Hindi!
27 RUFUS: Right, right, right. You . . .
28 VANESSA: We should be doing English.
29 RUFUS: We basically had two options. One was Hindi and English,
30 and then we have an English-only option as well, which got
31 away from the Hindi.
32 VANESSA: Mm-hmm.
33 RUFUS: So that takes the Hindi away and puts back the English.
34 VANESSA: Okay, I think we should do . . . that.
35 RUFUS: Okay! And you know what? That's the debate that we had
36 internally as well, because at the end of the day, it's going to be
37 published and released in the Asian Indian publications, with

Based on the client's research and recommended strategy, Asian Ads knew to do an English-only execution but drifted away from that decision. Even Sunil, in his creative review call with Jayshree, Andrew, and Jun Yi (excerpt 2.6), recalled the client's recommendation to use English but decided to nonetheless create a headline in Hindi. Realizing that they had ignored Vanessa's recommendation to do the ad in English, the compromise, as Rufus put it, was "not making Hindi the hero" (line 12) but using it in a subhead (under the headline) rather than as the central copy in the ad (lines 14–16). Indicating that they had an English option as well, one that "takes the Hindi away and puts back the English" (line 33), Rufus did a skillful job of reassuring her by relaying that they had the same debate internally and that they had come to the same conclusion "at the end of the day." Actually the account team had not come to that conclusion, but ultimately they agreed with Vanessa and her research, conceding that there were enough in-culture elements and a media placement strategy to offset the use of English (lines 36–39). Even when ad executives found the bilingual execution to be a better transcreation, they deferred to the client.

Regardless of the parameters clients set, ad executives can challenge them only so much without seeming difficult and potentially losing business. This is the least desirable outcome and rarely happened. Still, doing transcreation within the parameters of market research that they may not completely agree with did not absolve them of doing great creative and ensuring that brand message was effectively conveyed. In the print ads I discussed earlier, in-language copy worked with visual elements as qualisigns of diversity, signaling to clients and intended audiences that an ad had been transcreated and tailored to a specific ethnic audience. The specific configuration of in-culture and in-language qualisigns contributes to assemblages of ethnoracial diversity that are intended to resonate with particular types of Asian consumers. Ad executives and clients were both attentive to language choice for in-language transcreation, but ad executives were additionally attuned to how these elements were structured to convey message.

Poetics, Sound, and Accent

My discussion thus far has focused on how in-language transcreation re-lies on the structure of narrative and the selection of language varieties and how lexical items are paired with visuals to convey intended creative affect. Poetics are another integral part of creating message for advertis-ing. Roman Jakobson identified the importance of how words sound when they are put together and how the acoustic shape of communication af-fects not just indexical meaning but also aesthetic experience.[30] Wordplay through sound, rhyming, punning, and other means has been a tried and true approach in advertising. Specificities of poetic patterning contribute to assemblages of ethnoracial diversity because they make ads potentially memorable and subject to reiteration and circulation. Whether copy is set to the tune of a catchy jingle or chanted in verse, or a brand or logo is paired with an acoustic soundscape in which seeing or hearing one conjures the other, the materiality of form is instrumental. For instance, in a print ad for an automobile maker that had released a G series of sedans, the copy for Asian Indians featured the clever pun "G is for *josh*." The copy would be meaningful only to Hindi speakers who recognized the phonemic play on *josh*, meaning "fun" or "enjoyment" (pronounced "jōsh," not like the English word josh, pronounced "jash," which means to joke around or play but has a different connotation). This in-language transcreation relied on a well-educated bilingual Asian Indian population that would relish this type of wordplay and enjoy the camaraderie of this insider humor with others in this target audience. Puns, idiom, and other language-specific markers like this one exemplify how important aspects of poetics can be in advertising when done well.

The broader poetics of advertising language, as copywriters explained them to me, should be above all clear and easy to understand. Wordplay is welcome, as copywriter Jody suggested, but nothing that is too difficult to understand: "Good writers don't have to be excessively deep. Consumers shouldn't have the responsibility of trying to understand what you want to tell them."[31] Putting the burden of communication on the speaker is in keeping with the communicative norms of American English, and adver-tising is no different.[32] "You need to catch their attention, since they don't spend a lot of time understanding," Jody added, reiterating that messages should be clear and easy to digest so as to not lose consumers. Ad execu-tives emphasized that quick and catchy language was important, as was anything that makes people revisit the ad. "Five words max" and similar parameters were imperatives for slogan creation, with golden exceptions such as the U.S. Army's six-word success "Be all that you can be" held up as exemplary. "Short and punchy" and "Make the consumer think" were other guidelines that copywriters were asked to follow, in hopes that they would create winners like MasterCard's "Priceless" and Visa's "Life takes Visa."

Writing great copy in one language is difficult, but having it gloss well in two or more languages simultaneously is quite a challenge. Translating brand names in a market whose audience would also experience a brand name and identity in English is a risky proposition. An Rong explained the dilemma: "I think the Chinese have different degrees of English capability. Some Chinese cannot read English well, so if you leave the brand name [Allied Country] as is, sometimes they may not be able to connect well. Also if the names are difficult to pronounce, they are not easy to remember." The underlying assumption is that in order to create identification with consumers, brands need to be easy to grasp, make phonetic sense in-language, and be easy to pronounce, even for English-speaking Asian Americans. While these consumers may understand the brand names they read, if there is no easy way to connect to them, then developing brand loyalty is less likely. For example, the structure of Mandarin words, which are logographs (characters that stand for words), has to be considered vis-à-vis the characters' relationship with other characters, as they modify one another. An Rong told me about a recent translation they did for their insurance and financial services client Allied Country in which the first two characters meant "abundant prosperity," while the third and fourth conveyed "mutual benefit." The notion of prosperity was important to convey the broader desirability of financial services—a message that did not come across in the general market brand name alone. An Rong added, "*Prosper* in Chinese doesn't have to mean monetary fortune. It's much broader, it's life in general, being abundant in your life." He admitted this process is especially difficult in logographic languages like Chinese, because they had to choose characters to represent brand identity but be sure they did not use characters that were already copyrighted under another brand. Moreover they had to ensure to not "overpromise," making claims that could be deemed false from a consumer regulatory standpoint. Terms like *prosper* seemed to be commonplace in Mandarin speech but connoted a larger financial promise in English—a tension that Asian Ads repeatedly experienced as they did in the creative for this client.

Debates about linguistic norms of use also arose in discussions about grammar and word choice. Rules of grammar were of course followed but could depart from standard norms of use to suit advertising copy. This is not unusual, as advertising copy in all languages tends to take liberties that bend rules of grammar, syntax, morphology, and phonology, especially when done in the service of brand identity. In one print ad conceit, copywriter Andrew wondered if he could use *Diwali* as a verb. In another, bivalent homophones in Chinese and English were used to ensure that all the main points were expressed using nouns. In one lengthy discussion with a client who had already turned down several creative ideas for a particular print ad, the client took issue with the in-language copy and the way it glossed with intended audiences. This client openly told Asian Ads that they used a group of South Asian colleagues who worked in the information technology department of the company as an ad hoc focus group for ads that were under client review. No one at Asian Ads knew the exact ethnic or linguistic background of the four gentlemen in question. The client simply referred to them as "Indian" or "South Asian," but the details of their linguistic abilities were not disclosed. Account executive Maya, who grew up in Mumbai and spoke Hindi, Marathi, and English, as well as Bengali, her mother tongue, took issue with the faceless feedback offered by this client on the grammatical correctness of the copy in question. After one client call, she expressed concern to her team that the Hindi headline "*Is haseen mausam* [This beautiful season], celebrate three decades of inspired performance" was being corrected to "*Yeh haseen mausam*." Thanking the client and offering to address the issue immediately, she ended the call and insisted that the client was incorrect. *Yeh*, which also means "this," is used for intransitive verbs, while *is* is used for transitive verbs and signals an action to follow. She explained to creative director Alan that both *yeh* and *is* mean "this," but that *is* would work better with the English that follows.

Within a few minutes a small crowd had converged in Alan's office, as creative Stanley summoned copywriter Jayshree and Maya called in Sunil and nodded at me to follow as she walked by my desk. Sunil explained that *yeh* is "without the action, and *is* is more time-sensitive. The word *yeh* has no action implied." Alan replied that he needed this written down clearly and wanted to confirm that neither is grammatically incorrect. In an earlier aside to me, Maya had expressed her frustration about this manner of client feedback, especially since they never disclosed who their South Asian colleagues were, what languages they spoke, how long they had lived in the United States, and the like. Such details, usually disclosed in market research to help ad executives better understand why certain approaches would be more or less apt for a particular audience, were here not available. Instead ideas and copy just kept getting kicked back to the team for revision, and the usually calm Maya began to get a bit riled. She recommended that Alan should "challenge" them and push for the use of *is*. Speaking not a word of Hindi, Alan, a native Cantonese speaker, was concerned that this could negatively affect their creative credibility. Sunil assured him that it would not, as both were grammatically correct. Of course, both would not enable grammatically the same actions and would make the statement either imply action (here the English word *celebrate*) or not (as an observation of the beauty of the season itself, but not necessarily connecting the copy and the visuals). Ad executives believed *is* indexed action in ways important to potential automobile consumers, linking the whole sentence with its Hindi and English halves to create identification and better build their client's brand. Ultimately the client went with the agency's recommendation, knowing that they would stand by their copy if focus groups or audiences criticized it.

The use of particular in-language words in combination with English can sometimes create a powerful message. In a brainstorming session for a print ad for money-transfer company Send Cash, Jayshree suggested a series of headlines about *munna*, a colloquial term for "boy" in regions of North India. While not a perfect analogy, *munna* is used in ways that I understand the term "Bubba" is used to refer to boys in regions of the American South. Familiar, affectionate, and regionally inflected, *munna* refers to a boy in the family (other than one's own son) and is used as a term of address as well as a term of reference. It was the latter usage that Jayshree found to be appealing here, as she paired *munna* with "upgrade," a word of significance in the South Asian context. Apart from meaning "to improve" something, it also has a strong professional connotation of technological improvements that play on the centrality of South Asian Americans in high-tech in Silicon Valley and elsewhere, as well as airline promotions from economy to first class, the mark of a powerful business traveler. The copy that Jayshree wrote, "Your gift upgrades *munna*'s future," suggested that those material benefits would be successfully transferred to loved ones in the homeland, "because you are living the good life in the U.S." An Rong required further contextual information about which little boy specifically would benefit, if it was not one's own son. Jayshree explained, "Usually for IT, they come here when they are like twenty-seven or something and join an IT company here, but when they need to get married they go back and have an arranged marriage, and then after six months they bring the wife here."

2.7 Spot for an insurance ad aimed at Chinese American consumers featuring in-culture and in-language transcreation (2010).

From the looks of puzzlement and curiosity on An Rong's and Jun Yi's faces, Jayshree deduced that they were unfamiliar with this immigration pattern, and she provided a small but informative overview on the migration patterns of South Asian high-tech workers and what distinguished them as consumers. Emphasizing the white-collar nature of this scenario, Jayshree added that *upgrade* could also work for other conceits she envisioned for this campaign, featuring a computer or IT guy, as it seemed to do important in-culture work in conjunction with *munna*. Andrew remarked that he liked the *upgrade* idea for the South Asian market but that "*upgrade* for Filipinos, it would be too white-collared a word. It's too . . . it's up there. It's a white-collar word." Emphasizing the importance of choosing words that work in-culture but also index the correct class status, Jayshree agreed that it wouldn't really work for blue-collar images but that perhaps *munna* could work across class background, and an equivalent to *munna* in Tagalog could be effective as well.

Lexical choices and gestures thus had to correlate properly with the intended audience in order for the ad to work well. In one insurance ad, for instance, an insurance agent transforms a routine outing into a hyperstylized trip to a nightclub, with the translation "He is awesome!" accompanied by one of the young men giving him a fist bump (fig. 2.7). It was trickier, however, to preserve deictics in-culture when using English. Henry told me about a campaign for an insurance company that featured a moving red dot that served as "a visual cue, sort of like a map," in which people stood in different points on the dot and shared events that connected locations with experiences.[33] The conceit that connected all the dots was the phrase "I'm so there," repeated in each spot. Henry explained, "The idea is that the insurance company understands your situation, where you are in life, and is right there with you. We were asked to align as closely as possible to that." That double entendre of *there* did not work at all for Chinese and Korean speakers, so the agency was able to offer a satisfactory in-language transcreation. Jody explained that "being there for you" is not a common turn of phrase in Chinese, and she recalled loosely transcreating it to "You will be reassured every day." She elaborated that in Chinese the notion of "being there for you" would be better conveyed "physically, not mentally, like, 'We'll be by your side.' So having someone on your left-hand and right-hand side means they have people to help them." It is somewhat expected that such idiomatic uses would not translate neatly from English into Chinese, and having a cultural gloss on the concept would align the copy with Chinese ideologies about individuals and society while still preserving brand identity. The real trouble came when they had to change the copy for Asian Indian. Even though it was in English, Henry explained that they had done some testing and the phrase did not resonate. Oliver, the creative who had worked on the spot, explained that if the tagline does not relate to the culture, then "you have to completely change it, otherwise they'll understand the English, but it won't resonate with them."[34] Regarding the tagline "I'm so there," they spoke to coworkers and friends, and the consensus was that the tagline was "so very American." So they decided to change it to "I'm here," which Oliver said "made it more emotional, and we tried to infuse the physical crossing of 'I'm here' with the emotion that it carries." Ultimately they were able to work with the client's strategic team to stay on message and use the visual with the copy "I'm right here," which "did test stronger than the general market work."

Another effective approach to in-language transcreation was the use of accent, either for varieties of Asian English or for discernible regional accents in Asian languages. Details about accent were not always specified in the creative, but creatives did elaborate on what might work best for a concept to help accomplish the tonality of an ad. For the 2007 Nationwide Asian Indian campaign I mentioned earlier, each ad featured a voice-over about the brand delivered in South Asian Received Pronunciation, a distinctive accent that indexes a high level of education in English medium schools and universities. While in-language accents are generally not criticized for being "wrong" for a specific ad, they are sometimes scrutinized for their authenticity. Authenticity is a complicated concept, especially in an era of global capitalism in which different cultural and linguistic forms such as accents can be differently valued, depending on speakers and listeners.[35] For example, questions of authenticity surfaced in an automobile ad created by a Los Angeles Asian American agency. Copywriter Jody explained that she coached the young men featured in the ad on their Mandarin and Cantonese accents. They had lived primarily in California but were heritage speakers of these languages, and they needed some assistance with their pronunciation and diction. Jody justified the decision to cast heritage speakers who were bilingual in English rather than native speakers for whom Mandarin or Cantonese was their first language by explaining, "Every young kid has a hard time pronouncing Mandarin or Cantonese. Our kids cannot speak one hundred percent perfect Mandarin, they have the [American] accent." For Jody the slight American accent in the Mandarin or Cantonese evident in the speech of these young men lent credibility to the notion that they live in the United States. Moreover it differentiated them as Asian Americans whose speech differs from Mandarin or Cantonese speakers in China. Viewers seemed to be highly attuned to this subtle accent, and numerous comments were posted about the ad on YouTube. Henry, the account executive for the ad, recounted that according to the comments posted, the ad worked very well with the younger audience, but not all responses were positive. There were a number of people who criticized the accents in general by saying "they suck." Henry reiterated Jody's point that the ad was oriented toward "Chinese Americans, and of course we would use guys with that accent because most Cantonese ABCs (American-born Chinese) identify with that accent and would find a fluent accent too formal." Accent here was intended to create generationally specific identification, and while they incited some controversy, these ad executives believed that the comments were not so negative or extreme that they would detract from the overall efficacy of the ad.

In a different ad in this campaign, however, accent worked perfectly as a qualisign of diversity, along with in-culture casting and wardrobe. This thirty-second spot featured three young South Asian American women exiting a yoga class with rolled-up mats and wearing stylish yoga clothes and flip-flops that epitomized South Asian American youth in California (fig. 2.8). The first woman giggles about how another woman in the class pushed her during the yoga pose "downward dog," and the second woman utters the word *karma* when the pusher's parked car is found to have a dent. Her pronunciation of "CAR-ma" is decidedly American and is in clear phonetic contrast to the Sanskrit-derived pronunciation "kuhr-

2.8 Transcreation featuring second-generation Asian Indian talent, in-culture with American-accented English (2010).

muh." The three young women, as well as the slightly older insurance agent who appears later in the ad, speak American-accented English, the younger women with a Valley Girl lilt. Here the use of American-accented English did not draw criticism, perhaps because the entire assemblage of three young South Asian women going to a yoga class conveys a plausible yet diverse scenario. Noteworthy, however, is that other aspects of the in-culture transcreation raised questions during audience testing, such as whether the inclusion of a cricket player and a Bollywood star in the ad seemed to have too many in-culture qualisigns. Since the women had most of the speaking parts, accent worked well to carry the ad and convey brand. Accents that index first- or second-generation migration status broaden the reach of transcreation while preserving brand identity.

English Back-Translation, Puffery, and Copyright

In-language transcreation required explanation to clients, usually along with an English back-translation, or EBT, as ad executives abbreviate it. This English translation of in-language copy was loosely based on the original English copy or brand name in the general market campaign. The complexities of this translation sequence were manifold and revealed broader dynamics of negotiating ethnic and linguistic difference in the whiteness of corporate America. Recall George the client from the opening vignette of this chapter, in which he apologetically asks for further glosses on the copy that will make sense to his "English-speaking brain." Making translations sound fluid in English, not "overpromising" or making overblown claims about a brand's merits, and complying with trademark are all interlinked aspects of this process.

A large part of what ad executives wish to explain and clients aim to understand through back-translation is tonality. Susan explained that regardless of the tone they set for the ad, the client is "relying a lot on the direct translation that is provided by us or any other advertising agency" to get a fuller sense of the intended message. Angela, who handles much of the production and legal details for Asian Ads, noted the difficulty of hiring what she called "A-list copywriters" for all five Asian ethnic segments who can also create well-worded back-translations. She explained that Filipino and Asian Indian EBTs usually offer glosses on English terms or translations for words or phrases in Tagalog or Hindi, respectively, and these are easier for clients to understand. By contrast, it is far more difficult for copywriters to make Chinese, Korean, and Vietnamese EBTs sound fluid and retain their in-language poetics. Morris, a creative at a Los Angeles agency, similarly told me that it is difficult to find people who are fluent in both languages and cultures. He suggested that if they are proficient in-language, usually their English is "so-so," while those who "are good at English and understand English culture—can they come up with a really good headline?" In other words, there are not many bilingual speakers who can write great copy in both languages and want to be an advertising copywriter at a multicultural agency. Reiterating how difficult it is to do a good in-language transcreation of a headline, he declared, "The translation **always** comes out weird." Taking this a step further, Asian Ads creative Fen laughed that the English back-translation often sounds like it is "lying" because it is so awkward and strange in English: "The client has to trust [Asian Ads] to do good translations, but very good clients will do their translating research."

Creatives in several agencies remarked that they found it difficult to make English back-translations sound as effective in English as they did in-language. After a difficult back-translation, Angela expressed concern about clients losing respect for her agency's in-language work because "it sounds too Chinglish. They will comment on your English and ask, 'Why is it written that way?'" Angela's description of English back-translation was similar to a variety of English common in advertisements and other media in the late nineteenth and early twentieth centuries, known as "Yellow English." Sometimes called "fortune cookie speak" because of missing articles, incorrect subject-verb agreement, or phonological irregularities, grammatically incorrect English back-translations suggest illiteracy and potential incompetence. Even when Angela warned clients that such a degree of specificity may make the English sound awkward, she complained, "that's what they want. And then sometimes we do that and then their supervisor says, 'Oh, I can't send that to legal, I cannot show it to my boss because it's too Chinglish. It has to be written better.' So even though this English copy would never be published, we still have to do our best English copy." Remarking that they sometimes have to work "twice as hard" as the general market, she sighed, "They get so used to A-list copywriters, but my copywriters are A-list in Chinese or in Japanese or in Korean. And then to have both A-list? It's very hard." Perhaps for this reason some agencies tried to do impression management on this front. Oliver, a white creative who learned Mandarin in college and in China, was hired at one Asian American agency in large part to "smooth out those transcreations and back-translations and communicate to the client what was being said." Such an intermediary role proved to be important to maintain client relations as well as acquire necessary approvals from a client's legal department. Oliver recalled that the tagline "We'll help you get there" for an insurance client "sounded like it was about assisted suicide and dying when translated into Chinese." Yet the alternative sounded too similar in English to another company's campaign, even though it was not similar in Chinese. Although these English back-translations never circulate publicly and are seen only by agencies and clients' legal departments, they nonetheless require client approval. Copywriter Andrew told me that sometimes they have to do ten to twelve exchanges of a translation proof before the client approves it and that such editing can result in their losing the original creative idea behind the copy.

Issues arising from English back-translations were a routine part of calls with clients. In one Asian Ads creative review phone call with an automobile client, small translation details led to broader questions about grammar and norms of use in Chinese for the body copy and descriptive details for an automobile ad. Ella the client questions the in-language copy, and Alan and Debbie attempt to address her concerns.

Excerpt 2.8. It doesn't matter

1   ELLA: There's one thing I noticed, that I don't know how it
2   translates to Chinese. In the copy it's "a sleek redesigned
3   interior and the newly expanded exterior." Shouldn't the "the"
4   should be "a"?

5   ALAN: "A"?

6   ELLA: "A."

7   DEBBIE: Okay.

8   ALAN: Okay.

9   ELLA: But how does it translate from Chinese? I have no idea,

10   maybe I'm

11 DEBBIE: =It doesn't

12 ALAN: =It=

13 DEBBIE: matter=

14 ALAN: =doesn't, yeah.

15 DEBBIE: Doesn't matter

16 ALAN: = English does not. Yeah.

17 DEBBIE: Right.

18 ALAN: The Chinese grammar does not have a definition that way.

19 ELLA: Okay. (0.6) Really?

20 ALAN: Yeah. But we-w-we'll change the back-translations, yes.

Here the client found a small grammatical irregularity in the English back-translation in lines 2–4, and Alan had to reassure her that there was no analogous irregularity in the in-language copy. Disbelieving that such differences would not matter (line 19), Ella required several rounds of reassurances that continued beyond this excerpt. She finally believed Alan when he explained that Chinese does not have gendered articles. In a moment of clarity, she exclaimed, "Yeah, English doesn't either." Skillfully sensing that he had finally reached a moment of understanding, Alan added, "Yeah, English does not either, but you can still feel it a little bit!" and diffused the tension with a bit of metalinguistic humor. For the most part, however, Asian American ad executives did not have the grammatical knowledge to explain, for example, in this case, the lack of English definite and indefinite articles in Chinese and had to rely on other ways of assuring the client that grammatical mistakes in English did not mean that the same existed in the in-language copy.

Some back-translations expose the tension between the legalities of trademark and the aspiration of brand identity. The following is an excerpt from a conference call to review the Chinese copy and its English back-translation. Concerned with semantics, the client's legal team had conducted a search of each Chinese character individually, which would ostensibly affect their meaning, because, as ad executives explained to George the client, Chinese characters modify one another.

Excerpt 2.9. Prosper?

1   GEORGE: Before we go on, can we talk just a little bit more about
2   "prosper"? Because that was a real hot topic for us. I mean hot,
3   like you would not believe the fighting that happened. We in
4   our advertising cannot make promises to people that if you do
5   business with us, that you will financially prosper. We hope that
6   with our processes and our financial advice and our planning
7   that you will come to prosperity, but from an advertising
8   standpoint and from a regulatory standpoint, whether it be
9   the stock exchange commission or whether it be the insurance
10   departments, we have to be very careful about what we say
11   to the consumer at large, so as not to mislead them, okay? So
12   when the discussion around "prosper" came up, it was like, "So
13   we don't use 'prosper' for anything at all, and now you want
14   us to make an exception for you, for a brand-new marketing
15   program?" So it kind of went from there.
16 AN RONG: So in the Chinese translation, we talk about "prosper"
17   or "prosperity," but that doesn't physically equal "fortune." In
18   Chinese, prosper could mean "Your life prospers," meaning you
19   are abundant. That is why it is a good phrase in the financial
20   industry, for financial capital.
21 SHU MEI: . . . I think the challenge here that I find is that in
22   English, words present certain meanings. In Chinese, however,
23   in order to present certain meanings, two characters have to
24   be together, but the legal team is looking for the translation of
25   what each character means, so it really doesn't relate it to what
26   you said before.

As Shu Mei explained in lines 21–26, the act of pulling characters apart
to translate them individually changes their meaning. Separating characters takes them out of context, and translating them in isolation from one
another could make them seem more persuasive than they do in Chinese.
Here writing Chinese copy that connoted prosperity in a general but not
necessarily a financial sense got muddied in the process of back-translating
the copy and veered into the dangerous advertising territory of overpromising. As George indicated, not "misleading" the consumer had become a
regulatory issue (lines 10–11). Richard Parmentier has written that this
type of advertising language, "puffery," is problematic precisely because
"puffs" such as this have shifted during the course of American advertis-

ing.[36] In the past there was little regulation of what could be claimed in advertising, but fraudulent claims and duped consumers led the FCC to take a far stronger hand in curtailing overpromising. Parmentier notes that this action actually resulted in a more complete shift in the consumer mind-set than was perhaps warranted, in that the ideology of regulation suggests that there is truth and honesty in content and that consumers can take ads at face value. However, Chinese American consumers are not necessarily expecting this degree of regulatory control of overpromising, as An Rong indicates in lines 17–20. Moreover the in-language copy did not actually overpromise, as Shu Mei attempts to convey in lines 22–26. Of the various types of media censorship in place in China, puffery does not appear to be a pressing one.[37] In fact removing any notion of prosperity could lead to underpromising and, potentially, consumer disinterest.

George, however, further explained that for trademark purposes his legal team had to examine each character on its own: "What they do when they go back in, they start looking for the trademark, they go looking for each symbol individually." He offered an example: if a symbol was created for a cigarette company but subsequently became part of common use, for legal purposes it must still be identified as a symbol for the cigarette company.[38] An Rong pointed out, however, that although two or three characters together form a particular meaning, when pulled apart those meanings change. George indicated that he wanted to avoid "transposing characters in ways that change the meaning, and then that exposes us in a way that we can't protect ourselves. If for some reason somebody were to step up and say, 'Well wait a minute, we use that for an airline company' or 'We use that for our tires.' So that's kind of what we're talking about here." Just as the Asian Ads team began to look very discouraged, George told them that they had 90 percent of what he was looking for; he just needed a bit more to pacify his legal department. Encouragingly, he continued, "Now the beauty in all this is that I thought you did an excellent job of explaining it, that the language is contextual, it can mean just about anything you want it to based on the setting and the situation." Stating that such breadth would work in their favor, he repeated his request for something concise to show "a legal department looking for concrete assurances." Reviewing each logograph and how they would represent the "literal meaning," George declared, "We need to have that captured on a single piece of paper!" Managing this complicated meaning with a single sheet of paper epitomizes the complexities of in-language transcreation, especially as it is subject to processes of trademark.[39] As much as George wanted to approve Asian Ads' back-translation, he could do so only when they had convincingly demonstrated that their copy did not infringe on already trademarked copy, and in a way that his legal department could readily grasp.

TOWARD ACCOUNT SERVICES

Creative at Asian American agencies centers on generating in-culture and in-language transcreations that further brand identities. As brands continue to play a far more central role in the work of the new economy and in the everyday lives of consumers, the ways that they are adapted and glossed by niche ad executives shed further light on how brands may operate semiotically.[40] In-culture creative generates indexical icons that convey aspects of the Asian American experience that extend beyond iconic signs of Asia in the American imagination. Ad executives use indexical icons that they hope will act as qualisigns of diversity to their clients while they also establish affective connections with intended consumers. The linguistic materiality of in-language copy contributes substantially to this process, through the form of sound, its interaction with visuals, and the poetics of words combined with the creative affect of an ad's tonality. All of these elements, including the process of vetting and negotiating in-culture concepts, in-language copy, and English back-translations with clients, contribute to ethnoracial assemblages of diversity. Yet, as I will discuss in the next chapter, qualisigns of diversity are not always legible as such to clients, especially when they are not conveyed iconically. The communicative work required to "sell it in," as they call it, forms the basis on which they perform "intercultural affect" with clients, to negotiate and gain approval for their ideas. This work furthers the construction and recognition of brands for multicultural audiences, ideally in ways that are consistent with general market brand identities. My emphasis on the minutiae of in-culture and in-language decision making is in part to illustrate how the racially naturalized Asian American model consumer is crafted by these mundane choices of region, religion, language variety, register, accent, apparel, and so on. These choices, which can appear arbitrary and at the whim of account executives, over time begin to form patterns that contribute to the emergence of idealized Asian American consumers.

CHAPTER 3

Account Services

The next round of client review for the creative concept had been scheduled, and the account executive had sent his team's "deck" (presentation slides) the previous day. Dialing into the conferencing center, they awaited the moderator with tempered optimism. Having already completed a few rounds of presentation with the client, Allied Country, the team was fatigued and hoping the client would approve the creative conceit and copy this time. Even though the client liked the visuals, the copy was a source of ongoing concern for both the Chinese and the Asian Indian ads. The first was dismissed as "overpromising," while the second did not align with the recommendations of the client's focus group. As the call started, the client read aloud the creative in the deck. Hearing the client stumbling over the central ideas, Sunil and Andrew threw their hands up in disbelief that the client still did not grasp the concept. In a flurry of signaling and nodding, creative Jun Yi jumped up to scribble talking points on the dry erase board. Revealing none of his frustration to the client, Sunil instead reviewed the "key consumer insights" he had sent in the deck, summarizing these as "financial independence and self-sufficiency. That's what Allied Country is able to communicate to those target consumers, and that's the brand image we would like to create." The client countered that English might be more appropriate based on their market research and planning. "How about I take out the Hindi copy and make the whole thing in English?" Sunil offered. This seemed to please the client. Adding that the copywriter would send modified copy for the Chinese print ad once they had finished altering visuals from the general market ad, the Asian Ads team looked at one another, wondering if they had finally pleased their client. Apparently they had not, as their client told them, "Don't hear me as critical, but I don't get this." Sunil let out a stiff but friendly laugh and tried to strike a lighthearted tone as they launched into a more elaborate explanation of their in-culture and in-language creative, this time correlating it even more closely with their market research data. The client appeared to recognize Asian Ads' efforts and offered a conciliatory comment that seemed to indicate approval: "This is like a good wine. You have to let it sit there for a little while, and just sip on it to really appreciate the complexity of what you're doing." The client assured Asian Ads he was close to approving the creative.

In this chapter I examine tensions that arise between cultural and linguistic meanings that advertising executives believe to be important, how they sell them to the corporate clients they serve, and how this process contributes to racial naturalization and ethnic formation in multicultural advertising. Advertising agencies operate as collectives of experts, each performing different roles as creatives, account executives, media, planners, and others.[1] At Asian American ad agencies, ad executives claim to have advertising and marketing skills as well as ethnic and linguistic expertise based on their Asian heritage culture and language. In order to display their expertise to clients, they employ a number of strategies that illustrate how race and racialization are negotiated in capitalism. I look at how Asian American advertising executives do the work of "selling it in," getting clients to approve their creative concepts, through modalities of affect, use of certain registers, and displays of expertise. These ad executives objectify aspects of specific ethnicities and languages when relevant and downplay them at other times in favor of displaying their expertise about how to reach Asian Americans as a broader category in multicultural advertising. Like many other minorities in multicultural advertising, they are expected to embody and perform their ethnicity and language as experts. Accordingly, they index diversity and act as qualisigns in many of the same ways their creative is expected to. Especially given the paucity of broader public discourse about Asian Americans apart from the model minority stereotype, advertising executives position themselves as best able to shape the public image of this category in ways that further brand identities and Asian American consumption.

Asian American advertising executives train one another to be ethnoracial experts and undertake the creative and affective labor of selling their work to clients. In corporate American workplaces that place a premium on cheerful, conflict-free interaction, such as the tense but pleasant exchange featured in the vignette, performing affect is an integral part of modern labor. To lead clients to buy into the broader project of Asian American advertising work, ad executives navigate "intercultural spaces" of capitalism. Fred Myers uses this term to refer to formations of art collectors and artists in which value and ownership are negotiated; the concept is useful here to capture the differences of culture and language that are vetted in the advertising production process.[2] In chapter 2 I discussed how ad executives represent affect and tone in the creative work of their ads. Here I examine intercultural affect to more closely consider how these performances allow racialized capitalism to flourish in a corporate America where diversity is embodied by nonwhite people who do much of the labor of generating ethnoracial assemblages. Intercultural affect is embodied in different ways that further the communicative work of advertising and offers a lens through which to understand cultural and linguistic ideologies that prevail in corporate America.

AFFECT, RACE, AND WORKPLACES OF THE NEW ECONOMY

In workplaces of the new economy, performances of affect have become expected modes of conduct and interaction, so much so that they contribute to the success of economic endeavors.[3] Fordism was as much an affective form as an economic form, and so too is post-Fordism.[4] Michael Hardt has argued that while affective labor is not new in capitalist production, late capitalism has positioned "affective labor in a role that is not only directly productive of capital but at the very pinnacle of the hierarchy of laboring forms."[5] Affect differs from emotion, which operates at the individual level; it is materially, relationally, and corporeally based and can act as a way to understand what is conveyed, signified, acted out, and accomplished.[6] Intercultural affect can be viewed as another type of linguistic materiality in global capitalism. How ad executives modulate their voices, defer to clients wishing to pose counterpoints, and speak from an embodied ethnic or racial position that confirms their expertise further illustrates the linguistic materiality of capitalist production and its linkages to authenticity and value.[7] Relatedly Patricia Clough has identified affect as part of what she calls the biomediated body.[8] The biomediated body is relevant to my examination because it illustrates how U.S. Census data are combined with data from market research, demography, and history to construct the category Asian American for advertising. In multicultural advertising the Asian American biomediated body is conjured and made legible through the affective labor of communicative interaction in meetings, conference calls, and written communication. Intercultural affect and ethnoracial expertise rely on biomediated bodies that are conjured to serve a capitalist purpose. Regarding this process, Lauren Berlant has written that "the political gain expected of the affective turn—its openness, emergence, and creativity—is already the object of capitalist capture, as capital shifts to accumulate in the domain of affect and deploys racism to produce an economy to realize this accumulation."[9] The affective labor and expertise that are integral to this type of racialized capitalism contribute to assemblages of ethnoracial diversity. Assemblages are performed as much as they are produced, and are reperformed as they are reproduced. They contain different materialities, registers, affects, and circulations. Ben Anderson contends that "assemblage can reorientate understandings of race by focusing analysis on iterative performances of social differentiation in moments of encounter."[10] Such "iterative performances of social differentiation" abound in intercultural spaces and the type of work and communication that is accomplished in this arena.

In corporate America affect is negotiated in spaces where norms of whiteness prevail but that are also accommodating of ethnoracial difference. Race and ethnicity are not openly or easily discussed subjects in corporate America, and talk about these topics occurs under the heading of "diversity." Most general market agencies publicly emphasized their ongoing agendas of casting diverse talent in their ads and further diversifying their agencies by hiring more minorities. This was far less specific, however, than the explicit representations of culture and language that are the mainstay of Asian American advertising. Finding ways to communicate about these differences took considerable effort, usually from both the client and the ad agency. The spaces in which this communication occurs can be tense and charged, as illustrated in the opening vignette. As noted earlier, Myers considers how expertise is claimed and recognized in the cultural production of Aboriginal art and how concepts such as heritage are differently valued and understood in the intercultural spaces of art worlds.

Intercultural spaces, like the ones I discuss here, are zones of value formation and contestation.

In the intercultural space of Asian American advertising agencies and their corporate clients, most of whom have little or no cultural or linguistic expertise concerning Asian populations in the United States, intercultural affect enables the production of profit and underscores the conflicting ideologies of ethnoracial difference that can result in tension and discord. Clients commissioning multicultural advertising do so because they want to reach minority consumers through in-language and in-culture creative placed in niche media, but they often seemed uncomfortable questioning what ad executives presented for approval, out of concern for seeming culturally insensitive or inadvertently offending them. Asian American ad executives seemed to be acutely aware of this dynamic and took special care to never make clients feel uninformed or uneducated about aspects of ethnicity and culture. These carefully calibrated positions are managed through intercultural affect performed in the day-to-day conversations between ad executives and clients. Asian American ad executives embody and perform affect with clients and showcase their expertise alongside it to carefully and thoughtfully sell multicultural advertising to clients.

Expertise and Authority

Advertising is widely regarded as a professional field in which agency employees adopt the generic title "advertising executive," but what it takes to become an expert is less clear. Although advertising has emerged as a field of academic study and professional training in communications programs and business schools worldwide, many in this field have had minimal formal advertising education per se. Such a dynamic is epitomized in fictional depictions of 1960s advertising in the television drama *Mad Men*. Several characters who begin as secretaries and interns become expert advertising executives, and even the inimitable Don Draper, creative director and agency kingpin, was once a fur coat salesman. Advertising today may be entered by multiple paths and various certifications, and advertising executives who manage to excel in this field do so by successfully performing skills related to some aspect of the advertising process. For instance, generating original creative work is regarded as an innate talent more than a learned skill; account executives who keep campaigns on schedule and liaise with clients require excellent organizational and interpersonal skills, while media buying and production work call for technical knowledge in art design and editing. Experts from other fields, such as anthropology, may apply their ethnographic research skills to account planning,[11] while film directors may choose to work in production. In short, there is no one way to become an advertising executive, and the vast majority I met found their way into this industry through internships during and after college and worked their way up through agency ranks, switching agencies as it helped build their careers.

As in other professional settings where individuals are deemed experts, enacting expertise involves accessing a knowledge base that is extensive but available to the expert, one that is "authoritative." Such authority is critical not only to the day-to-day work of advertising development and production but also to broader claims about how the advertising industry is structured and the directions in which it may grow and expand. Similar to how Charles Goodwin argues that a large part of expertise lies in classification, in how individual distinctions are selected and heightened to create systems of values, Asian American executives organize census data in ways that naturalize statistics into racial and ethnic categories.[12] "Enactments" by experts for other experts, as well as nonexperts, underscore that expertise is not a static credential but a shifting one that is continually performed and contingent in each interaction, depending on the interlocutors.[13] In this sense current modes of corporate self-presentation position the self centrally, and advertising executives aim to sell a brand as well as "a favorable image of themselves."[14] Some advertising executives compel clients to commission their services, arguing that without advertising, goods and services industries would barely subsist, let alone thrive.[15] They alone know, for instance, that depicting their client's logo and goods in the Chinese art form of paper cutting would resonate well with their intended consumers (fig. 3.1).

Along with credentials, degrees, and other certifications, the use of specialized language confers power and authority.[16] One of the central ways advertising executives display expertise is by being able to talk the talk.[17] Creating specialized terminology, using it to discuss certain aspects of the advertising process, and encouraging clients to adapt to this way of discussing their work communicates their authority and expertise while offering easy ways to talk about race, ethnicity, and language. I see such specialized terminology as a product of late capitalist production, especially neoliberalism, in which certain kinds of intellectual labor are valued, especially when market forces confirm their demand. The 2010 U.S. Census count indicates that the total minority population has exceeded

3.1 Lowe's Chinese American print ad featuring in-culture paper-cutting work (2008).

100 million and is now a third of the overall population. Asian Americans are considered to be among the fastest growing of the minority populations, and the demand to reach them is accordingly increasing. Developing a set of terminologies that showcase their skills and talents helps Asian American ad executives enact their expertise in multicultural advertising. Bonnie Urciuoli identifies a rise in "skills discourses" that fetishize certain valued knowledge and abilities in different aspects of the new economy. She argues that these skills are not "a coherent semantic field" but rather a "loose associational chain" of "mutually enregistered uses."[18] Urciuoli's point here is that terms like *diversity* and *culture* connote different meanings to anthropologists than they do to advertising and other industries, but that the terminologies remain the same; for example, multicultural and general market agencies use terms like *diversity* to index more or less specific representations.

What I observed in multicultural advertising was the push to develop a unique set of lexical items and categories and ways of speaking about them. This process suggested preliminary evidence of enregisterment, or register (specialized language) formation, although my observations suggested that this register did not yet have the full range of phonological and affective dimensions expected of registers in general. Nonetheless these terms and ways of speaking about multicultural advertising created a sense of unity in their process and endeavors. Terms like *in-language*, *in-culture*, and *transcreation* are evidence of this emergent register, as are terms like *DMAs* (designated market areas), which are both specialized and unique to multicultural advertising. Leveraging this terminology imparted authority to Asian American ad executives and allowed them to further differentiate their work from general market advertising—a distinction that has become increasingly important for multicultural advertising as general market advertising has sought to ramp up its efforts to reach minorities. Intercultural affect and stance are hallmark features of multicultural advertising discourse as it becomes enregistered. Asian American ad executives adopt accommodating stances even when their clients are wrong about cultural or linguistic facts and gently redirect these clients toward their viewpoint. Suggesting to clients that all ideas about culture are potentially important and valuable, they prefer to educate and explain rather than argue or assert aggressively.

When done effectively, multicultural advertising discourse and education do the double work of making the labor of this advertising easily describable and legible to clients and also make nonwhite linguistic and cul-

3.2 Email flyer for 3AF "Boot Camp" event (2013).

tural difference accessible in white corporate environments. In everyday client calls, presentations, meetings, and industry events, Asian American ad executives display their expertise by informing clients and their general market colleagues about the Asian American market, the ethnic groups it includes, and those they are expanding to reach. They hold private and public forums to make cultural and linguistic differences about Asian Americans accessible while also reinforcing their importance. Each year the Asian American Advertising Federation holds a marketing summit for agencies, clients, media partners, and potential entrants into this world. They even offer "boot camps" for those uninitiated in the marketing potential of Asian American audiences (fig. 3.2). Throughout the year they hold workshops in regions with large Asian American populations to bring together agencies and clients and potentially attract new business. These types of educational events are sites where enregisterment of multicultural discourse takes place, increasing the visibility and legitimacy of Asian American advertising. Notably this approach to diversity fits exceedingly well in neoliberal corporate culture. In an era of diversity training, HR-led sensitivity workshops on how to acknowledge difference, and a profit-driven push to appeal to minority consumers in ways that do not offend them, corporate clients, media outlets, and even some general market ad executives see the value in this type of education. Becoming conversant in this type of discourse allows clients to make suggestions and requests without fear of offending Asian American ad executives, even if they sometimes inadvertently do.

Such client education also enables Asian American ad executives to speak about their audiences in a register specific to multicultural marketing in order to drive home the unique aspects of their work and their audiences. Terms such as *in-culture, in-language, transcreation*, and DMAs lend credibility to their work and place it at enough of an analytic distance to enable them to claim ethnoracial expertise. Asian American advertising executives project expertise with their cultural knowledge and linguistic abilities, which in turn play a key role in creating and maintaining an Asian American market. Convincing corporate clients of the importance of targeting Asian American consumers, demonstrating their expert understanding of and ability to reach Asian American consumers using relevant cultural and linguistic appeals, and of course making ads are the mainstay of their work. Acting as experts who are best able to address an audience, they are much like advertising executives elsewhere who do the work of keeping this world of innovative middlemen afloat. Indeed general and niche market executives both told me about how they "sell it in," meaning how they compel clients to accept a particular creative conceit as well as the broader social and linguistic assumptions on which it is based.

Selling It In

The process of selling it in is reliant on various elements that must work in concert. Watching clients' eyes, listening keenly to their affect on phone calls, and knowing how to interpret silences effectively were imperative to successfully convincing clients of the value of particular creative concepts and copy. Mandy, a general market account executive, told me about a particularly tricky campaign she had worked on. While the client appreciated her team's work and efforts, for weeks "they didn't have that aha moment — 'This is it!'" Reenacting the enthusiasm she saw in her client's face when an idea finally clicked, she told me that the creative concept the client really liked and approved for production later created public controversy. When I asked if anyone foresaw this response, she admitted, "To be honest, I wasn't in the meeting to see in the clients' eyes what made them gravitate towards that, or what discussion took place to sell it in." Actually tracking clients' eyes to understand their attraction to one creative idea over another underscores how central affect and embodiment are to advertising development and production. Asian American ad executives likewise read embodied and voiced responses of their clients and tried to steer them toward concepts and strategies they thought would have the highest return on investment. Account executive Steve explained that, like other multicultural segments—Hispanic, African American, gay and lesbian— "you have to help create an argument almost for clients to see the opportunity and need to address this market specifically." He expanded on this concept when I spoke to him three years after our initial meeting in 2008, remarking that his agency had found great uses for the 2010 Census data "to help justify opportunities." As he put it, "It's not just taken for granted that this is who we have to sell to. You've got to help clients build an understanding, and almost make a case for the ROI [return on investment]." Such a stance was premised on presenting Asian Americans as model consumers who would be well worth the additional marketing budget.

One approach to displaying expertise and educating clients was linking Asian Americans to the ascendancy of Asia as a technologically advanced trendsetter. Highlighting digital and mobile technologies, media genres such as martial arts, Bollywood, and anime, fashion, fusion cuisine, and numerous other realms, Asia is "having a moment," as Asian American agency director Susan told me. The majority of niche ad executives had lived in Asia for some portion of their lives, while others were second-generation Asian Americans or had formal training in Asian languages and cultures. Thus they understood contemporary Asia intimately or could speak to the Asian American experience from a second-generation point of view. Either way, ad executives linked what they did to the prestige and cosmopolitanism currently associated with some Asian nation-states. Susan elaborated, "Lucky for us, we just happen to be hip right now. And we know that someday we won't be hip, you know it'll be Paris again, or it'll be Spain. Right now, thanks to China, I think, the whole world is watching the East." Emphasizing the expertise of her agency, she added that her ad executives are well versed in their heritage cultures and languages, have been to Asia numerous times, and have maintained numerous business contacts, friends, and family there.

The worldwide popularity of Asia, as Asian American ad executives saw it, reflected positively on Asian American heritage. Susan explained that "[Asian Americans] are saying, 'Hey, you know I'm proud to be an Asian American!' So when we're reaching the so-called Asian American market, we're very cognizant that we have to be a little more up to speed about the psyches of these Asian Americans." This knowledge of Asia was especially valuable in offsetting other areas in which some Asian American ad executives struggled. For instance, if their English was accented or they required visa sponsorship to work in the U.S. advertising industry, Asian American ad executives could gloss these as a profitable extension of a rising Asia and, by association, a rising Asian America. Being a first-generation Asian immigrant in the United States in this industry need not index the "foreigner" or "outsider" status once linked to this position. Rather it could mean being on the pulse of what is trending in Asia now and harnessing such cultural knowledge to promote brand awareness to Asians in the United States. Asian American ad executives characterized themselves as being several steps ahead of their clients and general market ad executives with this knowledge, and at least one step ahead of their audience, who may be aware of Asian trends but require an Asian American perspective in order to reframe aspirational identification for their lives in the United States.

Undertaking this education, then, created grounds for legitimacy and belonging in corporate America and for claiming a space outside the whiteness of general market agencies. The very linguistic and cultural knowledge that would have no clear purpose in a general market agency enabled these ad executives to claim to be experts on Asian American audiences. Ad executive Joyce suggested that clients are open to such convincing and that

> sometimes you have to just **show** your client, you have to educate them. We keep doing this because they're not familiar with the market. When you talk about the Hispanic market, everyone knows that they are the largest minority group. But for the Asian market, they know it but they don't really understand it. So it is constantly our job to keep educating them. And of course clients will have their own subjective opinions, but you have to find things to show them. Because they want to make sure that money they spend will pay off.

Asian American advertising executives emphasized their cultural knowledge and linguistic abilities, which in turn played a key role in creating and maintaining the Asian American market. One way ad executives created opportunities was to make differences that were not obvious explicit to clients, which did not always go smoothly. Speaking about frustrating moments in which clients did not see the originality or relevance of their creative choices, one creative told me about the work she has to do to impress on the client the broader cultural importance of those choices. She offered the following illustration: "Say, for instance, this is the year of the ox, but next year's is going to be the tiger. So we have to make [the clients] understand that it's **totally different**, it has totally different meanings every year when we come up with ideas, even though it's [part of the] Chinese Zodiac." As this ad executive's view suggests, even those clients open to exploring Asian American advertising may bring to it reductive ideas about culture and language.

To address these challenges, Asian American ad executives enacted expertise in several ways, including constructing Asian American as a meaningful category, performing essentialist identities outside their areas of industry expertise when called upon to do so by clients, displaying expertise about a particular group within the larger Asian American category, and training novices to become ethnoracial experts. One of the primary ways they made Asian American a meaningful category was to embody it in their interactions with clients. In their day-to-day agency lives, they affiliated far more with their particular ethnic or linguistic heritage and seldom used the broader term *Asian American*. With their clients or with other multicultural agencies who expected them to embody the category of Asian American, however, they acted accordingly. In addition to promoting themselves as an Asian American advertising agency, Asian Ads responded enthusiastically when addressed by clients and ad industry colleagues as "our Asian friends," the "Asian neighborhood," and even the "Asian gang." These names added credibility to their standing as experts of a particular niche in American advertising.

The actual process of selling it in was primarily accomplished during presentations to clients, in which executives emphasized how unique and important expert insights could be. Asian American advertising executives presented their knowledge about an ethnic group as a key cultural insight, and clients asked them a variety of general questions about Asian ethnic groups in the United States. Prior to one client call, account executive Sunil explained to others on his team that the client was asking for websites frequented by Filipinos: "This is part of our Asian expertise, and we have to recommend it as the best solution. It is part of our in-language cultural expertise." Likewise ethnoracial expertise about cultural and linguistic preferences was important when ad executives advised clients about how to allocate a finite budget across segments in ways that would correlate with ROI. Depending on how well they believed a brand or product would resonate with a certain Asian ethnic group, they advised clients on which segments to target. Depending on the product or service, putting money into certain segments could yield higher returns than others. For example, meat-based fast food is not heavily marketed to South Asian Americans, who are believed to eat less beef than Chinese Americans. In fact because many clients assume Chinese Americans make up the largest U.S. Asian population, they routinely target this group, while the smaller Korean American population is more selectively included, depending on the product and how results might be tracked. In many of the campaigns I observed, ads for the Chinese American market were commissioned first and other segments followed, based on performance (fig. 3.3).

For Asian American ad agencies, defining the object of their expertise was effective only insofar as they could educate their clients about current U.S. demographics. They used specialized terms to create racial order out of perceived ethnic chaos and to present their approach as accessible yet specialized. Asian American executives "pull data" and organize census information in ways that naturalize it into racial and ethnic categories. This can include simplifying the seemingly confounding variations contained in the category Asian American. Suzie, an Asian American account executive, offered this example: "The client will be asking, 'Oh my god, you have [five] segments, more than that, how do you really do that?' I think the answers are simple. One is that you have pockets of people . . . on the East Coast, West Coast, basically the coastal lines. So they are very easy to locate. . . . Secondly, they share some common values among the [five] segments . . . such as that they all value family and education to the extreme." Suzie's discursive strategy to make the answer simple and self-evident enabled her to demonstrate effective control over and reach within the Asian American market. The confusion of the novice she voices is nicely juxtaposed to her logical, reassuring expert knowledge. Such performances reinforce the dynamics and conditions that enable this niche advertising to flourish.

As the term *Asian American* became more commonplace, replacing the earlier *Oriental* and *Chinese* to refer to a broader group, advertising executives used the term in their formal introductions and communications. Even as recently as 2012, when I was finishing this research, clients and ad executives alike used the shorthand *Asian* to refer to Asian American. This seemed somewhat analogous to the way *Hispanic* is still used in advertising, though younger generations, as well as politically aware individuals, tend to use the term *Latino*. One common strategy that I observed

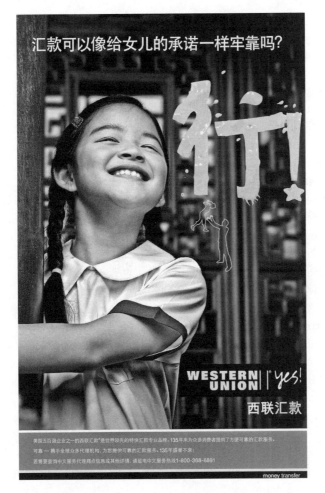

3.3 Western Union Chinese American print ad featuring in-culture and in-language elements (2009).

and that executives articulated to me is to emphasize that the category of Asian American contains a great deal of ambiguity that only an expert can decode. For instance, rather than treating Chinese Americans as a group that has little in common with South Asian Americans, executives choose to highlight points of similarity and confluence. Some ad executives present different groupings as "corridors," such as "the South Asian corridor," that can encompass a broad category or be parsed according to nationality, religion, or class. Such reformulations are important because they assign specific cultural and linguistic meaning to Census Bureau groupings that could be vital for successful advertising. The Asian American ad agency CEO Neeta Bhasin found it helpful to educate clients about the postcolonial partitioning of the Indian subcontinent into India, West Pakistan, and East Pakistan, the last of which became Bangladesh in 1971.[19] While clients usually listened politely, she said, they are not particularly interested until she uses this history to make the claim that South Asians are the largest ethnic group, larger than even Chinese Americans. The success of this narrative and the actual marketing goals she has been able to accomplish by operationalizing the larger South Asian American audience have enabled her to enter a multicultural advertising world predominated by East Asian, primarily Chinese agencies that have been in the market longer. That, along with the increasing visibility of South Asians, Bollywood media, and other forms of diasporic South Asian culture, has allowed her tack to succeed. Despite their apparent upward mobility, this group constitutes a socioeconomically diverse market. Neeta happily reminded me that not just luxury goods will do, because "when you're selling detergent or paper towels or toothpaste, forty-five percent of hotels are owned and operated by Indians!"

Part of selling the creative concept to the client includes elaboration of "consumer insights," which work dialogically to illustrate the overall message. Consumer insights can take the form of knowledge about the consumption habits of a specific ethnic population, about a language variety, or about the spatial orientation of Asian communities in the American landscape and being able to leverage social networks to most effectively reach them. They include consumer trends specific to one ethnic group, those that cross-cut several groups, and those that vary generationally. Consumer insights are most effectively conveyed when they are executed by creative. During a creative presentation to a client, copywriter Andrew presented both of the headlines he had developed: "This holiday season, everything sparkles brighter in the home" and "Decorate your home with all the joy the holiday season brings." When his cheerful delivery was met with dead silence, he took the opportunity to steer the client toward the first headline, which he disclosed was his preference, and justified his choice with a cultural insight: "The Filipino mentality has a strong Hispanic influence, in which everything sparkles and becomes more exciting, more flashy during the holidays. This is why they refer to everything being sparkly and better and brighter. This has a more festive feel." The client, who seemed to have no idea which choice would work better, thanked Andrew for his explanation and went with his recommendation. This was not always a smooth process, but with some clients and accounts, it certainly could be.

In other instances clients had numerous questions about the cultural and linguistic aspects of the creative, even when back-translations were provided. Here consumer insights offered glosses on back-translations, especially when the English seemed to be a poor fit. In one client presentation of the copy for a holiday-themed print ad featuring the back-translation "usher in," the client grasped the consumer insight but couldn't understand the use of the phrase. Account supervisor Alan explained, "It's common in the Asian mentality to talk about seasonal change as transforming, as bringing the holidays into the home, and [brand] can help celebrate and add to the festival." The client rephrased it to be sure he understood it properly, and asked, "So it's more of a, 'helping you bring the holidays to your home'?" Alan enthusiastically agreed and assured him that it made perfect sense in this usage while also assuaging his concerns that what seemed like "a lot of body copy" was "not a bad thing. Asians tend to like to read, and they don't mind having slightly more copy. Yes, it's more copy, but we don't want to lose the message." These enactments of ethnoracial expertise worked to promote the creative work of the agency and also supported broader goals of acknowledging and representing Asian American diversity in advertising.

As this example illustrates, selling it in is a collaborative effort that can take a good deal of narrative work. In the next example, featuring a creative presentation to the client Allied Country via speakerphone, account executive Kew realized she had to go beyond consumer insights to weave narratives and embellish them until they were able to sell it in. Kew began by filling in details about the target consumer so that the client could develop a sense of who they were trying to reach:

We know that our target consumer is in the San Francisco area, first- and 1.5-generation Chinese, and they are married with children, and their household income is slightly high, 75K or more. They tend to own their home and be bilingual in Chinese and English. The key consumer insight for those target consumers: they are looking for security overall, financial independence and self-sufficiency. That's what Allied Country is able to communicate to those target consumers. The brand personality. This is what we think it says to a person: it is a very approachable and experienced guide and advisor who works with you and puts your needs first. That's the personality and brand image we would create.

Kew painted a brief portrait of the target consumers—where they live, their immigrant generation, about their household income and language use—and identified a key consumer insight that is relevant to this financial services company. Reaching this audience would involve altering the general market brand identity to also address these insights. Kew continued by outlining how they would go about doing this by going "back to the Chinese consumer mind-set." Selling it in here involved matching the mind-set of the consumer with the visual and linguistic attributes they wanted to showcase about brand, including the brand's circular logo as part of the creative conceit. Kew continued to illustrate this: "Most Chinese families, they think about their life journey, at every step of their life. You know, it's like, the circle of life. So they are looking for completeness, to fill their lives, fulfill their dreams. The round circle has a good meaning in the Chinese family. So, what Allied Country means to them is how they do their planning and fulfill every step of their dream. That is the concept."

When Kew completed her narrative, there was pin-drop silence on the other end of the speakerphone—rarely a positive sign. Everyone in the agency conference room seemed to understand that some work needed to be done to manage this intercultural space. A scramble began, with much signaling, nodding, and scribbling on paper. Sunil pointed to one of the creative executions on the boards and scribbled notes to help Kew further explicate the concept, circling and underlining as a way of directing the conversation without undermining Kew's expertise with the client. Kew was eventually able to convey the overall conceit to the client, but only with considerable group effort. The team's support of her presentation allowed her to maintain expertise and authority in her intercultural affect, as having several ad executives bombarding the client with explanations would have created a potentially awkward and confusing dynamic.

A less contentious type of expertise involved leveraging social networks and demographic knowledge to locate and reach Asian Americans in DMAs.

Finding Chinatowns on a map or simply knowing that New Jersey has a sizable South Asian American population did not make them easily reachable, especially to clients who were trying to establish a brand presence with a new population. Here ad executives offered entrée into seemingly closed ethnic communities, often positioning themselves as insiders. In the following excerpt, Sunil responds to his clients' (Vanessa and George) request for public relations and marketing by offering his personal social networks, especially after their initial strategy of running a press release in regional media did not go as planned.

Excerpt 3.1. *I'll use my personal connections*

1   SUNIL: I want to update you on the Asian Indian ad, I think we had
2   three newspapers that we pitched the story to
3   VANESSA: [Mm-hm.
4   SUNIL: And of those three only one has carried the story, because
5   it was uh (1.6) Diwali season, right?
6   VANESSA: Right.
7   SUNIL: So all the space was full, and ah, you know they were
8   extremely full, but one of them carried (1.7)
9   VANESSA: Well that's good, I mean considering that we're not
10   really known in that market yet?
11 SUNIL: Right, exactly.
12 VANESSA: That's good.
13 SUNIL: We got them to carry, so
14 VANESSA: [Yeah, mm-hm.
15 SUNIL: And for future ads
16 GEORGE: Mm-hm.
17 SUNIL: Ah, I'll use my personal connections to make sure the story
18   is released, so.
19 VANESSA: Great.
20 SUNIL: No problem, okay ((laughter)).

Sunil had several options at his disposal, including booking media earlier and doing a public relations event. Instead he promised to use his "personal connections" to work on the client's brand identity, to "make sure the story is released" (lines 17–18). Likening this brand launch to a story in lines 4 and 17 seemed to please the clients, as did his offer to use what he touted as his extensive social networks as an expert means of marketing.

Enacting expertise in these ways reveals some of the processes that underpin the development and production of Asian American advertising, especially meeting the demand to generate insights that clients can trust. Much of these insights are born of training and experience in Asian American advertising and marketing, but some are drawn from personal knowledge about heritage language and culture. Indeed the very ethnic and racial identities that contribute to the expertise of Asian American ad executives are sometimes thought to be traits possessed by anyone of this Asian heritage. Acknowledging one's ethnoracial background as a source of expertise was something Asian American ad executive Alice called "native intuition." She defined this as a phenomenon in which people who identify as an Asian ethnicity are expected to speak authoritatively about all aspects of this category. Alice identified a tension between market research and recommendations agencies may make based on "understanding, because we are Asian." By this logic, if second-generation Asian Americans do not consider their cultural knowledge "native," and such socially acquired knowledge is not intuited but learned, the neoliberal notion of diversity that people can speak as experts because of who they are seemed to prevail here, as in other sectors of the advertising industry. Broad generalizations, as well as specific insights about ethnic groups, were taken as social fact when reported by someone of that population.

This was both a selling point and a stumbling block for Asian American advertising. Ad executive Steve explained that his team of experts is composed of "the right blend" of people: a Korean who understands Korean Americans, an Indian who understands the South Asian market, and so on. "Collectively, as a team, the collaboration allows us to create something that has the nuances, the right language touches," he said. This assumption was certainly why I was asked to provide a "consumer mind-set and cultural cues," as I discussed in chapter 2. Answering as an anthropologist, I offered several possible answers for each question, correlating them to relevant gender, class, social networks, and so on. When I realized that this seemed to frustrate the account planning team, I instead offered one definitive answer, which led to more positive reactions. In theory I was happy to help, especially given how generous they had been with their time and accessibility, but I found the questions I was asked, including the following, incredibly broad and varied: How do South Asian Americans purchase insurance or cars? Who has the last say in a household? Which tone is better: humorous or serious? Do parents of young children return to India? When parents retire, do they live with their kids? Is the caste system still important? Is it important to have an insurance agent in-language, as it is for Chinese and Korean? Is a referral from a friend or family member important? How does shopping work—are Asian Indians brand loyal, price conscious, or both? The questions went on, each suggesting that there was in fact one correct answer that would become an authoritative cultural insight and be treated as expert knowledge. Much like the South Asian IT colleagues of one client who were solicited for their expertise, being a member of this group meant I could speak as an expert.

What is common across all of these examples is that the information framed as "consumer insights" is treated as established, authentic group traits that contribute to assemblages of diversity. Taken as social fact rather than a set of observations, these ideas about ethnic groups and racial categories become reified into set characteristics that can carry beyond their original creative contexts. This seemed to happen in all segments of multicultural advertising, where Asian American, Latino, and African American agencies were routinely asked to speak for their segment as if these populations were uniform and easily reducible to a set of preferences and trends. In conference calls in which other multicultural agencies were present, executives from these agencies were similarly asked how to raise a client's profile by linking a brand to an event, such as the World Cup for the Latino agency. These marketing insights, which all three multicultural marketers were asked to produce, are emblematic of the overly simplified ways diversity is operationalized in advertising and marketing, and the more complicated and problematic differences they tend to erase. Ultimately these seemingly small insights contribute to naturalizing select ideologies about race, and ad executives train new experts to apply these approaches to cultural insights and expertise to "emerging segments" of the U.S. minority population.

Creating New Experts

As this discussion of expertise has illustrated, Asian American ad executives aim to grow and expand in whatever ways are available to them. During the 2008 recession, for example, some agencies aimed to reach "emerging segments" of the minority population. Which ethnic groups are included in the category of Asian American and which lie outside of it are certainly shifting, but many Asian American agencies were not concerned about the limits of their expertise. Rather they tried to corner emerging markets by using their market research and ethnographic skills to effectively reach them and by identifying and training new experts. Cultural knowledge about Islam, for instance, allowed some ad executives to make claims of expertise about the Muslim world, including having connections with immigrants from North Africa, the Middle East, South Asia, Southeast Asia, the Philippines, and other regions. While separate, targeted messaging would need to be developed for each, ad executives grouped them together as a geographical unit about which they displayed knowledge and insight.

Cultural insights about emerging markets comprising specific ethnic and linguistic knowledge were generated by individuals from those ethnic groups who spoke the language. At Asian Ads they periodically hired individuals from ethnic groups not on staff to conduct ethnographic research and build their knowledge base. These individuals were usually recent immigrants who were finishing college or looking for work in advertising and marketing. These consultants were paid on a contract basis and hoped to build social connections and make inroads into multicultural advertising. In the development of a new pitch for a money-transfer company for emerging markets I observed in 2009, Asian Ads had already done some work for this client, but not with the newer ethnic groups the client hoped to reach. At a staff meeting the account supervisor Sheng Li explained that the client welcomed pitches for U.S.-based populations hailing from regions included in the acronym EMEASA, currently served by their top competitor. Sheng Li read the puzzled looks on his account executives' faces and took a moment to elaborate: "We are pitching for EMEASA right now, which stands for [Eastern] Europe, Middle East, Africa, and South Asia" (fig. 3.4). Noting that the agency already had experts for South Asia, he stressed that they needed experts in the other areas, a process that he predicted would be "intense and challenging, and definitely time sensitive." Confused and uncomfortable glances were exchanged by those charged with this task, and Sheng Li dismissed the group except for the senior account executives and the copywriter. "I am worried about EMEASA. We have no staff or consultants from those ethnicities," he confided. Reiterating the looming client deadline and reminding them of the importance of new business after the 2008 financial crisis, he instructed them to begin searching for cultural consultants through "college organizations, the community, and Craigslist," and added that personal contacts from these groups would be welcome.

Beginning with the supposition that individuals from particular ethnic groups are best suited to serve as experts, Asian Ads searched for individuals to interview, hire, and train as consultants. Finding consultants from

3.4 Citibank print ad, Russian American promotion (2009).

these markets would not be a problem, Andrew the copywriter assured me. He explained that the challenge would be getting those individuals to ask people in their communities questions, get into the fabric of their lives, and possibly take video "that would be great to enhance the pitch." Angling his computer monitor toward me at our long shared workstation, he showed me a dedicated Gmail account that was filling up with responses to an ad seeking consultants that he had placed on Craigslist. Andrew wrote the ad to solicit consultants for Eastern European, Middle Eastern, and African markets but did not specify racial backgrounds, to avoid any legal trouble. The plan was to screen consultants and then dispatch them to the nether regions of New York City, to the far reaches of the outer boroughs of Brooklyn and Queens, where many of these newer immigrant communities were concentrated. When I asked if they had to be members of those communities themselves, he confirmed that people from each of those cultural groups, however conceived, would be preferable. Ad executives then looked at résumés to ascertain countries of education and work experience and conducted interviews. Successful candidates would be trained to collect data that would be used in the Send Cash pitch for groups encompassed in EMEASA.

On a mild October day soon after, several consultants were invited to visit the office in small groups for interviews. All were women who had answered the call from Craigslist, a coincidence that account executive Sunil and copywriter Andrew both shrugged off when I mentioned it as we waited for the interviews to start. An African American woman in a blazer and jeans who responded to the ad for a North African consultant sat next to an Egyptian American woman in a flower-printed headscarf, pink Oxford shirt, and black pants who would serve as a Middle Eastern consultant. The pair listened intently to Sunil explain that they had been brought in to share their particular insights. Sunil's opening gambit was that he was an expert on South Asian American communities and would analogously consider them experts on North Africa and the Middle East, respectively. Noting that their ethnic background would help to an extent, he said he would pick up where their heritage left off and teach them the nuts and bolts of how to become experts. In the half hour that followed, Sunil laid bare the intricacies of how to be an ethnographer for hire: ways to ask questions, when to initiate conversation and when to remain silent, the level of familiarity required before videotaping, and what to record if given permission. All good advice, from where this anthropologist was sitting. "When you ask questions, you will need to put it in a format that clients understand," he emphasized. One of the women asked for clarification about whom to ask and what consumer perspectives Sunil sought. He told them to learn more about their interviewees' consumer lifestyles, including the media they watched and what they did for leisure: "Don't just ask which media, but *why* that media. Is it because they want to know what's happening in their home country . . . or is it only entertainment?" He also emphasized the broader goals of noting the spatial location of certain communities, asking them to make note of the "pockets" of blue-collar, white-collar, and other categories in each New York City neighborhood, down to the street blocks. This, he explained, would ultimately enable Asian Ads to do more effective marketing.

Sunil carefully described the end goal of gathering enough specific demographic information to create relevant categories, as well as glean group-specific insights that might be relevant. In underscoring their role as experts, he told them that they alone would be best positioned to make sense of their data, such as the relevance of differences of class and social status. Moreover only they would be especially sensitive to culturally specific insights and value systems to which others may be less attuned. This would enable them to create sketches of ideal consumers for their pitch, much like the ones Asian Ads had created for other groups. Sunil showed them the glossy collection of trifold marketing materials, in which characters of different class categories were depicted in their everyday lives, their consumer tastes and habits showcased prominently (fig. 3.5; see also fig. 2.2). Cautioning that this was merely an example, not a template, he told them that theirs could look quite different. Dutifully noting all these suggestions in her notebook, one consultant asked, "Do you recommend how we should approach?" Sunil expanded on his earlier instruction of categorizing people as they go along, noting that they should try to assess how busy someone is and avoid yes-no questions. He underscored the urgency of the project and that they should "make their numbers" by speaking to forty to fifty people in each market segment. The meeting with the second pair of candidates was quite similar, although one woman who had considerable experience from her work at Ogilvy in Latvia displayed a high degree of confidence in her marketing abilities well before Sunil's coaching. Acknowledging her interest in a full-time position, he remarked, "In the meantime, we would love to work with you as a cultural expert," and continued with the training session.

While basing each candidate's heritage in an ethnoracial group did not automatically make her an expert, it did seem to create the foundation

Asian American Values

Immigrant experience; **family security** is crucial

Stay **connected with their roots** is important

Believe **education** is 'pathway to success'

Family is central Close-knit **communities**

Saving is an important value/ virtue

Hierarchical - elders are revered

'**Collective**' cultures - emphasis on group vs. individual

3.5 Slide from a client presentation for Asian American advertising strategies featuring in-culture values thought to be shared by Asian ethnic groups (2009).

for gathering particular ethnographic data quickly for market research purposes. Steadily building the candidates' confidence, Sunil emphasized that they would be the ones to best identify what he called "emotional linkages" through their face-to-face interaction. Remarking on the limited nature of survey tools, he made eye contact with each consultant as he explained that these instruments rarely provide the "in-person, emotional, feeling thing. You never get that in a survey. *You* need to interpret face-to-face." Echoing what he and his colleagues do with clients, he urged them to act as the cultural translators for their groups. He explained that eliciting goals and aspirations and having the interviewees articulate what is important to them about their families and American life are all vital because sending money is an emotional transaction—how often they send it, how much they send, and for what reasons would be very helpful to understand. To illustrate this point, he offered an example from the South Asian research on *hawala*, a preferred system of money transfer in some regions, in which fees are relatively low and there is no public transaction record or taxation. Explaining that it was through Asian Ads' research that they understood the intricacies of hawala and accordingly created their strategy and message, he reminded the candidates that they were best positioned to find similar insights. When one candidate suggested that Africans "can be guarded," Sunil reassured her that she should not approach those who seem so, complimenting her on her insight by exclaiming, "You will know, so don't do it!" When a second candidate raised concerns about videotaping Middle Eastern immigrants who believe in the "evil eye," Sunil beamed and remarked, "Thank you! I didn't know that, and it is great to know!" Puffing them up further, he leaned in to concede that even his office full of experts could not interpret data on these communities as well as they could: "Even if we're there in front of them, we won't know what the smile means. Which is why we need you on our side, right?" With this lesson in symbolic anthropology complete, Sunil seemed content that his candidates were ready to start the process. He led them out of the conference room and waved them forth to the outer boroughs of New York City.

Sunil's transformation of these Craigslist respondents into experts proved effective, as these newly fashioned ethnographers diligently returned to the office within days, bearing bits of video, a handful of diaries, and many cultural insights with emotional linkages. Sunil reviewed the data with each and invited them to guide him through the next stage of analysis, in which they were asked to offer suggestions on how to "change [their interviewees'] behavior to be more aligned with the brand," as Sunil put it. He remarked that the right "consumer insights" would be showcased in the Send Cash pitch in ways that would appeal to clients and other ethnoracial experts alike. Training processes like these underscore that ethnoracial background alone is not enough to create multicultural adver-. tising and that more specific skills are required to generate the type of expert strategy that will make a pitch or a campaign successful. Much of the work that ultimately led to success, however, was accomplished interpersonally, in the day-to-day work of building agency expertise and successfully performing intercultural affect.

INTERCULTURAL AFFECT AND RACIAL NATURALIZATION

Claims of expertise abound in professional and skilled realms of work everywhere and are absolutely vital to multicultural advertising. Expertise, however, is only as useful as how it is deployed and the extent to which both parties acknowledge it. Intercultural spaces are sites in which expertise is negotiated, both in the creative work and in the embodied presentation of expertise by multicultural ad executives. Intercultural affect was especially important because geographic distance, shrinking advertising budgets, and downsizing have made face-to-face visits for anything other than new business something of an anomaly. Most business was conducted via phone or video conference, and most seemed to favor the former. Usually a set of slides to be viewed as a PDF or PowerPoint file were sent in advance of a call, and each party gathered around a speakerphone in their respective conference rooms; additionally some people called in from remote locations. Such an interactional format was ripe for minor misunderstandings and communicational miscues between clients and agencies, even when concerted efforts were made to find a cultural middle ground about what a successful business conversation should sound like. In this section I look at aspects of intercultural affect, especially advertisers' metacultural and metapragmatic assessments of their own performances with clients. The stances they take during friendly as well as tense interactions with clients suggest that intercultural affect plays a role in racialization, specifically the racial naturalization of Asian Americans. Doing small talk, performing conversational routines to which they may not be accustomed, and otherwise adapting to the interactional norms of white corporate America worked to soften the "forever foreigner" stereotype. Indeed consistently enacting pleasant intercultural affect, even during tense encounters, was an important way for agencies to maintain business relationships and build collegiality with one another.

Building Rapport through Intercultural Affect

Dedication to the client was paramount for Asian American agencies, and they demonstrated their loyalty to client brands among themselves and to their clients. In addition to the standard industry practice of working on only one account in each product category at a time, Asian Ads, like other Asian American agencies I spent time in, went further to make clients' brands part of their everyday lives. They aimed to consume their clients' brands whenever possible. This was easier done for some brands, such as using a money-transfer service, drinking a certain brand of coffee, or eating a new sandwich introduced by a fast-food client. Some products would arrive at the agency courtesy of the client or the account executive in charge, who pushed creatives and others to have an experiential relationship with the product. At Asian Ads this often happened at the weekly agency-wide meeting. With everyone in the room, account executives would review the progress of different campaigns and ads, while upper management would encourage brand identification. This ranged from inviting people to try a new food product attractively piled on a platter in the center of the conference room table to reminding people to consume a certain soft drink or bank with a particular financial institution. Reporting back to clients about their consumption usually elicited very pleased responses, which often furthered their relationship. Displaying client dedication could also involve larger commitments, such as when office manager Paul tried to incentivize his ad executives to drive a car made by the agency's automobile client. Tempting them by offering to pay one monthly payment whether they chose to buy or lease, he anticipated his roomful of New Yorkers' response by adding, "Besides the discount, I'll teach you how to drive the car." His executives were genuinely amused but not interested. Paul conceded that he made the offer to demonstrate his dedication to the client.

All of these ways of pleasing clients were an integral part of account services and of maintaining and growing a small agency. Larger displays such as buying a car were supplemented by smaller ones such as gestures made to clients themselves. The agency sent seasonal gifts during major Asian festivals, especially attractively boxed moon cakes for Lunar New Year. Occasionally clients were not allowed to accept gifts, but for the most part they enjoyed these little treats, which seemed to perform the additional role of providing fodder for small talk on phone calls. Such strategies enabled ad executives to build and extend client relationships—an accomplishment that never seemed to be taken for granted in this niche of the advertising industry. Such material gestures were coupled with an active interest in the clients' lives. Many ad executives aimed to establish a positive, deferential affective stance at the start of the call, beyond exchanging greetings. Some engaged in extensive socializing before business began. This was more easily accomplished with longtime clients with whom Asian Ads had a standing weekly conference call. With some clients Asian Ads could spend over ten minutes simply chatting on a call scheduled to last thirty minutes.

Performing intercultural affect well required just this type of friendly stance, and making casual conversation was never wasted time because it furthered personal connections with clients and could lead to more business. During one such call with a client, there was much to catch up on because the marketing director had just returned from a long vacation. The team asked friendly questions about his trip, how his family was doing, and so on. When the client shared that the airline had lost his luggage, the Asian Ads team conveyed appropriate dismay, followed by requisite relief that it had eventually been returned to him. The client, who seemed to want to continue this friendly line of interaction, changed the topic to inquire about one of the Asian Ads executives who had been expecting a baby. The team happily reported the birth of her baby, adding, "She sent pictures to you too, but they bounced back." The conversation took numerous other turns, including details about the delivery and how the new mother was doing. After ten minutes of laughing and chatting, creative Stanley and account executive Maya seemed unable to carry on without at least wordlessly acknowledging the humorous nature of this conversation. With every new topic the client introduced, they were almost unable to contain their laughter, and began to make hand gestures indexing the chattiness of the client and the rambling nature of this opening portion of their weekly conference call. It all seemed to be in good humor, and the Asian Ads team welcomed these pleasant conversational exchanges as they did the important work of building and maintaining long-term client relationships.

Moreover such exchanges built a strong foundation for times of critical feedback. Clients who had good relationships with Asian Ads executives met them halfway in their friendly demeanor, and they went to considerable lengths to present themselves as supportive and helpful interlocutors. They performed interest and curiosity, as in the chatty conversation that brought Maya and Stanley to quiet giggling, and conveyed gratitude and praise whenever warranted. In some instances there was enough rapport and trust for lighthearted joking and teasing as well. In the following excerpt from a call with their longtime client Allied Country, Rufus provided status updates on several ads in progress, and Vanessa the client seemed genuinely pleased. Rufus followed with questions that he should have known the answers to himself, and Vanessa took the opportunity to poke fun at him.

Excerpt 3.2. *Great great great*

1   RUFUS: Okay, great.
2   VANESSA: ((laughter))
3   RUFUS: Great. Great great great.
4   VANESSA: Great! Sounds fantastic.
5   RUFUS: All right.
6   VANESSA: ((mumble))
7   RUFUS: I have one question. I'm sorry to be taking so much of your
8   time.
9   VANESSA: **Noooo** I'm here for **you.**

10   JUN YI: Oh wooow

11   ALL ON CALL: ((laughter))

Vanessa's playfulness came through in the reversal of roles (line 9), as the agency is the party commissioned to serve the client, not the reverse. Vanessa's "**Noooo** I'm here for **you**" flipped this dynamic and allowed her to have a bit of fun at Rufus's expense. As in past conversations, Rufus took advantage of being relatively new on the account by asking her questions instead of finding those answers on his own. Despite Vanessa's gentle barb, which stunned Jun Yi and elicited laughter in others (lines 10–11), Vanessa confirmed that she was simply being playful with Rufus when she concluded the call by telling the team, "You are the best team in the world!" Both parties performed intercultural affect, and Vanessa preserved a pleasant tone while still being clear that they were behind schedule. Her gentle reminder, "Yes, the legal team would have wanted it last week, but Friday is fine," was an affective stance that further endeared the team to her, and she in turn seemed to be able to cajole a higher degree of service out of them. This sort of rapport is an ideal that many account executives strive for but cannot take for granted, especially if the client takes a different affective stance. Even though Asian Ads remained deferential, Vanessa had no culturally or linguistically sensitive content to discuss and so could risk joking with Rufus without fear of offending him or the agency. In this example, both parties seemed to understand the humor, that Vanessa's remark was meant to amuse and was successful because Asian Ads laughed along.

In other conversations clients tended to steer clear of making jokes, especially about creative content, because they wished to avoid comments that could be construed as mocking. Back-translations are one area that can bring clients to outright laughter, about which they usually apologize, and ad executives have little recourse but to laugh along. In the spirit of fun and humor, such laughter is not intended to be offensive in intercultural spaces, especially when an apology is proffered after the laugh. Usually such amused feedback occurs when copy that works in-language is translated awkwardly or in an overly dramatic fashion. Some clients attempt to share a laugh with ad executives rather than simply laugh at copy and back-translations, but ad executives are not always attuned to why a back-translation might seem humorous to a native English speaker. Overall, however, ad executives seemed to value humor highly; even though many were cautious about how to deploy it in ads, they nonetheless infused everyday interactions with humor.

Being able to say things to each other that would be too impolite or politically incorrect to say in front of clients allowed ad executives to find common ground and diffuse tension; for example, ad executives sometimes joked with their team about insider stereotypes about each ethnic group.[20] One such exchange occurred while an account team sat in the conference room ready to deliver a presentation, waiting for their conference call to start. With pleasant hold music on in the background and polite directives to wait for the conference moderator, Andrew decided it was a good moment to hit the group up for a donation for a 2009 earthquake relief fund to aid victims in the Philippines. Sunil asked if he would also be collecting for Pakistan, as it had also recently experienced an earthquake. "Okay. Yes, in different envelopes," Andrew replied. Sunil didactically explained that he was making a human gesture, that people are people, and exclaimed, "Oh, is that racism or what?" Flustered, Andrew explained that they have to be separate envelopes but are both important. When Sunil identified the two envelopes as proof of Andrew's racism, Andrew turned bright red and everyone laughed. Sunil assured him that he was only joking and that he was a good guy, and Andrew was saved a response because the conference call moderator came on the line. Andrew recovered as his colleagues smiled at him while they began making small talk into the speakerphone. Creating common frames of reference for laughter and humor served as opportunities to practice and hone intercultural affect and made shared humor with clients more fluid and natural.

Such rapport was essential to selling it in, which was not always an easy process. When both parties performed intercultural affect, ad executives could work more easily with clients who seemed anxious about appearing insensitive when conveying feedback about in-language and in-culture transcreation. In the following excerpt the client George is exceedingly cautious about offering criticism and makes the rare move of assuming the burden of communicative responsibility. The Asian Ads team had sent their creative deck to the client and just finished presenting their recommendations for the brand, when George responded.

Excerpt 3.3. Don't hear my comments as being critical

1 GEORGE: I love the idea, don't hear my comments as being critical.
2 AN RONG: Oh no, no, I think that your, your comments are very
3   valuable.
4 GEORGE: Let's talk about concept two. I like the idea of going

5 through different life stages. I think it is a great idea to use a
6 life map. It was a little bit difficult for me to grasp the concept
7 of connecting the dots with these visuals (↑). Although I like
8 what you're trying to do here, I'm not sure that the concept
9 of connecting the dots comes across as strongly. Now, it could
10 be that, now please, tell me, tell me if this is not the case, but
11 when you guys went about creating this, did you create this
12 first in Chinese, in-cultural, if you will, and now what we're
13 looking at is the back-translation?
14 AN RONG: Yes, correct, we created it in-culture, with the visuals
15 and wording, that we can we use to inspire a Chinese family.
16 And you look at this, actually it is, uh, a back-translation.
17 GEORGE: That's what I wanted to try to clarify, because for me, and
18 I'm trying to adjust my thought processes, I'm looking at this
19 and I'm trying to uh, I'm trying to um, make the, consume the
20 concept in my English-speaking brain (↑).
21 TEAM: ((uneasy laughter)).

George does a great deal of accommodative work throughout this exchange, as does the team presenting the concept. George opened with his positive regard for the concept, having asked the team to take his feedback in stride (line 1). Asian Ads matched his tone by welcoming his comments as "very valuable" (lines 2–3). In what followed George shifted his prosody to end many of his utterances with an uptick in his voice to signal his tentative stance—a trait not present in his statements prior to this critical feedback (lines 6 and 20). This intonation shift softened his delivery of feedback and rendered the comments as suggestions rather than the required changes that they were. Reiterating that he liked what they were trying to do, he suggested that any shortcomings in the back-translation could be attributed to his "English-speaking brain" (line 20). The laughter that followed this comment was strained and awkward, revealing the team's failure to communicate to the client cultural insights through the creative. Even if the intended audiences of the ad would not encounter this disconnect, until the team made the creative easy for the client to grasp, it would never reach those viewers. In this exchange the affective work of both parties allowed them to work through this process with minimal intercultural tension. The solution arrived at after a lengthy discussion was that Asian Ads would create a summary of the back-translation for George's legal department, with a decidedly simpler approach and tone. To reiterate the importance of clarity, George gently suggested how they might tailor the document: "So yeah, if you were explaining it to a five-year-old." This time the laughter was genuine, as there was a clear plan of how to move forward with this idea and explain its in-language and in-culture intricacies to the client. Both parties had adopted the same intercultural affective stance, and both seemed to regard the process positively.

Sometimes selling it in was difficult because of the absence of properly executed intercultural affect. Indeed moments of tension underscored that intercultural affect was not a natural disposition but a learned, embodied stance that ad executives have to be trained to take. Senior executives were especially attentive to how junior ad executives performed intercultural affect and corporate American conversational routines that were essential to communicating with their mostly white client base. For the most part ad executives and clients were exceedingly accommodating, but more experienced ad executives saw room for improvement and routinely counseled junior employees about how to communicate, especially making sure they were willing to please clients but not overpromising on what they could deliver. Many a conference call I observed included a conversation afterward in which senior executives offered feedback about how junior executives could have communicated better and how doing so would improve their skills and benefit their overall agency reputation. After one such client call, Asian Ads senior account manager Alan remarked that the client had been "too nice" to his team, that she should have been more critical. While his junior executives stared uncomfortably at the conference table, perhaps wondering why Alan was concerned about a relationship that seemed to be going well, Alan elaborated that he thought the client was actually just being polite in accommodating their awkward performances as ad executives. To Alan it seemed that the client was performing intercultural affect in ways that masked her discontent with Asian Ads, which could ultimately result in a loss of business. It was also possible that the client was less concerned that Asian Ads perform white corporate American conversational routines, but this did not stop Alan from issuing metapragmatic and metalinguistic feedback.

While it is unlikely that a series of small communicative missteps will culminate in the demise of the Asian American advertising industry, professionalization lessons like these indicate how carefully calibrated intercultural affect ought to be to keep the entire process moving smoothly. For Alan and other senior executives, getting intercultural affect right was part of thriving as an Asian American ad agency. Alan advised against "exaggerating," as he told account executive Maya after one call: "Don't over glorify it, or you will make it out to be bad for the agency, and the community. Choose your words carefully." He additionally advised Maya to speak slowly and not omit any key points, especially during phone calls. An ongoing area of improvement was to do a better job of helping clients understand the lexical items common to multicultural advertising discourse and ensuring that clients followed when the team used such terminology. Longtime clients were usually conversant in this discourse and needed no assistance; new clients, however, needed far more elaboration. In the following excerpt from a client call, creative Fen casually uses the word *transcreate*, a process that refers to transforming general market brand identities for a specific ethnic group by using in-language and in-culture signs.

Excerpt 3.4. Wait, wait, what did you do?

1　CLIENT: Wait, wait! What did you do? You . . . **transcreated**?
2　　What?
3　FEN: Transcreated. The, the ((slowly)) "inspired performance," to
4　　be in synch with the branding (2.3) branding. Ah, uh (2.3).

Using a routine Asian American advertising agency term, Fen became flummoxed when her client required clarification (lines 1–2). The client cut her off midsentence with "Wait, wait!" (line 1). Fen paused awkwardly as she proffered an explanation (lines 3–4), caught off-guard by the client's lack of familiarity with the term and her own inability to explain it on the spot. Later in the conversation she recovered to talk further about the creative and how it is "in synch" with the general market branding, and the client seemed content. After the call, however, Alan told her that she did not offer a clear enough gloss and that she should be able to define the terms she uses. A master of intercultural affect, Alan did not correct Fen while she spoke to the client or interrupt her to offer his own definition. Instead he gave her the opportunity to explain the term and preserve her credibility as an expert. He did, however, stare intensely at her as she tried to communicate more effectively with the client, suggesting his displeasure even though the client would remain unaware of it. Fen, however, stared at the tripod speakerphone and never looked up. She seemed to be wholly focused on maintaining her composure and sounding authoritative as she defended her creative. As a native Taiwanese speaker, her English-speaking ability was excellent, but her cadence became halting when she struggled to explain a technical term that was so routine she probably had not defined it in some time. Seeming to realize that she was not offering a clear meaning, she instead attempted to illustrate it through her team's approach to the creative and to building brand identity.

Conversational exchanges like this one, where an ad executive scrapes by and minimal damage is done, are considered less than optimal. Afterward Alan told Fen in a frustrated tone that she had both misused the term *transcreation* and did not clarify her misuse effectively when pushed by the client. Speculating about the effects of Fen's error, Alan exclaimed, "It's raising questions for them. She might not say it, but she might have to go get a second opinion now, because of how you have defined it. **I** would question it because of the way you said it." Suggesting that the magnitude of her error could lead to a rejection of their creative work, Alan considered moments like this to be valuable for reviewing intercultural affect overall. His broader concern was his junior ad executives' communicative competence in corporate American conversational norms. As excellent speakers of their native languages who worked at an Asian American ad agency, he recognized that they had likely had only a limited amount of experience with white corporate America, and it was his role to offer metalinguistic feedback so that they could more effectively perform the expertise he believed they possessed. The following excerpt is from a reprimand he delivered to Fen and Joyce immediately after this difficult client call.

Excerpt 3.5. Howya doing!

1 ALAN: When you guys communicate with the client, you have
2 to really train your overall voice and manner. (1.8) From the
3 beginning, we open the phone call with a greeting: ((positive
4 tone)) "Hello! Howya doing!" (0.6) All the tones are very (1.9),
5 not business-like, okay? (0.9) You all need to try. You don't just
6 jump into it. Let them know who you are, okay? **At least** to get
7 some connections. When the client says something, you don't
8 need to repeat it again, okay? Listen to what they are saying
9 and then only recap if necessary, right? But you have to, you
10 have to control the whole conversation from beginning until
11 you hang up the phone. The energy, the tone, the enthusiasm,
12 and the **confidence**. What's really, really missing from both of
13 you is the confidence. You are not one hundred percent sure

14 what you're trying to communicate. The message was kind of
15 (0.6), the client said, "Oh, I got it, I got it," and then you're
16 still repeating something that she already got, okay? You both
17 have to work on it. It's getting worse than last time, than I
18 remembered. ((attempt at an inspirational tone)) Prepare
19 yourselves, get into it, regardless of what it is. Pick up the
20 phone, first thing, loud, happy, business-like, okay?

Alan paused frequently to let his words echo in his subordinates' ears. In this lengthy monologue, he focused on what he identified as a critical part of the client services process in Asian American advertising: intercultural affect. Setting the correct tone by exchanging pleasantries (lines 2–4), keeping things cheerful, and managing the client's emotional state the entire time were elements of successful interaction. Alan offered critical feedback to this effect, much to the discomfort of all present. He began by reviewing the basics of what he understood to be corporate American conversational norms. Rather than getting right to the business of the call, which Joyce and Fen both seemed to think was a preferred way of doing business based on the conversational norms of their work time in Singapore and Taiwan, respectively, here they were being asked to do things differently. Implying that their tone was too serious, Alan coached them to do small talk the American way and modeled the cheerful affect he wanted them to emulate, going so far as to smile brightly when saying "Hello! Howya doing!" Even though clients would never see that smile through the speakerphone, a full embodiment of intercultural affect was required to stay in control of the conversation. Confidence could be projected in this way, and being "loud" and "happy" were just as important if not more important than their "business-like" stances. So important was intercultural affect here that Alan himself realized that he needed to model a more positive, upbeat tone in his monologue if he expected his employees to do the same, and he shifted to a softer, more hopeful demeanor to deliver his closing lines (line 18). As this process of correction suggests, there were payoffs and challenges to managing intercultural spaces. Intercultural affect, as Alan performed it, combined his own beliefs about what American small talk sounded like, with an emphasis on efficacy in the advertising process. As far as he was concerned, the latter would simply not work without the former.

Embodying Intercultural Affect

Clients who wish to reach Asian American consumers rely on multicultural advertising executives to be experts on a wide range of topics. In reality most ad executives simply do not have expertise about every facet of their heritage language and culture along with marketing insights and media placement strategy. This expectation is especially challenging for those who joined Asian American agencies after working for an agency in an Asian country, where they were rarely expected to possess enough cultural and linguistic knowledge to speak for an entire country, let alone a continent. Yet in an Asian American context, clients expect ad executives to be experts in a number of areas pertaining to their ethnoracial background. The following example is an excerpt from a phone conversation with a client in which the account team had just completed a creative review of ads for Chinese and Asian Indian audiences. Maya, an ad executive, had not worked on these ads, but because one of the ads featured in-language copy written by a freelance copywriter, the account team asked her to be present for the call. Not introduced at the start of the call, she had to step in as the call was ending to answer questions about the copy.

Excerpt 3.6. Asian Indian expert

1   CLIENT: Jody?
2   JODY: Yes?
3   CLIENT: Who else is with you?
4   JODY: Who else is with me? (1.8)
5   CLIENT: Yeah, thank you guys=
6   JODY: =oh, oh, oh Fen! Yeah, Fen and Joyce, a bunch of people
7   here. And Stanley, and Maya, our Indian expert. ((Laughter))
8   CLIENT: Yeah, okay: (1.2) I'm glad there's an expert over there in
9   Asian Indian, cause=
10 JODY: =yeah=
11 CLIENT: =we
12 JODY: We do have Asian Indian staff here.
13 ((laughter))
14 CLIENT: Good. (2.5) All righty. You're located in New York, right?
15 JODY: Yes, we're in New York, New York City.
16 CLIENT: Okay, are you, are you all creative or just media?
17 JODY: Oh, everybody's here. We're in the same office.

18 CLIENT: No no no, the person that you just said for Asian Indian.

19 JODY: Oh, she's right here, she's right here with, with us. Maya,

20   you want to say something in Hindi?=

21 MAYA: =Hi. I

22 JODY: =in Hindi! ((laughter))

23 MAYA: I'm actually an account, I'm an account executive. (1.0)

24 CLIENT: Ah. Is, is *Indian Express* a good mag—ah, publication?

25 MAYA: Yes, *Indian Express* is a very good Indian newspaper ((Jody

26   gestures to Maya to stop talking))

27 CLIENT: Okay, that's all I want to know. Thank you.

28 MAYA: It's very um, good.

29 CLIENT: Okay. (1.8) Perfect.

30 MAYA: All right.

31 JODY: Okay, thank you all.

In this exchange the client's line of inquiry was not immediately apparent to Jody (line 4). After initially thinking the client was simply trying to thank the entire room, she realized that the real intent was to find the "expert over there in Asian Indian" (lines 8–9) which led her to excitedly announce the presence of the "Asian Indian staff." Further misunderstanding that the client wanted to solicit more advice, it took Jody a moment to introduce Maya directly. After these missteps Jody attempted to make amends by urging Maya to display her expert status by speaking in Hindi (lines 20 and 22). Maya sheepishly responded in English that she is an account executive, not a media buyer. Despite this, the client solicited her opinion on an Indian publication, which Maya was able to remark upon but not expertly assess as a media placement venue for an advertisement (lines 25 and 28). The client was satisfied with all aspects of this exchange, and Maya effectively displayed expert knowledge. Because she is a member of the ethnic group for which this advertising was being created, her opinion was valued more than those of the senior creative and media executives who were also on the call.

In these moments intercultural affect seemed to entail minority ad executives embodying the diversity about which they were expected to be experts. Clients viewed these minorities as qualisigns of diversity and treated them as experts sometimes simply because of their ethnoracial heritage. Especially when clients did not have the knowledge to assess in-language or in-culture creative, clients turned to others around them who could. The notion that everyone is a consumer led to the constitution of ad hoc focus groups of coworkers. Indeed these minorities seemed to act as additional assurances for clients that the transcreated work they had commissioned was striking the correct tone and that the in-culture and in-language executions were being done correctly. In one lengthy and contentious conference call between an Asian American ad agency and their automobile client, there was much debate about the possible connotations of the in-language copy featuring a Hindi phrase used alongside English. Both parties had struggled with this copy. With the account team exhausted and the client frustrated, both parties moved to end the call. Rebounding to a more courteous affective stance, the client thanked the agency and continued, "Okay, you know our normal thing with Asian Indian . . ." Polite laughter ensued from the account team before the client had even finished his sentence about showing the creative to his Asian Indian colleagues. He continued, "Because, I'm having trouble really getting, engaging with this. So I'm curious . . . Asian Indians, what [do] they think about it? In the office right next door to me is my office focus group, so I will try and run this past them." The account executive cheerfully responded, "Okay, okay, that's good." Acknowledging that doing niche advertising could involve clients not accepting their creative despite commissioning them as experts, ad executives had no choice but to perform intercultural affect in ways that signaled understanding and acceptance.

Performing the correct affect of "the client is always right" sometimes meant deferring to their experts instead of moving ahead with the creative their client paid them to make. Ad executives on the call knew that the office focus group was not a collective of advertising or marketing professionals, but four men who worked in the company's information technology department and whose offices were adjacent to the marketing director's. Yet knowing that their own sources of expertise were not so different, they had no choice but to momentarily concede that ethnoracial expertise could be drawn from one's heritage as much as it was a combination of actual skills and experience in advertising. They were not in a position to suggest that clients disregard their coworkers as experts in the advertising process, primarily because they occasionally claimed expertise on these very grounds. Advertising executives likewise treated others from these groups as experts, such as the consultants they hired to expand into emerging markets, or me as an Indian American anthropologist. Finding some assurance among their coworkers seemed to be the norm, and this has not changed despite the growth and diversification of Asian American advertising. In 1995, for instance, Elliot Kang, who founded two highly successful Asian American ad agencies, told a journalist that "more than once he has had to wait for clients to ferret out the only Asian speaker among their employees."[21] In this sense, minorities function as qualisigns of diversity for advertising by embodying expertise whether or not they know anything about advertising layout, copy, production, or media. Their ethnolinguistic heritage is the foundation for their expertise, and this seems to hold great importance in an otherwise white corporate American workplace.

Embodying ethnoracial diversity seemed palatable to ad executives when they were asked to make media recommendations, like Maya in excerpt 3.6, or in acting as an expert on advertising copy. Yet other moments revealed that expectations about embodiment were not easily delimited, and clients occasionally crossed the line into what ad executives found culturally insensitive. In the following excerpt Alan's team has just finished a lengthy discussion about a creative concept that the client decided required further work, and this resulted in an intense back-and-forth between the two parties. Once they agreed to revise and resubmit the concept for another review, both parties seemed interested in quickly diffusing tension and ending the call pleasantly. The Asian Ads team had not departed from a deferential stance of intercultural affect during the call and eased into what they expected to be an uneventful close. The excerpt begins with Fen picking up on something Ella, the white client, said earlier in the conversation about a National Public Radio (NPR) story.

Excerpt 3.7. Chinese belly dance instructor

1. ELLA: You never know. Asian men! Alan . . .
2. FEN: Okay, did you guys hear about this guy who is a belly dance
3. instructor in China?
4. ALAN: ((laughter))
5. FEN: He's like, super popular.
6. ELLA: Well that's the point. Asian men are **very** connected to their
7. **feminine side**.
8. ALAN: ((awkward laughter))
9. JODY: That's true.
10. ALAN: Well, it depends. ((laughter))
11. FEN: I hear it's super popular, I heard about it today on NPR, you
12. should check out the story about=
13. ALAN: =Oh.=
14. FEN: =the Chinese belly dance instructor.
15. ELLA: Okay.

16 ALAN: Wow. Okay.

17 ELLA: Good luck.

18 MANY: ((Laughter))

19 ELLA: I would like to have a man belly dancer. ((Laughter))

20 ALAN: Is it on *Entertainment* [*News*]?

21 ELLA: (1.1) What's that?

22 ALAN: Is it on *Entertainment News*?

23 ELLA: I don't know.

Ella tries to diffuse tension in line 1, but does so in a way that is awkward for the Asian Ads team. The two women, Fen and Jody, have no choice but to align with Ella, at Alan's expense (lines 9, 11, and 12). Fen helps Ella to neutralize the negative tone of the conversation (lines 11, 12, and 14), but in a way that allows the women to share a laugh about Asian men, largely at Alan's expense (line 18). At first Alan tries to laugh along, but his affect becomes strained as he realizes that his only way into the conversation is to embody the "Asian man," a connection that Ella makes for him (lines 6–7). Alan's "Wow. Okay" (line 16) is met with laughter by all three women, leaving him no conversational opening except to inquire further about the source of the story. Despite Fen's reference to NPR, Alan asks Ella if the source of the story is *Entertainment News* (lines 20 and 22), but she does little to help him find a way into the conversation. In this performance of intercultural affect, tension is successfully diffused but at the expense of Alan. Moreover the racialized nature of this diffusion is apparent in the uncomfortable silence that followed the call. Having to occupy a dispreferred stance in this exchange, Alan unwillingly embodied a feminized Asian male for the sake of client relations. He was left in a far more docile and subservient conversational position than his client or his female subordinates in the room.

Such exchanges test the limits of intercultural affect and draw attention to the unspoken norms of white corporate America, where such remarks may not elicit similar discomfort. In the interactions I witnessed, ad executives remained deferential and polite, but their stunned expressions revealed offense that they had little space to address during the call.

TOWARD PRODUCTION AND MEDIA

Ethnoracial expertise is constructed through several approaches, including managing the perceived demographic chaos of the category Asian American, training novices to become ethnoracial experts, successfully performing intercultural affect, and embodying diversity and withstanding insult. The success of selling in-culture and in-language creative to clients relies in large part on the ability of ad executives to promote the merits of multicultural advertising. Even when budgets are tight, the importance of diversity remains a strong push for clients to continue to invest in Asian American advertising and brand promotion. Asian Ads sought to be more than simply ethnoracial experts, even though that was their main charge. They also wanted to be regarded as competent, loyal industry professionals. Yet differences in vantage points and orientations were evident in the intercultural spaces of the advertising development process, signaling the gap between the whiteness of corporate clients and the ethnoracially marked space of the Asian American ad agency. Intercultural spaces are sites in which ad executives had to find common ground between their enactments of ethnoracial expertise and corporate American norms of language and culture. Ideally Asian American ad executives performed intercultural affect through a polite, deferential, explanatory stance that enabled in-language and in-culture concepts to be discussed with minimal awkwardness. As corporations have increasingly included some talk or training about diversity for their employees, a certain willingness to be educated about difference seemed to be built into intercultural spaces. Likewise Asian American ad executives anticipated helping their clients understand audiences from their worldview, vis-à-vis the ethnicity, class, and other categories they put in place. When both parties participated, multicultural discourse allowed ad executives to demonstrate expertise while also allowing clients a way to offer respectful feedback.

Assemblages of ethnoracial diversity encompass intercultural affect, expertise, and embodiments of ethnoracial difference. This commercially commissioned cultural and linguistic representation can be produced only when the requisite affect is performed. Without intercultural affect by both parties and deferential stances by Asian American ad executives, their work could not be produced in the spaces of white corporate America. Stephen J. Collier and Aihwa Ong emphasize that assemblages are "material, collective, and discursive relationships" in which "forms and values of individual and collective existence are problematized or at stake, in the sense that they are subject to technological, political, and ethical reflection and intervention."[22] Assemblages of ethnoracial diversity encompass this set of perspectives and tensions, as they require a version of what Anthony Giddens has identified as specialized social expertise for modern institutions.[23] The structure of the advertising development and production process brings together multiple competing players and agendas, and the kinds of assemblages that arise from these visions are shaped in the communicative exchanges of intercultural spaces.

Moments of harmony as well as rupture reveal the underlying assumptions and expectations participants bring to these intercultural spaces, especially the work that diversity is to do in the neoliberal workplace. Intercultural affect and embodied diversity seem to be required to serve the client. Tense exchanges underscore that intercultural affect can run the gamut from humor and pleasant accommodation to racist remarks and embarrassment. Even though Asian American agency team members sometimes deployed stereotypes among themselves as part of friendly banter, the same stereotypes were rarely pleasant when introduced by a white client. Some clients accommodated and participated in restoring a polite tone, while others seemed oblivious to the offense they had caused, leaving the ad executive to manage his or her feelings without drawing attention to any offense. Such racist exchanges did not excuse ad executives from continuing to perform intercultural affect, and they generally did so until the awkward moment had passed. While these were not a daily occurrence, I observed enough remarks and exchanges of this kind to understand that they were not unusual. Rather they were part of the work of intercultural spaces that contributed to Asian American racial naturalization while also harkening back to yellow peril ideologies that characterized Asian American men as effeminate. Being able to take jokes at one's expense and having deep reserves of patience for clients who were slow to grasp the creative or quick to dismiss it were ways of keeping multicultural marketing afloat and maintaining the value of one's position as an ethnolinguistic expert. It is the only way to move the creative through the development process and into production and media.

CHAPTER 4

Production and Media

On a humid summer day in New York City, a small photographer's studio just west of Chinatown was buzzing with activity by 9 a.m. The Soho studio was one of many on a long hallway on the sixth floor of this Broadway building and was the location of a photo shoot for two of several Allied Country print ads approved for production in this campaign. The Chinese American photographer was a longtime colleague of the Asian Ads CEO; they had met through business and social networks in New York. Account director Sheng Li was present to oversee the shoot, and creatives Jun Yi and An Rong would give specific direction to maintain creative control over the artwork Asian Ads had commissioned. The session was to photograph an infant for a print ad. This one featured baby Eric, who arrived in a postnap haze in his well-appointed stroller. Eric's mother was Chinese American, his father white, and he was the nephew of someone in accounting, who gladly volunteered him when word went out in the agency that they needed a baby for a photo shoot. With no hair, makeup, or wardrobe needs, baby Eric simply had to sit in his mother's lap and produce an open-mouthed smile. For this ad the creative concept was a pacifier featuring the Allied Country logo. The baby would be photographed up close and edited as needed in Photoshop, but eliciting an appropriate smile took an entire roomful of cajoling and cooing adults. Eventually baby Eric's small face spread into a grin that captured the room, and An Rong was very pleased with the thirty or so rapidly clicked shots the photographer took.

As the photographer uploaded the photos to a site for Asian Ads to access, An Rong and Jun Yi conferred about the media placement and page layout that would work best, and Jun Yi emailed the media department the specs from his phone. As they gathered their belongings to return to the agency, An Rong requested an update about the remaining ads in the series. Jun Yi admitted that they were not going as smoothly as they had hoped, since the Asian Indian bride regalia was far more complicated than the white wedding dress and gold band they had acquired for the Korean American bride shoot. The in-culture transcreation required details of wedding *me-hendi* (henna), head jewelry, forehead decoration, and costume to be coordinated to fit a particular region of North India, and they had yet to decide which region. Reading his creative director's annoyed expression, he quickly added that it would be done by week's end.

In this Asian Ads campaign, each of the print ads for the creative conceit had to be individually planned and executed to cater to the ethnic groups the client wished to reach. Print ads required considerably less production coordination than television commercials or "spots" but nonetheless contained myriad decisions to be made about the minute details contained within. Creatives like Jun Yi involved themselves in production to ensure that their vision was properly executed through the choices of casting and direction, but others, such as clients, account executives, production directors, and art or film directors, could also weigh in, making production one of the most painstaking and time-intensive aspects of advertising. Production activities can be quick and straightforward, like the photo shoot described in the vignette, or quite complex, involving days of auditions, director searches, location scouting, travel, and sound and film editing in postproduction. Production and media encompass the interlinked processes of creating or buying art for ads, editing sound, and securing the media in which the ads will appear. Beyond envisioning a media placement for a print ad, spot, radio ad, or other communication, production decisions are based on where the ad will "live": the periodicals or television channels, regions of the country, frequency of appearance, and other factors. The politics of production, especially what the talent (actors and models) should look and sound like and how these messages circulate, are critical facets of assemblages of diversity.

All broadcast ads require strategic media placement in print or on TV, radio, or the Internet and may be supplemented with digital marketing, contests, giveaways, and public relations events. Especially in the absence of dedicated television stations like Univision, Telemundo, Black Entertainment Television, and the like, Asian American ad agencies increasingly rely on the Internet, social media, and location-based digital technologies to supplement cable television, periodicals, and radio shows. Current technologies that enable ad executives to track consumers and map their movement through city streets and suburban malls offer new mechanisms of surveillance and audience feedback to the process of multicultural marketing. Neighborhoods are envisioned via social media and digital technologies as spaces that draw potential Asian American consumers, and digital technologies anchor Asian American communities in regional landscapes. Together production and media contribute substantively to assemblages of diversity that bring together meanings of racial and ethnic difference, understandings of language and culture, and the time-delimited ways they appear and endure in media and space.

PRODUCING ASSEMBLAGES OF DIVERSITY

The concept of assemblage that I have drawn on throughout this book is especially useful in thinking about production, as it is the phase in which finer aspects of message vis-à-vis bodies, sound, and affect are all carefully selected, vetted, and finalized. As Gilles Deleuze and Félix Guattari explain, assemblage involves culture as impermanent constellations of referents that are open to a range of perspectival meanings.[1] Because of their ephemeral, subjective nature, assemblages are unstable in their spatial and temporal orientations. They can offer a time- and context-specific snapshot of the multiple, competing agendas at work to make diversity commercially viable and to make ads that look and feel "normal" in general market advertising. George Marcus and Erkan Saka argue, "The assemblage is productive of difference (non-repetition). It is the ground and primary expression of all qualitative difference."[2] Assemblages are useful here to determine what constitutes "normal" in advertising, especially general market advertising, and as a term that is often used in creative to refer to a seemingly objective set of values about social life and language use. Production and media are sites of decision making where notions about what is normal become exposed and ideologies underpinning them are articulated.

That definitions of normal have changed in the years since I began this research in 2008, and will no doubt continue to change after the publication of this book, underscores that these values are temporally and spatially bound and depend on when and where they circulate and are consumed. The consumers advertising executives imagine, the ways they project aspiration, and the medium in which ads are placed all come to bear on how normal takes shape in advertisements. Qualisigns of diversity have to be materialized in some way, and here they take form in the bodies that are cast to represent diversity, in the language varieties and accents evident in their speech, and in their overall demeanor and presentation. Ad executives are deeply attuned to these details, and their production decisions are careful and deliberate in ways that reveal what diversity can mean at particular moments and how it is to be represented in general and multicultural market agencies. Assemblages are also helpful to understand how ad executives see creative concepts circulating in different media, as they might appeal to intended audiences. Marcus and Saka point out that assemblages can encompass the process of becoming or the act of perception, both of which are important when considering assemblages of diversity with regard to production and media, where assemblages of diversity come to life through activities of casting, shooting, and editing as well as in how they find homes in media landscapes. The mobilities that media creates, as well as the worlds they may conjure, are instrumental to how assemblages are produced and consumed.[3]

Inside Production

Production is, first and foremost, about brand. "When an idea needs to be brought to life and it's going to come off the piece of paper, that's when production gets in. It's very much about personality, it's very much about expertise. People who manage production are brand keepers," production director Lucy told me as we sat in her modernist corner office at a large general market agency.[4] As the "keeper of a brand vision and the keeper of a creative vision," she characterized the producer as "the UN, keeping all parties engaged and on the same page as to what the vision is for that idea." As advocates for the creative idea, producers "bring it to life in the spirit of what the concept is meant to be." Producers cycle through detailed questions to ensure that they can bring creative to life properly. They consider many factors, including these that Lucy voiced to help me understand this process: "Where's this going to live? Where's this supposed to live? What do you want this to look like? What should it feel like? Does it have people or does it not have people? Does it have graphics? Is it animated? Is it shot on film? Is it shot in a real location? You talk about every single nuance that makes the idea." As Lucy's questions suggest, the creative affect and tonality that creatives want audiences to experience are brought to life in production. This work is not straightforward or simple; accordingly the smallest of details can become topics of lengthy discussion between creative and production teams. Greg, an account executive at a large general market agency, recalled numerous lengthy conference calls of this kind:

> You'll get off an hour-long call and be like, "I can't believe we just spent an hour talking about that person's haircut and beard, and what that says about the spot and what that says about the brand." We'll be arguing about "Should we make them get a haircut, or should we make them shave their beard, or should we take this person over that person, or what would **that** person's back story be like?" You really are training a very specific eye on things that may or may not get noticed in the final spot.

Audiences do indeed notice the finer aspects of what an ad looks and sounds like, so spending time on the small details seems justified.

At its core, production is about making concepts look and sound perfect. For Asian American advertising this meant doing excellent in-culture and in-language transcreation. "Like quality control, we have to be experts about all these little things," said Fumiko, a production director at an Asian American agency. Fumiko's work centered on art direction but also included oversight of the in-culture and in-language aspects of the production process.[5] Some of her clients, for instance, commissioned one shoot and overlaid copy or voice-overs in different languages. Other clients preferred ethnically specific executions aimed at each group, and it was up to Fumiko and her team to get the small production details just right. Especially when viewers post feedback beneath spots on YouTube and other websites that provide space for comments, the minute details of production can make or break an ad. Fumiko recalled an ad for Chinese American audiences in which a handheld fan was a prop: "The client brought it, so we used it. And the fan is Asian, right? So we thought that was going to work, but some people saw the fan as more Japanese than Chinese." Here an object intended to index Asia in a general sense and used in deference to a client ultimately indexed the wrong Asian ethnicity. Fumiko confirmed that small details of this nature routinely created large production glitches. One Korean ad director decided the bamboo selected for his ad was "too Vietnamese" and demanded new bamboo before he continued with the shoot. Dismissing the bamboo on set as being "too curvy," he sent the production team in search of the straighter Chinese bamboo. In another execution featuring an orange to index happiness and luck for Chinese and Vietnamese audiences, the Chinese director argued that they could not use the "very round American orange, it is the wrong shape. It has to be a tangerine." Fumiko laughed, acknowledging the occasionally absurd level at which these details are parsed, especially when directors get involved and producers are expected to be real-time, expert problem solvers.

Print ads, as Cheryl, an art buyer at a general market agency, observed, have fewer parts to coordinate in actual production, and much can be altered in postproduction using Photoshop or similar tools.[6] Auditions are rarely required, and models are chosen from portfolios. Details that are not perfect can be altered graphically, making the format far more forgiving and easier to manipulate and control. For either medium, however, the high-pressured time frame can stifle creative concepts. Moreover viewer engagement with any medium is difficult to predict. For some in advertising production, the format of television spots seemed quite constrained. Art buyer Cheryl put it like this: "On a TV commercial, you're seeing what they want you to see, and you're hearing what they want you to hear. You could look at a print ad for forty-five minutes if that's what you choose to do, and take in what you want. If you like it, you look at it. If you don't, you flip the page, but no one's telling you how long or what information to take in." Cheryl's reflections on the temporality and spatiality of viewership emphasizes how attuned ad executives are to the contingencies of advertisements and suggest how, as assemblages, ads' consumption cannot be easily regulated.

The centrality of brand never disappears in this equation, and at every step production managers like Lucy keep the broader goals in mind: "Who are we selling to, who are we building a brand to, who do we want to call to action?" Noting that all stages of production work are done with these goals in mind, she underscored how affective dimensions of advertisements can come through in small production details of lighting, camera angles, editing, and media placement as much as they are scripted and conceived of in creative. All these details are carefully calibrated with the goal of building brand, or "a call to action," as Lucy put it, as well as maintaining brand image with loyal consumers. This is why many producers believe that giving the director what he or she wants will yield the best ad, and they try to do so whenever humanly possible. Greg, a general market account executive, summed up the process: "You want to make sure that everybody feels good about it and you understand as many different layers of meaning as you can." Greg's attention to layers of meaning is a reminder of the deliberate ways ads are assembled and how they account for a variety of audience readings.

Production may appear to be a random collection of details and schedules, but it is about making *art*, the term production people use to refer to the content they produce for television spots and print ads. Many producers liken the spot to a short film and consider the production process as loosely mirroring motion picture production. They divided the process into stages of *preproduction* (pre-pro): casting via live auditions or model portfolios, location scouting, hiring directors, finalizing scripts, collecting bids, and getting client budget approval; *production*: shooting, filming, or recording on location; and *postproduction* (post): editing, sound mixing, and adding graphics and visual effects. Ad executives consider this timeline in terms of how their audiences interact with different media. Account executive Greg explained that the length of a television spot was something he took into account when making production decisions. The spot can be "a thirty-second film medium" or only fifteen seconds, requiring ad executives to "turn the dial up on things a little more, and you communicate really, really fast." This is certainly different from feature films and television programs, where there is far more time for narrative and character development.

Time is always of the essence in production, and time frames tend to be short and intense. General market producer Roger described his role in making ads: "Sometimes creatives bring me into meetings just for a consult, like 'Hey, we have three weeks to do this. What type of idea can we get produced in three weeks?' Especially if a client has a schedule of marketing aims, getting an ad produced in time is vital."[7] Oscar, a producer at an Asian American ad agency in Los Angeles who used to work with a small Japanese production company, also based in LA, was drawn to the creative freedom in this intense process.[8] He painted this picture of the production process once the creative is approved: "You've got your walkie-talkies and there's a chain of command, it's very military. Our production is actually very military. You're looking at maybe three weeks to a month of production, and then about three weeks to a month of post." They adjust this time frame according to the urgency of the project, but it nonetheless follows the stages I outlined earlier. Oscar's colleague Hannah handled the daily production schedule; she commented that a campaign that had just been approved for production was "going to be hectic!" Each thirty-second spot usually took two days of filming, but "could take longer if the director requires daylight or specific weather conditions." Hannah explained that finite periods are allocated for the preproduction, production, and post-production of each ad in order to be ready by a campaign's scheduled media debut. For the campaign she was scheduled to work on next, she was awaiting client approval for the four-week shoot that included two Asian Indian ads, two Chinese ads, and print ads that were to be "consistent in message but not artwork." Noting that this was a very short time frame for four spots and print ads, she stressed the importance of having them ready for the client's launch date. Multicultural advertising often synchs the launch of campaigns with the general market; in this campaign, the Asian American, Latino, and African American launches were to be synchronized, requiring everyone to stay on schedule.

For each spot to be filmed, a storyboard is generated to correlate dialogue with each visual shot, generally sketched by an artist and followed by the director (fig. 4.1). For print ads, mock-ups with stock images are used as a model to be executed as original photography. Each type of product is governed by its more or less firm set of specifications; ads for food are among the most rigid. Elaine, a producer at an Asian American ad agency in Los Angeles, told me about a recent shoot she had done for a fast-food company.[9] She had to take extra care to coordinate with the director, the talent, and the food artist to be sure the food looked appetizing throughout. In order to comply with regulatory rules, they were not allowed to use models of food or make the cardboard container in which the food is served look any fuller than the actual product would look. She explained that when actors bit into the food during the spot, it had to look fresh, which meant that the talent had to be in wardrobe with hair and makeup ready when the food arrived for the shoot. For this shoot, the art director had sent the casting agency a request for Chinese, Korean, and Filipino American talent, so they searched for a pan-Asian look. They rented a location they believed would work for the creative concept—an empty loft in downtown Los Angeles. The shoot went well, and the mild March weather made managing the food far easier than during hotter Los Angeles days. When I marveled at all the details that had to be coordinated for

Man on a business trip is in his hotel room checking his cell phone. His face glows as he watches the lovely video message he just received from his wife and newborn baby.		DAD: "I'm here where I promised to give her the best and to protect her, but I have no clue where to start." 我在這裡， 發誓要給她最好的， 盡全力保護她， 可是不知從何開始？
Mother holding in her hands what looks to be a typical Chinese protection charm. Her daughter is leaving on an outing and simply brushes off her mother's request to carry the charm with her. Mother looks with both frustration and worry.		MOTHER: "I'm here, where I worry about my daughter being a new driver, but I don't really know how to help her." 我在這裡， 擔心剛學會開車的她， 卻一點都使不上力。

1

4.1 Storyboard for the production of a commercial for Chinese American audiences (2008).

this thirty-second spot, Elaine smiled and told me about shoots for department stores that she had to do after the store was closed and had been cleaned. These shoots usually begin around 1 a.m. because most stores do not like to close off portions to consumers during business hours.

Much of the look and feel of a spot is based on location. The LA-based agencies I visited did the majority of their production in California with union talent. The large Asian American populations combined with actors drawn to television and film make it an ideal location to search for talent. Northern California agencies seem to adopt this model as well and do their shoots and their postproduction in-house "so it is more under our control," explained Morris, a producer at an Asian American agency. If they do not have the editing technology, they take the work to one of their vendors in San Francisco or Los Angeles. Oscar similarly told me that production is generally not outsourced in his LA agency because "people don't want to travel as much and there are logistical complications, though you can save a lot of money that way." For Asian American agencies that have social and professional networks in Asia that can handle production, however, casting, filming, and doing postproduction in Asia can be a cost-effective, appealing option. Steve, an account director at an Asian American ad agency in New York, relayed the success of a campaign they produced in India in 2007, stressing the wide range of talented actors from which they were able to find just the right comedic and dramatic personalities for certain ads. He added, "Sometimes we don't find the right talent here in the States. It's easier sometimes to find a richer talent pool overseas."

When asked to develop and produce a new soundtrack for an ad for their automobile client, Asian Ads had neither the budget nor the time to fly the Taiwanese pop star they wanted to New York. Flying a team to Taipei was also pricey, and less convenient than the other option: using social networks and directing the recording session via Skype. Fen, one of the creatives on the project, has a sister who manages a recording studio in Taipei and was willing to work with the New York office. A recording session was scheduled late at night in Taipei so that creatives and producers could Skype in from New York early in the morning and direct from there. Two versions of the song, an American rock ballad rewritten with Mandarin and Cantonese lyrics, had to closely resemble the original English version. When I arrived early one Monday morning, the session was already in progress. After each take, creative Fen offered feedback and direction on behalf of the whole account team to her sister via Skype, focusing in particular on his prosody, pitch, and ability to make certain consonants sound enough like the American original.

Even with a continuous Skype feed, it was difficult for creatives in New York to exert control over the session. Fen quieted her coworkers when they were murmuring about the singer's pitch being out of range, reminding them that the singer had won the Taiwanese equivalent of Grammy Awards. A wave of oohs and aahs permeated the room when the singer finally nailed it, and praise poured out for Fen's sister for being a great vocal coach. This seemed to come as no surprise to Fen, who declared, "We have to let her do her thing." Doing her thing, it turned out, would be guiding the singer on how to hit the high notes exactly right, how to deliver lyrics in the correct cadence in Mandarin and Cantonese, and how to interpret and convey the emotion of the original version of the song. As the lead creative, however, Fen could not help but insert herself into the process as well. Standing and gesturing in front of her computer like an orchestra conductor, she frequently tried to direct her sister to instruct the singer about his voice. This was only occasionally successful; Fen's sister had to angle herself to see Fen on the computer, and primarily did so when she spoke to her at length. The singer could not see Fen at all, so her direction was delivered via the sister in the recording booth. As with the other directors Asian Ads has hired, Fen ultimately deferred to her sister and trusted her to produce a great track. She remarked that she could make small adjustments to the recording in postproduction, where the soundtrack would be "cleaned up," laid over the commercial, and combined with voice-overs that had already been recorded in New York. The coordination of multiple individuals, locations, and creative agendas intersected to assemble a particular creative vision. Whether or not those viewing the finished spot would understand the spot the way these ad executives and the talent did was beyond their control, but it was intended to index ethnoracial diversity to the client and audiences.

Casting for Diversity

Casting is technically a preproduction activity, but it seems to dominate the overall tone of the ad, at times overshadowing the creative. In an agency world where whiteness is the norm and ethnoracial difference is marked, normal is not a simple concept. What makes an actor or model "the best" for an ad certainly has something to do with the individual's overall appearance, acting abilities, accent, and relevance to the brand and creative conceit, but all of these benchmarks are set by white corporate American standards. For general market agencies, "normal" seems to index a person or combination of people that will make their creative work seem less like an ad and more like a work of art or a short film. This advertising strategy furthers three racial ideologies. First, it champions white middle-class values and features well-educated, well-groomed individuals. Second, it reinforces whiteness as aspirational norm in the United States, and accordingly in advertising. To be represented as white, or "normal," is the most flattering and effective of all consumer aspirations and ideals. Third, it suggests that racial differences are naturalized to a point where they no longer matter and that America is in a postracial era. If this were the case, then using actors of different races would ultimately not change the meaning of the ad, but would potentially broaden social identification. This varied significantly according to the creative, but even for those ads that featured "real people" (nonactors) or represented a unit such as a "family," creatives and production directors seemed to have a clear sense of what constituted normal and what would disrupt this vision. In general market casting, then, normal plays a significant role in shaping how diversity looks and sounds. Actors and models act as qualisigns of diversity and are strategically deployed to create audience identification.

Ad executives often operate on the conceit that viewers will identify with brands by being able to envision themselves using a product or service, and casting the right talent does a great deal of work in creating that identification. In general market advertising, casting is a time-consuming, inexact process in which advertising executives and clients aim to find a middle ground.[10] Roger, a producer at a general market agency, described casting as "time-intensive" and potentially requiring multiple rounds of decisions that can take several weeks. Casting companies hold casting sessions, "where they just bring tons and tons of people in," Roger explained. These auditions result in a short list generated by the casting company and director, and creatives further winnow this list for callbacks. The next round usually involves the director and creatives watching live call-backs and gauging how actors respond to direction. Roger elaborated, "You know, is the one thing you saw on the tape the only thing they can do? If you're looking for something a little bit different or you're looking for a variety of reads, are you going be able to get that?" Roger zeroed in on an important aspect of what made someone right for a particular ad: that he or she can respond to live direction and produce a variety of affective stances and emotions in a register appropriate for that brand. Based on this vetting process, ad executives made recommendations to the client, with which the client usually agreed.

Casting is one of the few activities in corporate America where blunt discussions about race and ethnicity occur and demographic categories are named and described in depth. Fara, the director and co-owner of a casting company, told me, "Some clients state the exact ethnic mix they want in their commercials, which on average is twenty to thirty percent."[11] The "mix" refers to nonwhite characters, not the 70–80 percent white cast. If the characters are to have a speaking role, they should speak American-accented English, and the most "normal-sounding" accent is chosen. I took this to mean an accent with minimal regional association or heritage language inflection. Fara explained that these decisions are usually driven by account planning data about the intended audience for the ad, or by the creative. As one account executive confirmed, those data and concepts help define what kind of actor or model would be best for the role. Production director Lucy emphasized, "Truly you should be casting for who is the best performer. Male or female, who is the best actor for this?" Lucy confirmed that she adheres to this approach, even if the gender of the role has to be changed according to the talent they find. Echoing this sentiment, general market account executive Greg told me, "In most cases, it really comes down to finding the right people to bring the idea to life, and then sort of picking up on the subtle nuances of meaning as you get more and more into the process. And then you can start building up the story and the backstory a little bit more in your head, wanting to make sure that it all makes sense in a way that reflects the idea of the ad and reflects positively upon the client." According to Greg, the creative idea itself drives the process, and the best talent can help execute a vision and promote a client in a way that benefits all involved. Greg added that based on the lead they "fall in love with," or the one who emerges as "the best," other roles are cast accordingly. When we spoke in 2008, he explained that a white leading woman in a creative concept who required a family would lead to casting a white husband and children, an Asian women with an Asian husband and children, and so on—a situation that has shifted somewhat since then.

Minority talent is sought after as well, but they have to look and sound a certain way in order to emerge as "the best." Nonwhite talent bring diversity to the ad, but for the most part they dress, act, and sound just like white people in the ads. They share the same ways of speaking, sense of humor, and social worlds. In short, they embody versions of diversity valued by white corporate America, in which racial selection is governed by standards that have become naturalized to the point where they are thought to no longer matter. As Greg explained, "It's not about what they look like— what color, what size, what race, what gender—but who's best for the job." For Greg and others in general market advertising, "best" seems to be the talent that performs most effectively according to these questions: "Do you buy it? Is it real? Is it okay? Is it going to work?" When minority talent gets selected from open casting calls, it is because they fit this unmarked norm of whiteness to an extent that they can carry off a mainstream white notion of what is "normal" or "entertaining." Greg called these moments "happy accidents," when the best actor for the role was a minority who could perform a role without being "hacky and fake-sounding."

Successfully casting for diverse talent is certainly valued, and some general market agencies I visited described their diversity agenda as a point of pride. As experts of general market audiences, most ad executives realized that it was important to offer the client several talent options, even when diversity was not specifically requested. Greg explained that, with rare exception, casting is "usually kept pretty open. 'Cast for open ethnicity' or 'Look for diversity' is what we tell the casting agency, and then it comes down to figuring out which talent is going to make the spot the best." "Open as to race" is how they usually announced the casting call, unless creatives explicitly asked for certain characters to be of a particular race. Greg said that most casting calls today seem quite open. However, some ad executives read this openness as vagueness, leaving them wishing for more specificity. Nick, a general market creative, put it like this: "Clients rarely, if ever, say they want half of twenty percent of people in an ad to be a certain race, unless they are only trying to reach a certain market, which is hard to do with these general market ads." Greg elaborated, "If we produce five commercials, the client doesn't want five commercials that are jam-packed with only white people." He recalled that one client asked his colleague, who had cast only white people for a campaign, "You got something against black people?" For this reason, ad executives strive for a balance of ethnic and racial diversity in casting, which usually means 20 to 30 percent nonwhite. Depending on the creative, diversity is tailored according to the account team's expert recommendation as well as the available pool of talent. One account executive told me about a theme park ad she had worked on for which her team made a concerted effort to make the ad diverse: "We tried to build families that come from diverse backgrounds because certainly the people that come to our parks are from diverse backgrounds. We try and make sure that's representative, but can only build family situations from what we have available at the shoot." Her colleague Cheryl, an art buyer, also mentioned this account to me, explaining that they had to hire professional talent from a nearby major city to diversify the ad because "there wasn't a lot of ethnic diversity" in the regions surrounding the theme park itself. Diverse talent was brought into this on-site shoot to more accurately represent the broader theme park clientele according to ethnicity and race.

Through casting and art design, general market agencies can, when the need arises, tailor ads for specific ethnic markets. Art buyer Cheryl recalled modifying a general market campaign for Latino audiences by graphic adjustments. Beginning with the original artwork of a man eating an apple, she told me, "we had the illustrator make him look Hispanic by giving him darker skin, slightly different-shaped eyes, and black hair." In other instances, general market executives are asked to make ads explicitly for a multicultural audience. While clients wishing to reach Latino or Asian American audiences in-culture and in-language usually use a multicultural agency, those wishing to reach black audiences still use general market agencies. Since the 1950s general market agencies have created in-house departments that target "urban markets," which here refers to black consumers. The creative for urban markets is generated in these departments or simply tailored during production by casting black talent. Cheryl told me about a soft drink account she helped to produce in which the client wanted to target the African American community. The product had tested as selling best among black consumers, and every aspect of creative and production was tailored accordingly. The agency made sure all the talent and production staff were black: "I had a black photographer, a black art director, a black copywriter, I had all black talent. It was like, 'This is your market, and this is what we're going for.'" Cheryl elaborated, "We bought all the media in *Ebony* magazine, *Jet* magazine. We didn't put it in *People*." Adapting a similar approach to multicultural marketing, this general market agency work stood out as being very targeted, and the ads were not intended to reach general market audiences. Unlike Latino and Asian American advertising, however, questions of language and cultural nuance were thought to be effectively handled in-house, an approach that most ad executives do not want to risk for other segments of the multicultural market. Based on the casting and media placement, this campaign was not considered to depict a "normal" scenario or reach mainstream audiences and differed from a mainstream ad that featured nonwhite talent.

General market executives did mention instances when clients were clear about not wanting diversity, usually because they regarded their brand as skewing white and male. Cheryl remarked that a luxury car account she had worked on was "going for one market: white, upper-middle-class, male Americans." She added that ads for other car models by this automaker that skewed more female were treated similarly: "Like a vehicle they thought could be for the soccer mom. [It] was still in the same financial bracket, the same ethnic bracket." When I asked if this was unusual, she indicated that it was the norm for this company. As the worldwide art buyer for this brand, she revealed that they took this approach in other markets as well. She smiled knowingly when I told her I recalled seeing an African American couple in one ad for this brand and a Latino man in another. She knew exactly which ads I was referring to and politely replied, "Those were for the sale events. Because the cars were on sale." With full-price luxury brands like this one, upper-middle-class white men are the target audience, and the client considered diversity less beneficial for brand promotion; in fact it could work against brand identity.

As these examples illustrate, terms like *best* and *normal* seem to have some objective value, as if they embody universal standards. In practice they subjectively reinforce particular signs of whiteness that come to be taken as the norm. As ad executives cast for what feels comfortable according to their own ideals, talent who appear best suited for a role are those individuals who do not disrupt white corporate American cultural and linguistic norms. Production director Lucy elaborated on this idea of likability in her discussion of casting for testimonials, a form of advertisement in which a real person or a paid actor recounts his or her experience with a brand or product: "For testimonials, you have to **like** that person, right? You have to believe in that story, and the authenticity of that person. So even if it's an actor retelling that story, you have to be engaged in them to listen to what that whole story is." Lucy emphasized the importance of audience identification for the ad to work effectively, and here identification would happen through dominant standards of likability, which she did not spell out. Based our conversation, which included illustrations of creative work that she considered to be well executed, Lucy seemed to indicate that audience identification would come from casting white talent or other talent that could speak American-accented English, perform affective stances that were consistent with white middle-class culture, and talk about the product in a manner that was clear and convincing but not aggressive.

Like most ad executives I spoke with in general market advertising, Lucy did not spell out why audiences would love a person in a testimonial, or an ad for that matter, because much of this was assumed to be understood among ad executives. Much of my gentle prodding for further detail and exemplification was met with the response, "Well, you know," which would either lead to my nodding in complicity or create an awkward dynamic that signaled the end of the conversation. For the most part I chose the former because ad executives did not want to be explicit about their underlying assumptions, and I was able to develop my own sense of them by spending time in their agencies. Likewise Lucy did not extensively discuss why audiences may not love a character, but it seemed to be because anything that stood apart from being normal could detract from the efficacy of the spot. Looking unfamiliar, foreign, or unkempt or speaking accented English could all index values outside the range of normal. These values were certainly not limited to nonwhite talent, but the mainstream here was quite narrowly conceived.

Defining and casting for diversity, then, is largely left in the hands of agencies. Greg summarized the approach of most of his clients: "We want to exhibit diversity throughout our commercials. We don't really care how you guys achieve that." Yet he pointed out that sometimes clients do care when whites are not adequately represented, echoing Cheryl's remarks about the luxury car campaign. In a few instances when his agency cast mostly minority talent, Greg admitted that the client became "uncomfortable. The client asks, 'What does my customer base look like?' So to have this cast that is dramatically overrepresented in diversity groups or minority groups would not work as well." Overrepresenting minorities posed a different but perhaps even more urgent set of concerns than underrepresenting; that is, such a representation could alienate white audiences. Running the risk of not connecting with white consumers in general market ads is a major concern that few clients left unaddressed. Greg summarized the dynamic: "It really comes down to entertainment value **and** what makes it feel the most real. I guess sometimes those are not the same, but sometimes they are." Entertainment value is not to be compromised in general market advertising because it is vital to promoting brand. Entertainment value is promised in the creative and ensured by casting good talent but can still fail to be realized if it the ad seems "fake," as Greg put it. "Fake" in this context meant overcompensating for diversity by casting "a representation of each one, of each possible ethnic diversity in each role," as Greg explained in his critique of a Benetton ad (see fig. 2.3). Such an approach to diversity could seem overwrought but does not have to be if properly executed. He added, "You're trying to make it feel like America, you're going to see a nice array of different-looking people." The particular assemblage of the nice array recruited to represent a certain brand contributes to whether the ad succeeds in looking "real" rather than contrived and "fake."

Making diversity look normal is also tied to issues of miscegenation, specifically which races can be put together in a heterosexual couple. Lucy recalled doing a very open casting call and finding an African American man and a white woman who had great chemistry. When she told her African American client that her agency wanted to "do something interracial," he responded, "That's not appropriate for the market. We're not ready for that in this advertising yet." Interestingly it was the African American client that in this case did not want a white actress paired with a black man for a black audience. The specific concerns he voiced to Lucy included "That's not typical. That's not what the relationship would be. That's not what the dialogue would be like." In addition to the default position of the client being right, in this case Lucy accepted that he was in a position to understand these visual and linguistic nuances better than she. His expertise indicates certain types of knowledge because he belongs to the racial group of the target audience.

4.2 Cheerios spot for general market featuring a white mother, a black father, and a mixed-race child (2013).

These orientations toward miscegenation have certainly not disappeared since the 2010 U.S. Census, but they have shifted a bit. Census data indicate a rise in the number of individuals who self-identify as belonging to two or more races, and this has furthered a representational shift from what I observed when I spoke to general market executives in 2008 and 2009. During this earlier period general market producer Roger identified this tension as a "white-black thing. I don't think anybody would be as uncomfortable with Asian and white, or Asian and Hispanic, or black and Hispanic." He emphatically added, "It's **never even brought up**, so there's some sort of trepidation about something." In 2013 and 2014 major brands cast black-white couples featuring a black father, a white mother, and an interracial child. The breakfast cereal Cheerios made a 2013 spot with this configuration of talent, with a white mother sitting at a kitchen table, a black father napping on a sofa, and a child that moves between the rooms (fig. 4.2). The two adults do not appear in the same frame but are clearly connected by the child, who refers to them as "Mom" and "Dad." The spot was considered a success for the Cheerios brand despite eliciting some racist comments on YouTube and other Internet discussion boards, and the company continued using this "family" in 2014. Debuting the first Super Bowl spot for Cheerios, the brand featured the mother pregnant with her second child, seated in the kitchen with the father and daughter. This brand seemed to succeed in representing something "edgy," as Roger and other ad executives put it, by drawing largely positive viewer responses, rather than being "controversial" and drawing negative responses. From my perspective, the choice of talent is certainly a break from the previous decades that seemed to anticipate responses to black men–white women couples as only "controversial," but the creative in the ad epitomizes "normal." Set in a middle-class home and speaking American-accented English, with a little girl eating Cheerios and asking for a puppy when her younger sibling arrives, this scenario would be quite similar if an all-white middle-class family had been cast instead. This assemblage of diversity successfully indexes racial difference through talent alone, rather than using any indexical icons that might create other types of identification for black viewers. For the most part a similar approach is taken with contemporary casting of Asian American talent in general market ads.

Asian American Talent as Diversity

That Asian Americans are featured in ads as "normal" characters is not simple or coincidental, despite Greg's earlier characterization of this phenomenon as "a happy accident." Another way of looking at this occurrence is through the lens of racial naturalization and how Asian Americans' increasing visibility as upwardly mobile consumers does a good deal to explain why they can be considered normal. Creative director Ron at an Asian American agency remarked that he sees many more Asian Americans in general market ads but that they are integrated to the point where he does not quite notice them: "It's not like, 'Hey look! We've got an Asian guy in our spot!'" Compared to earlier negative depictions or periods in which Asian Americans were not included in general market ads, today Asian Americans are increasingly naturalized as a normal part of the American populace. In fact one creative suggested that even more Asian Americans would appear in general market ads if better Asian American talent appeared in casting sessions. He attributed the low visibility of Asian Americans in ads to this low audition turnout, which keeps talent from emerging. An alternative reading of this phenomenon is that the actors who audition do not often fit the criteria for "best" or "normal." Some creative seems to be a better fit: Asian Americans overwhelmingly appear in campaigns for technology, retail electronics, and financial services. Best Buy, IBM, and Samsung are just a few brands that have prominently featured Asian Americans in speaking roles (fig. 4.3). Asian Americans often appear in financial services ads with voice-overs; other brands have cast Asian American talent in supporting roles, such as in office or department store

4.3 IBM spot for general market featuring Asian American talent (ca. 2010).

settings. Rarely are Asian Americans featured in beer commercials. These trends suggest that currently Asian Americans are considered to be technologically savvy and upwardly mobile, if not entirely carefree and fun-loving, but this could certainly change over time.

Casting an actor who can be identified as Asian but not from a specific nationality is a desirable approach to including diversity without disrupting an overarching narrative of whiteness. An example of this is an ad for an online auction website featuring a young Asian American woman who could be Chinese, Japanese, or Korean. Greg, the account executive, explained that the conceit for the ad was a "fox hunt"–style chase for a kitschy lunchbox that would serve as a metaphor for the online auction process. He reflected that during the creative and casting process, the account team asked themselves, "Well, what kind of person is chasing the lunchbox?" Deciding that this person would have to resonate with the properties of the object itself, they wanted to ensure the brand had a "kitschy but not old-fashioned" look. He described the rationale to me:

> The first thought was that it would be some middle-aged, collector-looking guy. But that was a little too stereotypical, too old. All right, so then the thought was, "So maybe it's a hip, young, stylish person who has sort of an ironic kind of collection of these lunchboxes." And we looked at men, women, white, black, Asian, you know. I think a lot of different people came back and there was just something about her look that said "young, cool, hip, design-y," and I think the fact that she was Japanese-looking helped that story a little bit, because I think often-times the young, hip Japanese design kind of look is something that, certainly in New York, we see a lot.

Greg concluded that his team was able to "communicate something very clearly with the person's appearance. And there was a real interest in not making fun of that person." Here the inclusion of a young, hip Asian American woman fit into a broader New York design aesthetic of someone who would have an ironic collection of kitschy objects but was not a social recluse or social outlier. Rather this Asian American hipster, who seemed Japanese to Greg but whose actual Asian heritage did not seem to matter, was chosen to represent this mainstream brand identity because she was the best talent for the spot.

Casting Asian Americans in interracial couples and families draws positive feedback. Ron, a creative in an Asian American agency, told me about an Asian American actor he had recently cast for a niche ad who was also in a general market ad. In the general market ad the Asian American man was dating a "Caucasian" woman: "He walks into her apartment, obviously on their first date, and he sits down on the couch. What's shocking to me is that it's just kind of, not a big deal, you know, the interracial thing. And I think for the general market, I think it's probably safer to show than a black guy and a white girl." Ron's description illustrates how casting for diversity has neutralized any cultural or linguistic signs that might be brought out in the multicultural advertising or might simply exist in society. In order to seem normal, the Asian talent was not distinct in any way but his appearance and could easily have been replaced with an actor of any other race. Asian Americans who are depicted as racially naturalized like this seem to most often be paired with white talent, making the white-Asian family visible and normal. The electronics giant Samsung features this combination of talent in a series of spots for their interactive television product. In a 2013 spot the Asian American actor plays the mother, wife, and daughter-in-law, speaks American-accented English, and seems to fit naturally in a multigenerational white family (fig. 4.4). In another, the mother and daughter are aligned against the son, father, and grandfather, who have been watching television for an extended time. Their children look neither like the white father nor the Asian American mother, suggesting that the agency cast biracial talent. The creative features a "normal" white middle-class American scenario of males watching television while women are attending to other matters. With the two white men and biracial son as the object of humor, the Asian American woman and her daughter are made to seem natural and like white American women.

Even a few years ago actors of Asian descent were featured in ads performing Chinese and other accents—a trend that seems to be waning. Still,

4.4 Samsung spot for general market featuring an Asian American mother, a white father and grandfather, and mixed-race children (2013).

for some spots, general market ad executives wonder if they are reproducing ethnoracial stereotypes, even if no one is complaining. Showing me three spots he had just completed for a large electronics chain, creative Nick told me he wondered whether the racial configuration of characters in the ad was offensive, but he did not pursue it when the client and others in the agency did not voice concern.[12] In one ad a black man is a store employee helping a white family, and in another an Indian American man acts as a GPS, directing the white family to their destination. "Do they look servant-like?" asked Nick. He similarly scrutinized the third ad, in which two Asian Americans on a boat are avidly videotaping with camcorders, and reflected, "I thought the boat was inappropriate, that they are coming over in a boat like boatpeople, and that they look like typical Asian tourists with video cameras." The ads aired as planned and there was no public outcry, suggesting that for general market audiences, these representations of diversity fall within the scope of normal, even if they push the limits of this category.

As these examples illustrate, much has shifted even in the past decade with regard to casting Asian American talent. These casting decisions are largely the result of how ad executives issue casting calls and how clients direct them to create audience identification. Sometimes ad executives cast actors of different races and ethnicities based on work the agency has already done for that brand. Account executive Greg described a campaign for a major electronics chain in which he cast an Indian American in one ad and an East Asian family in another: "I remember asking specifically for African Americans, Asians, and Indians, because we hadn't cast an Indian in any of the previous TV spots. So I offered the specifics and kept it diverse as well." Similarly casting director Fara said that in her experience, casting has become much more diverse, and pan-Asian is a category they use a lot more: "With Asian casting, they may want someone who is Japanese, Korean, Chinese, Filipino, whatever, or they may want someone where it is hard to tell." This casting strategy is apparent in a 2009 spot for a mid-range automobile that includes a variety of racial and ethnic talent. When Asian Ads was asked to make a Chinese version of the ad by overlaying a new soundtrack and voice-over, they found it helpful to learn more from the client about the actors who were cast. Account director Alan remarked to his team about one actor, "There is an angle in which she looks Asian," but he couldn't be sure because the scene was very brief. Broaching this topic carefully during a client call, Alan said, "She looks Asian, I thought." The client quickly responded, "Yes, she is! The first one is Asian." "What about the last one in the ad, is she Asian?" queried Alan, about a woman with similarly long, dark hair. "No, but the first one was cast to be Asian. That was purposeful." The client seemed pleased that Alan was able to detect the Asian talent they had intentionally cast and that he identified a second actress who might be Asian.

While the use of the term *pan-Asian* in general market advertising indexes individuals identifiable as Asian American, other designations make identification intentionally complicated or even impossible. General market executives prefer the term *ethnic ambiguity* to describe a look that indexes diversity but not in ways that are specific to any one racial category. Art buyer Cheryl reported a rising interest in this category when we spoke in 2008: "In the past couple of years, for casting, 'ethnically ambiguous' is the terminology that we're using, which means not necessarily Latino, not necessarily Hispanic, not necessarily African American, but could be something that a group of people would relate to. That covers everything. I get Asian women, I get pan-Asian women, I get Middle Eastern women. It's across a broad spectrum, and then they find the one or two people that no one can really pinpoint what they look like, and they market to everybody else." When I asked why that was desirable, she replied, "It's a little bizarre. I honestly don't understand. Are you afraid to have a Japanese-looking woman in your ad because a Korean woman wouldn't relate to her? If you have a Middle Eastern woman, would a northern Russian woman not . . . I don't understand it, but that's the terminology. Ethnic ambiguity. It's a term that we use all the time now." Ethnic ambiguity, as Cheryl explained and others confirmed, is powerful because it allows ad executives to create consumer identification with multiple ethnoracial groups using the same talent, such as the woman in the car commercial Alan could not categorize. Confirming this point, one Asian American account planner at a general market agency described his recent spot as featuring a romance between two ethnically ambiguous young people. When we spoke about this 2011 ad that year, he recounted that it was virtually impossible for his focus group to tell if the actors were Hispanic, Middle Eastern, South Asian, some combination, or something else. For him the racial and ethnic backgrounds of the actors are not important because the ad "accomplishes the kind of broad potential for consumer identification that we hope for when promoting brands." Ethnic ambiguity holds great potential for broad audience identification. This strategy is particularly effective when characters do not have speaking roles and their appearance alone acts as a qualisign of diversity.

By contrast, ads that feature copy based on ethnically specific humor typically require talent who can be identified as a specific race or ethnicity for the joke to make sense. Each year this seems to wane in popularity as a strategy. Playing on stereotypes or characteristics linked to specific ethnic and racial groups usually involves recognition based on how people should speak and act based on how they look. Regional accents, signaling how people from "the South" or "New York City" sound, do not differentiate along racial lines and so are more acceptable. For instance, one ad executive described a Domino's pizza campaign in which people who are clearly from distinct ethnic and racial groups speak with the same Brooklyn accent. The joke was at the expense of a region, not a group, and indexed the authenticity of the pizza style featured in the ad. The use of accents particular to an ethnic or racial group is rarely regarded favorably. Creatives and production executives assured me that they were never intentionally trying to have fun at an ethnic group's expense, although some acknowledged that the risk of offending was always a possibility. Roger, a producer, remarked that humor can be risky but is not off-limits because it can be so effective:

> It's funny because there are those things that are kind of stereotypes in and of themselves, not that black women are traditionally comic foils, but you could go to the route of, "Oh, if a fat guy falls down, it's funny." Is it right that we're having the fat guy fall down? I don't know. And

then you get into the cultural thing, and then you just go, "It's funny!" And I don't know, sometimes it's funny, sometimes it's not, sometimes the skinny guy falling down is funny. It's tough when those kind of things come up.

To illustrate this mixed set of responses, Roger recalled a spot set on an airplane, in which a man opens an overhead bin and a suitcase falls out onto a large black woman. He conjectured that her angry reaction is part of the intended humor in the ad but is not racist: "I'm sure the client never thought anything other than that it was funny. Even if somebody had brought up, 'Is it right that we're doing this?' The question goes to, like, 'All right, if we can't hit a black woman in the head, is it better if we hit a white woman in the head? Or is it better to hit a black man in the head?' Because when you open up that can of worms, then it's just like, 'What do we do next, we can't have a joke at all?'" In his reenactment of a conversation that Roger suggested had occurred on numerous occasions, the question "Can't we have a joke at all?" draws attention to the fine line between humor and offense in advertising and the broader issue of where that line should be drawn. Anthropologist Jane Hill has deftly illustrated this point in her identification of the use of "mock Spanish," which includes uses of Spanish by non-Spanish speakers for levity or dramatic effect.[13] Hill's point is that racism need not be intentional but can nonetheless thrive in the repetition of "jokes" that rely on reductive ideas linked to race and ethnicity. In advertising, the classification of these representations as jokes and their use for entertainment value underscore the power held by those who might prefer these depictions, especially if they come at the expense of and insult others.

Some ads have received nearly immediate community and media condemnation for being racist. One was the "More Flags, More Fun" campaign for Six Flags amusement park, in which a talking-head Asian host periodically appears in the corner of the screen, offering a rating of up to six flags for unusual activities destined to be less fun than a theme park ride, which is consistently given six flags (fig. 4.5). In an AM New York article that summarized the views of Asian American watchdog groups in New York, those protesting the ad alleged that the halting, accented English spoken by the disembodied Asian head, along with the overall quirky nature of the ad, was prejudicial toward Asian Americans. The AM New York article described the character as "a screaming, thickly accented Asian man" and quoted Margaret Fung of New York Asian American Legal Defense and Education

Fund as saying, "It's a pretty offensive ad, not only because of the thick accent, but also because someone is screaming at you." According to the article, the Legal Defense organization received several email complaints and suggested collective action could be effective, but none was taken. Perhaps not all found the ad objectionable; the article also noted that Councilman John Liu (D-Flushing) had not received complaints. Liu characterized the ad as annoying but not necessarily racist. Still, Aimee Badillo from the Asian American Justice Center in Washington, D.C., was quoted as saying, "It's always that fallback of the stereotype of the perpetual foreigner. There's still very much that image of [Asian Americans] as foreign and still not belonging to this country." This ad eventually faded away, but social media outlets such as Facebook and Twitter have intensified the speed and volume of response to such ads, as can be seen in the reaction to the actor Ashton Kutcher's 2012 "brownface" viral ad for the snack brand Popchips. Using stereotypes as the main point of humor, Kutcher dons a variety of guises as different bachelors for a dating site, including a Bollywood producer named Raj (fig. 4.6). Affecting an Indian accent that could have benefited from dialect coaching, Kutcher wears brownface, a thick brown mustache, and Indian wedding attire. The viral ad drew immediate and irate responses in the blogosphere and Twitter feeds, most of which were from young, hip, brown voices, including the South Asian American hip-hop group Das Racist and the comedian Hasan Minaj. Due to the swiftness

4.5 Six Flags spot for general market featuring "Asian game show host" (2008).

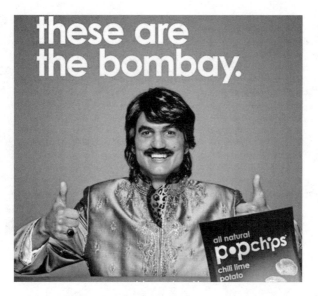

4.6 Popchips viral ad for general market featuring Ashton Kutcher in brownface (2012).

and intensity of this public response, as well as the offense taken, the "Raj" segment was removed from the campaign. This ad clearly crossed the line from edgy to controversial.

Asian American ad executives are well aware of how offensive these Asian American stereotypes are and call them out accordingly. Ron, the creative director at an LA-based Asian American agency, attributed these general market decisions to play on stereotypes as "creatives trying to win awards," meaning that they hoped that their sophomoric humor would catch on and become popular with audiences. Speaking in particular about the telecom company Metro PCS and its ads featuring two South Asian men who work at a call center, Ron remarked that the two characters spoke English with a heavy Indian accent and dressed ridiculously (fig. 4.7). Ron remarked, "It's not an agency head saying, 'Let's go make fun of East Indians and call centers and stereotypes,' but the agency is responsible for backing the execution, and I think it's horrible. I really think it's offensive, you know, 'We'll really make fun of these guys and we'll make them really, really weird and kind of wacky,' you know?" Creative directors and other executives are so attuned to these dynamics that they make it a point of public discussion. At the 2011 3AF annual marketing summit in Las Vegas, for instance, an entire session was devoted to discussing stereotypes of

4.7 Metro PCS spot for general market, "Tech and Talk with Ranjit and Chad," featuring Indian-accented English speakers (2010).

Asian Americans in mainstream media and advertisements; they also included the director of a nongovernmental organization focused on greater education and understanding of Asian American history.

As much as general market advertising values ethnic ambiguity, Asian American advertising veers toward ethnic specificity. Casting for Asian American advertising involves a different set of concerns shaped by issues of audience, media, budget, generation, and client expectations. Overall it is on a far smaller scale, and casting is dictated by ethnicity, gender, and age as warranted by the strategy and creative brief. In executions for which talent from a specific ethnic group is required, actors are cast in ways that index specific ethnicities and nationalities. Morris, a producer in an Asian American agency based in San Francisco, explained that they look for models or actors who appear "region-neutral" or a "mix between ethnicities" rather than someone who clearly looks to be from a particular region of an Asian country. The same was true for accents: "There are regional variations between dialects so we try to pick out the most neutral speakers. . . . Just based on customer feedback, we realize that people do notice these things. For example, people may notice that our language choice is representative of only Hong Kong or only Taiwan, and they tell us, or our clients. So we try to find someone representative so they don't alienate audiences." Even within a highly specific set of attributes, ad executives still identify signs of ethnic and linguistic neutrality that will serve as normal for Asian American advertising. When the principal characters don't speak, there is a bit more flexibility about how they can look. In a Nissan spot for Chinese Americans (fig. I.2), the woman cast in the ad is styled to look like an attractive suburban mother. She is dressed in a casual button-down blouse and pants; her children are dressed in everyday play clothes; and her dog travels with the family in the minivan. Everything about this suggests an everyday consumption scene, except perhaps the action sequence in which the shopping bags and packages she is toting arrange themselves neatly in the back of the minivan. The casting alone furthers the notion of Asian Americans as model consumers.

Like general market advertising, there is a degree of subjectivity about which model or actor would work best for an Asian American print ad or spot. For instance, the print ad photo shoot featuring the baby that I discussed at the start of this chapter was one of two that Asian Ads shot for this campaign. An Rong expressed his preference for the half-Chinese, half-white baby, praising his Asian facial structure, and pointed out that his team had the ability to "touch up the eyes to make them look more Asian." Saying, "The consumer looks at the ad, not at the process; they look at the final product," he emphasized that no one outside the agency would see anything but the finished ad, which could look as Asian as they wanted. Ultimately his team preferred a Filipino baby girl and recommended that photo to the client. An Rong insisted, however, that the ultimate choice to feature the Filipino baby was because she was "adorable" in a way that people could not resist, not because the boy didn't look Asian enough. In these and other campaigns An Rong stressed the importance of matching the creative with the correct look of the actors. He recalled a pan-Asian ad he had worked on for a luxury car client, in which the featured automobile model was intended to skew young (fig. I.3). Asked to make a spot adaptable for different Asian American ethnic groups, they cast models whom An Rong described as hip and attractive, who would "inspire our consumer." Even though he recalled that the ad did not look as "natural" as ads for specific Asian ethnic groups, his team decided that this collection of Asian American hipsters worked very well to appeal to Asian Americans as a broader category. In order to ensure this type of audience identification, they rarely cast non-Asian talent for their ads.

Overall, general market advertising has shifted away from ethnic humor in recent years, perhaps deeming it a less effective strategy for audience identification in an increasingly diverse United States with a black president. In a Best Buy spot that premiered during the 2013 Super Bowl, the Asian American actor Jake Choi stars as the friendly, knowledgeable

4.8 Volkswagen Super Bowl general market spot featuring Asian American talent and Jamaican-accented English (2013).

salesman who fields actress Amy Poehler's litany of tech questions (fig. 1.1). Choi speaks American-accented English and provides brief answers to Poehler's often absurd questions. As a comedian, Poehler is the one we are to laugh at, and Choi is a neutral presence. This calculus of risk and reward certainly does not lead to the absence of jokes but rather a more fine-tuned way of using accents and ethnoracial stereotypes. For instance, a Volkswagen spot that first aired during the 2013 Super Bowl features white and Asian American characters speaking in Jamaican accents. Set in a corporate office, the ad tracks the contagious happiness that comes from driving a VW (fig. 4.8). Characters' grumpy dispositions are reversed by a ride in the car, and the upbeat mood is confirmed by the Jamaican musician Jimmy Cliff's version of the song "Come On, Get Happy" as the soundtrack. To make this quirky scenario seem normal, the ad copy voices the question that viewers may have, which is whether the white male principal speaker is actually Jamaican. The man cheerfully responds to his co-worker that he is from Minnesota, "land of ten tow-sand leks [ten thousand lakes]." To break up office gloom, the man offers to take his Asian American colleague and white boss for a ride in the car. By the time they return to the office, the two passengers have also adopted Jamaican accents, a sign of their gleeful transformation. While cable news outlets like CNN argued over whether the ad was racist, VW marketing and public relations seemed to have anticipated these questions. In a Monday morning interview on CNN the day after the Super Bowl, Tim Mahoney, VW America marketing officer, cheerfully said, "We obviously did our homework to make sure that we weren't offensive. . . . The ad tested incredibly well."[14] They were even able to cite the support of the Jamaican tourism board, which declared that those alleging that a white man speaking with a Jamaican accent was racist were themselves being racist, as Jamaica is a multiracial nation. As further evidence that the campaign was not racist, the tourism board noted the inclusion of the Jimmy Cliff song, especially since Cliff himself had posted about the positive connotations of the ad on his Facebook page. Volkswagen's use of white and Asian talent and Jamaican music effectively quelled any controversy, and the company was praised for commissioning entertaining creative.

This ad and others that employ similar approaches suggest that "normal" can indeed include some carefully calibrated humor, provided it is set in familiar, controlled contexts of corporate offices and new cars. Public relations and other marketing tie-ins, such as the Jamaican tourism board, authenticated the ad's use of a Jamaican accent, and having a midwestern white man who epitomized "normal" in every other sense seemed to be the perfect embodiment for this accent. Contrast this to the botched effort of Popchips, whose ad featuring an Indian accent embodied by a racially altered Ashton Kutcher elicited a storm of negative feedback on social media and was taken out of circulation. Had Popchips done the audience testing, public relations, and other marketing tie-ins to music that VW had, they might have avoided the negative response. Both assemblages of diversity invite additional scrutiny and consideration of what can presently be considered normal and how certain renderings are praised for their entertainment value. Significant also is the media in which each was placed, which performed the additional contextual work of signaling legitimacy. Volkswagen purchased the most expensive media buy available by airing the ad during the Super Bowl; Popchips posted the ad to YouTube and other Internet sites so that it could go viral. The careful management of media, along with other types of public relations, does a great deal of work in making some assemblages of diversity seem normal while others are more vulnerable to consumer reactions.

Public relations, along with other parts of the marketing process, further brand identities, create consumer identification, and contribute to assemblages of diversity. For Asian American advertising, these are significant, location-specific venues in which to build brand recognition by linking corporations to community events, targeting advertising to specific neighborhoods, and altering retail appeal to certain ethnic consumers. Especially with the increasing use of smartphones and other wireless social media technology, these efforts add layers of meaning to creative and production, often in unknowable ways.

MEDIA PLACEMENT, PUBLIC RELATIONS, AND PLACE-BASED ADVERTISING

In advertising, *media* refers to the medium in which a completed ad will appear. A *media buy* is a block of time during a television program (during the second quarter of the Super Bowl, for instance), a full-page ad before the cover story in a magazine, or an Internet banner ad that appears with a certain frequency. All of these platforms are obtained at some cost, for a finite period of time, and are viewable by a general or subscriber public. Advertising is effective only when it reaches intended audiences, and multicultural advertising executives generally create "media plans" that combine a variety of elements. These may include *broadcast media*: television, radio, and print publications like newspapers and magazines; *out-of-home advertising*: billboards, signage, and ads placed on vehicles; *public relations*: events and messaging about a brand and its public perception; and *digital place-based marketing*: using GPS and other technologies to track consumers and push promotional content to them depending on their surroundings. This approach is in keeping with broader shifts in American advertising. Scholars have noted the changing uses of space and place,[15] and ad executives utilize spaces in urban and suburban landscapes for advertising and marketing. Whereas previously, ethnic neighborhoods were the primary places in which such marketing occurred through outdoor signage and in-store promotions, now other spaces are used to generate and circulate messaging for ethnic consumers, thereby expanding the scope and reach of multicultural advertising.

Broadcast media was once the primary site for all advertising, but the industry underwent a series of profound changes during the 2000s with regard to the platforms through which advertising agencies engaged with target audiences. First, the nearly ubiquitous use of the Internet introduced a variety of new modes of digitally based advertising, including banner and sidebar advertisements on websites.[16] Mobile Internet-enabled devices (smartphones, tablets, etc.) presented additional platforms for the dissemination of novel modes of digital advertising. Television is still thought to be the largest platform for advertising, and some studies of advertising spending and consumer product engagement have found that these new digital platforms have not outpaced TV and print advertising platforms.[17] But the increase in time spent on mobiles will soon force ad agencies to dedicate more effort and resources to mobile advertising.[18] Much has been written about the social impact of the Internet and shifts wrought by the information economy, including the effects of the instantaneity of information, the potential for connectivity, and new types of mobility that digital technologies can enable.[19]

Marketers fetishize information, and data are more highly valued than labor; this trend seems to be going strong, with new technological innovation increasing speed and reach. These new digital platforms for communication, consumption, and knowledge production are hallmarks of the new economy and illustrate the complex web of individuals, agendas, and capital that have been brought together in previously unseen ways. Such assemblages are temporally and spatially finite and provide a rich tableau for generating and circulating social meaning in ways that include consumers as well as advertising executives, marketers, and clients. When considering media placement and other types of marketing, it became evident that assemblages are actually located somewhere. Placing assemblages is a vital part of how the messages they are intended to convey can reach audiences. Not all media platforms are relevant to every product or service, but for Asian American advertising, advertising spaces as well as geographic locations are carefully considered as part of brand promotion. Asian American agencies consider the potential of designated market areas to further expand and transform these regions into marketing meccas. The addition of targeted promotions to retail outlets, developing ways to track ethnic consumer behavior, and mapping these onto urban and suburban landscapes through individual smartphone appeals or larger events sponsored by corporations all contribute to ethnoracial assemblages of diversity. The scope of my examination does not extend far into consumer engagements with these approaches, but I do consider how intended recipients of this message engage with this content through focus groups and audience testing. In an era of two-way content, media consumption overall has become far more interactive, and this provides even more ways to observe and track consumers. While new digital platforms certainly offer novel possibilities to reach specific target audiences, they also present a host of new advertising challenges not found in TV, broadcast, or print advertising. Advertising agencies are still learning how to determine the return on investment for the cost and placement of digital media, especially on Facebook, search engines, and online newspapers; research on these media suggests that the location on a webpage on which an ad appears remains important, even on the Internet.[20]

Broadcast Media

Media planners and buyers collect as much specific data as possible about broadcast media viewing platforms and practices of intended audiences. Ways of gauging Asian American viewership of television, radio, and periodicals are gradually becoming more precise, and ratings companies like Nielsen have recently commissioned studies about the "Asian American media consumer." Nielsen uses metrics that correlate income and education levels with viewing patterns such as hours of visual content viewed per day on television, on a digital video recorder, or streamed on the Internet, which allows media buyers to more effectively place ads. The cover of the Nielsen report itself conveys its findings: the Asian American consumer is "significant, sophisticated, and savvy" (fig. 4.9). Morris, a producer who considers media placement when making production decisions, remarked that Asian American media buyers developed their own metrics a long time ago, as they are too small to rely on large ratings corporations like Nielsen to price their advertising. Even with the limited data provided by Nielsen, which consists of top-line summaries and overall trends rather than weekly program ratings that would influence the cost of advertising, Asian American ad executives still rely on their own calculations of how much to spend on each type of media for a client. As new industries become interested in commissioning multicultural advertising for Asian Americans, they may also provide important market research and planning data. For example, although newer entrants such as the pharmaceutical industry cannot be relied on to provide extensive data, they usually do fairly extensive return-on-investment studies before spending to advertise, and these data are useful in specific accounts and could be helpful in developing other media buying strategies as well.

Identifying the dearth of specific media ratings data as an ongoing challenge, Asian American media buyers use data from third-party groups whenever possible to track consumption behavior to show clients that their audiences still rely on ethnic media and that ads are reaching them. Asian Ads media buyer Suzie explained that could mean relying on the data that media stations give the agency about their viewership—numbers that are not considered impartial and therefore are difficult to verify. Having

4.9 Cover of a Nielsen report on Asian American consumption patterns (2013).

such "hard data" is essential, she explained, because it allows her to "rationalize. To make our clients feel more comfortable about their advertising spending. So, **we** know ours is the best recommendation, but if you don't bring **them** the numbers, how do you prove it?" Suzie admitted that it is tricky to answer clients who question their ad placement by asking, "How do I know this program is popular?" Without precise measurements to track ratings, Asian American ad executives create some innovative ways to gauge the success of their ads. For service providers like insurance and financial services, one approach is to set up a dedicated toll-free phone number that appears only in those ads and staffing it with in-language consultants. If a different number is used for each medium in which the ad is placed, companies can gauge which one generates the highest volume of traffic. These approaches also help ad agencies understand the regions of the country in which the ad performs best. Automotive is the easiest to track because so much information is collected when people purchase and register a car. Jane, an account director who once worked in automotive marketing, confirmed, "When you register your car, your ethnicity is in the Polk data, so I would say automotive is the most advanced in terms of available data." Another is to develop a "microsite," a link from a brand's main website, that might be in-language, in-culture, or both. Such "click-throughs" measure consumer traffic, as do clickable Internet ads.

These small metrics aside, there are no weekly ratings for Asian television programs to set how much thirty seconds of advertising should cost, no shows comparable to general market price setters like *Two and a Half Men*. Asian American media buys are far less costly than general market ones, and even the most watched programs and events do not come close to the cost of a media buy for advertising during the Super Bowl. (Ad space for the 2014 Super Bowl sold out by November 2013, and a thirty-second spot cost up to $4 million.) Media is priced based on the estimated number of viewers, and the low cost of media is one of the selling points of Asian American advertising. But reaching consumers at a far lower price than general market media also means reaching far fewer consumers. In the absence of equivalents to Univision or Telemundo for Latino viewers, Asian American media buyers primarily place ads on satellite television channels, local access cable programming blocks, digitally broadcast national radio stations, and in-language and in-culture periodicals and websites. Copyright also plays a role in pricing, and the cost of licensing usage rights of a photographer's or director's work is determined by the geographic region in which the ad will be seen, the duration and frequency of the ad's run, and the platform on which it will air. Asian American ad agencies commission their own artwork and direction, striking arrangements intended to keep costs low and repeat an ad as many times as possible within a client's budget. Across the board Asian American television and print media cost a fraction of general market media buys.

Most Asian American media buyers I spoke with agreed that there was a lack of high-quality media platforms and not much effort to develop them. The Asian-centric channels that do exist usually air content developed and produced in Asia, which have a far higher production value and more widespread appeal than programs produced in the United States for Asian American audiences. Phyllis, a media buyer at an Asian American agency in Los Angeles, outlined an emergent dynamic that she and others experienced, in which Asia is regarded far more favorably than Asian America: "When a client looks at us as Asian American, you still feel a little behind.

But in Asia, it's a completely different story because the content is feeding in from India, China, and other countries. Any [station] that's feeding content from Asia is nice quality and clean. But anything that's locally produced here, you don't want to see. It's really bad, the quality and content."[21] Phyllis quickly added that it could be effective to have content tailor-made to life issues relevant to Asian Americans, to show "what happens in the community," but the standard of locally produced programming remains far below Asian programming. In what could be a partial compromise, digital radio seems to be able to harness hours of programming due to the ten- to twelve-hour time difference with Asia. Some media executives proposed that while Asia slept, this bandwidth could be harnessed via the Internet to provide content for listeners in the United States, creating opportunities for call-in shows in which Asian public figures connect with Asian Americans in the diaspora. One agency CEO in New York City, Sunil Hali, told me that he streamed about sixteen hours of music radio from India daily and did weekly shows focused on talk, business, and community.[22] For these he works with partners in India to interview celebrities while listeners in the United States call in, which "creates much excitement" about some of the featured guests.

Other ad executives reported that they have helped to create additional media platforms by lobbying digital and cable providers to import entire channels from Asia and curate content to suit Asian American audiences, thereby creating new media venues in which they could buy moderately priced advertising space that would reach their target audiences. Sunil emphasized how important this process was to connect clients with audiences in ways that would keep multicultural advertising afloat: "So when you look at all this, it creates this solution for what you are looking for, to reach the community as well as reach the market for our clients." Some media planners believe in-culture print media is an effective way to reach second-generation Asian Americans. While first-generation immigrants may gravitate toward in-language periodicals, identity-driven periodicals like *KoreAm* for Korean American youth, a bilingual magazine in Korean and English, like other thematically oriented magazines about fashion and golf published in the United States, effectively target second-generation youth who were born and raised in the United States. Regional periodicals like *Silicon India* in the San Francisco Bay Area, *Little India*, and *India Abroad* are also viable options.

Regionally specific media buys seem to work well. Asian Ads media planner Stacy reported that her team focused on buying media in the des-

4.10 Example of media monitoring in which ad placement is verified, documented, and sent to the client. Photo by agency (2009).

ignated market areas for their target ethnic groups. Especially in regions with a high density of Asian populations, such as areas of California and New York, measurements of media consumption were slowly improving. When I spoke with Asian Ads media supervisor Amado in 2009, he remarked that the agency focused on "those who need more in-language advertising, which would be Chinese, Korean, and Vietnamese." South Asians and Filipinos are considered English-proficient because "it's like a second language back in their own countries." For these audiences he primarily looks for in-culture sources. He considers the availability of print media for each group, whether they are heavy TV consumers, and if there are free radio broadcasts aimed at them. Another aspect of media buying is ensuring that ads look as the media buy specifies. Chris, a media buyer at Asian Ads, explained that although his department is reliant on any data they can find about viewing patterns for buying, it is equally concerned with how an ad looks once it is placed in print media. He and his team monitor whether TV stations air their ads during the correct day, time, and frequency of the programming block they purchased; whether their artwork is placed in the specified location of a periodical; and whether the ads look as they should. Each ad they place is carefully checked and archived for their own records, and a copy is sent to the client (fig. 4.10). "It's a lot of competitive monitoring too," Chris added, remarking that they track the type and frequency of media their competitors buy.

Media monitoring and metrics allow ad executives to create competitive buying plans for their clients but also to accurately tout the success of their work. Sometimes multicultural advertising performs exceptionally well in niche media; sometimes clients so highly regard the creative and production of an ad that they decide to air it on general market television as well. When large clients buy blocks of advertising time on a major network, they occasionally include a multicultural ad that they believe will effectively communicate diversity to their mainstream audiences. Asian American ad executives call these "crossover" advertisements and regarded them as points of pride. Asian American account director Steve told me in 2008 that such ads are proof that their creative was not simply "good enough" for the smaller media platforms of Asian American audiences but "actually good," so that clients were willing to pay top dollar to place it on networks and in mainstream publications. Steve told me about a couple of his spots that have enjoyed broader success than in the markets for which they were originally commissioned, including a sixty-second spot for Chevy that the client requested they cut down to thirty seconds so they could "air it during the Grammy Awards! They did a nice thing there. That year they had sponsored the Grammy Awards and bought a pod of advertising. So throughout the show you'd see different Chevy ads and ours was one of them. We re-recorded the voice-over in English and changed the end card so it would match." Changing the voice-over and end card, the screen of text and logo that appears at the end of an ad, was quite simple for the agency to do. Steve noted that such inclusion is not something Asian American ad agencies take for granted; it signals a sense of arrival and a chance for far greater exposure than would be possible on niche media.

Other campaigns Steve worked on required a more explicit spot with in-culture talent but were scripted in English to allow for easy and direct crossover. In one such spot for Nationwide Insurance in 2007, the once-famous *American Idol* contestant Sanjaya makes a spiritual pilgrimage to India, only to have his hair criticized by a "great guru." Sanjaya, who is of Indian American and white American parentage, was an ideal choice to appeal to both audiences. All the characters with speaking roles spoke English, and the ad overall played on the notion of a spiritual journey to India in which this wayward Indian American teen could connect with a higher spiritual power—a theme that had already become commonplace in a number of Hollywood movies and television programs. This crossover ad worked on two levels: it was diverse because India is a foreign land and Sanjaya is part–Indian American, and it was also mainstream because of Sanjaya's American accent, his *American Idol* fame, and his general appearance. Steve elaborated that crossover creative is relatively simple to do for automobiles, insurance, public health, and some other clients, but is a more difficult fit for other brands. He cautioned that multicultural advertising executives should be "careful that they aren't watering down the message to make it applicable to all segments. If we were asked to make it universally applicable, ads would lose their impact and flavor." In short, they would become general market advertisements with Asian American talent. Still, Steve identified important opportunities to cross over into the general market as well as to "the Asian market abroad. That's not unheard of. None of these spots happen to have made that journey, but that's certainly possible. You just have to be careful about the nuances." Playing up such nuances would allow these agencies to grow by reaching broader audiences and ideally be regarded for their creative, not just their transcreation. Generally multicultural advertisements are not expected to have an impact on general market creative, but occasionally they did. In one such instance, Asian Ads used their insurance client's circular logo as part of their creative conceit, integrating it into their artwork by embedding it in circular objects relevant to the creative, such as a wedding ring, a bird's nest, and a pendant. On a conference call the client remarked, much to the joy of the ad executives present, "We've never had anyone do this with our logo." He proceeded to praise the originality of the vision and the company's intention to suggest this visual approach for their general market ads as well.

Ad executives consider it fortunate when audiences and clients alike respond favorably to their ads because relatively few Asian American campaigns have the time or the budget for focus groups or audience testing. General market agencies leave this to chance less often; for example, part of Volkswagen's ability to stand by their agency's Jamaican-accented creative lay in the positive audience testing data they could cite. Production director Lucy told me that she often recommended testing even when her colleagues did not because despite looking "really beautiful and artful," a spot may not work for an intended regional audience. She elaborated, "We test to get a sense of who's responding to what. Are they understanding what the message is? Do they see what the product is? Do they know what we're trying to tell them? Is it too highfalutin? Is it too lofty an idea and not worthy of producing?" These rather focused questions are intended to save the client money and potential bad publicity if an ad is not received positively by an intended audience. Many Asian American ad executives see the value of testing, but others, like the Asian American ad agency producer Oscar, noted the potential downside of focus groups and screen tests: "A lot of times audiences say they like ideas that they really don't like, just to be polite." Should clients rely too heavily on focus group data, the creative "can become watered down because it is trying to please a wide range of people." Nonetheless his agency did focus groups or at least an audience screening whenever time and budget permitted. They also solicited feedback from any audience testing conducted by their clients once the ad had aired to apply these insights to upcoming work.

Digital and Social Media

For larger campaigns teams usually brainstorm to generate a more elaborate media plan budgeted for media buys on TV, radio, print, and other media. As I noted earlier, audience feedback is in some ways easier to track through the Internet, and nearly all clients expect larger campaigns to have well-developed digital components and social media aspects to aid with branding. Asian American ad executive Andrea, who specialized in digital, explained that her agency used to focus mainly on print and TV, but now everything has to have a digital component, generally in the form of a website, search engine ad, or social media ad.[23] These could include creating a microsite reached via the brand's main website that is in-language or in-culture, usually with an app for a mobile device. The interactive nature of these microsites varies according to the client and campaign. For example, in a brainstorming session for the digital component of a campaign, one account executive suggested interactive features such as consumers posting and voting on ideas for ads, with the top picks serving as the concepts for spots. The microsite could have a blog, he explained, and people could get involved by sending in their stories. The campaign would be active and participatory and get audiences involved, which seemed to be a widely desired outcome. Andrea, a digital executive, observed that in recent years digital had been "easier to push to the client. Some target audiences are so tech-savvy, everyone is online and sometimes clients even skip the TV spots!" She added that even when people come to the United States from Asia, they watch TV from other countries via the Internet, and this has led her to think about how to use these websites for marketing to U.S. audiences.

When speaking to clients, ad executives refer to Asian American consumers, especially those in the second generation, as tech-savvy. Phyllis, also in digital at this Asian American ad agency, tied this shift to generation and told me, "Traditional in-language media of print, TV, and radio target a little bit older audience. When we go younger we have to do more digital, and sometimes [it] crosses over with mainstream or general market stuff that we buy, like YouTube or ads on Facebook." This could include purchasing space during Internet sport broadcasts of cricket, buying space for in-language ads according to the language settings people set on their browser, and displaying in-culture ads for people who search for Bollywood gossip: "So whenever people search for certain interests, we try to buy those words and be sure our ad appears." The pairing of ads with keywords is a way of tracking that also monetizes the value of hobbies, interests, and other pursuits. Searching for certain words connects consumers to ads, provided executives successfully ascertain which words to buy.

One of the reasons ad executives have successfully pitched digital marketing to their clients is because they can discuss how effective it has been in Asia and how Asian Americans are already accustomed to it. Andrea explained, "There's a huge amount of technology, especially in Japan. The U.S. is so behind, so we are always encouraged to look at what is happening in Asia to see how it could be applied in the U.S." Account executives rarely present digital plans to clients by suggesting that the United States is "behind," which not everyone agreed with. Instead they focus on generating new ways of reaching clients via the Internet as well as out-of-home advertising. Out-of-home advertising used to refer only to billboards, ads on public transportation, and the like. It was generally reserved for densely populated urban areas and well-traveled roads. Angela, the media director at Asian Ads, reflected on growing up in New York City's Chinatown, staring at a Newport cigarette billboard on Canal Street: "Suddenly in the 1990s, the billboard became available and in-language advertising to Chinese Americans started there. Now there are Asian faces on that billboard instead of blond white people, and this is a definite change." Other spaces, such as bus shelters frequented by Asian Americans, ads in subways that service Asian American neighborhoods, and similar out-of-home placement, have transformed urban and suburban landscapes to reflect the public presence of Asian Americans as not simply residents but consumers.

Asian American advertising executives carefully consider advertising spaces as well as geographic locations as part of brand promotion. They also look to the potential of digital marketing to further expand and transform designated market areas into marketing meccas. Understanding how ethnic groups map onto the physical space of the United States is a skill that Asian American ad executives showcase as part of their expertise in being able to reach intended audiences. This includes targeted promotions to retail outlets, developing ways to track ethnic consumer behavior, and mapping these onto urban and suburban landscapes through individual, smartphone appeals or larger events sponsored by corporations. Place-based marketing (also called location-based marketing) geographically tracks select urban consumers and offers promotions in their immediate surrounding areas, and GPS technology is used to pinpoint suburban consumers. Ad executives envision urban neighborhoods as well as suburban regions via social media and digital technologies as spaces that draw potential Asian American consumers. Digital technologies map consumption onto spaces and anchor Asian American communities in regional landscapes. "Place-based advertising replaces 'lifestyle' with 'experiential'; it is now about one-on-one experience," proclaimed senior media buyer Grace at an account meeting in 2008 to a room full of colleagues waiting for elaboration. Asian Ads had paired corporate sponsors with community-level events, branding such festivals as Diwali and Lunar New Year when they were celebrated in Little Indias and Chinatowns. Yet for new brands, Grace asserted, such sponsorship would be meaningless to consumers without some prior introduction into their everyday landscape. Ad executives sought to locate and target consumers "at street level," as Grace put it, to draw them into retail outlets. In one campaign for a money-transfer company, I observed how Asian Ads considered how to best use new media to reach consumers in particular neighborhoods. During an internal brand strategy meeting, Grace asked the account team, "How will you connect the consumer to retail? What will help drive traffic and build awareness about the brand you built?" Much of this, Grace argued, should be place-based, in neighborhoods where there are high concentrations of foot traffic, like areas of New York City, in Jersey City, New Jersey, in San Francisco's Chinatown, and similar locations. The Chinatowns in Manhattan and in Flushing, Queens, were identified as neighborhoods that would be ideal for street-level campaigns.

In ethnically saturated neighborhoods location-specific campaigns lead consumers to nearby stores. Reaching consumers "at street level," as media planner Grace put it, was also important to draw them into retail outlets. Account executive Sheng Li excitedly took Grace up on her challenge, suggesting that they could implement street-level campaigns in the Chinatowns of Manhattan and Flushing. These could include actual deictic markers, like a pointer placed in a subway station, on subway stairs, and other places to direct consumers to a nearby store. Grace agreed that "anything that will point at a location" could be helpful in creating brand awareness for consumers, who could immediately visit that location, thereby linking consumers and their location in time and space. Different approaches were required for urban and suburban landscapes, depending on "whether you are walking or driving," Grace added. She painted a picture for those creatives who did not seem to grasp the scope of what she was recommending: "Consider Journal Square, the PATH train stop near Newark, New Jersey. It is just one block of Asian Indian stores, regardless of which direction you walk. You can see the whole block, all the way down. You could use that to brand. We could use these place-based spaces as branding vehicles. Like Jackson Heights, Queens, that's a multicultural area. All four corners have a different billboard in a different language— Spanish, Bengali, Tagalog, Korean." Significant in Grace's description is the way advertising executives map ethnic neighborhoods as dynamic marketing spaces and use language to do so. Leading consumers to actually visit a retail outlet, however, requires an experiential relationship with the brand, especially if consumers are unfamiliar with it.

Drawing in consumers not just to engage with an ad but also to have an "experiential" interaction at a point of sale is how place-based promotions can "draw traffic," media buyer Grace added. She continued, "The place-based ad is something that does not exist in that space and you create it, like a pointer, literally pointing in that direction. So it should direct traffic to that specific location." Besides actual signs, place-based ads may be holograms projected on sidewalks that direct individuals to local branches of major chain stores. Grace asserted, "The role of media is a space that will be seen by the right people at the right time. It will serve as a close connection to help generate traffic to the retail location. When I want to deliver that brand message, I'll go as broad as possible for my reach. Keep pounding them at the [television, radio, and print] level, and then at the street level. They already know the brand, here is the location of it." Extending promotions into the physical landscape of neighborhoods, outside of stores, is an approach that builds brand awareness while it also publicly marks neighborhoods and regions as those in which Asian American consumers are acknowledged and solicited, usually in-language and in-culture. Delivering brand message in this way used to rely entirely on broadcast media, but is now paired with branded promotions in actual neighborhoods and high-traffic areas where Asian Americans were likely to see them.

Digital, however, has added new types of "spaces" in which to reach consumers. Most effective is reaching consumers of specific ethnic groups directly and instantly. "New immigrants who have no visa, no green card, don't speak English, are here illegally—they all have a cell phone! It's none of our business how they get them." The ad team sat silently in the conference room, their thumbs scrolling over BlackBerrys and iPhone screens until Yang pounded on the table to draw his creatives and account executives back to attention. The cell phone, Yang proclaimed, was the next media frontier through which to reach people. Chiming in, Grace suggested that they should integrate a cell phone–based promotion to further the money-transfer company's brand in New York neighborhoods with a large Asian American presence. Consumers would receive "push" information via email and on their cell phones. Generating a cell phone registry, which Grace indicated is routinely done by marketers in China for various clients, was chosen as an optimal marketing strategy. Customers would share their cell phone number in exchange for a one-time offer of additional minutes and agree to receive promotional texts and other real-time messages when they are in the neighborhood. To reach multiple Asian ethnic groups, the team decided on an image-based coupon sent via text, which could be scanned and applied at a retail outlet right from a consumer's phone. In this assemblage of ethnoracial diversity, brands and consumers would be connected through the instantaneity of the tracking and zapping through digital platforms, so that the brand messaging could be delivered in real time, when consumers were in the precise location to avail themselves of it. It brought together, in time and place, a specific branded message. In this approach the push to provide interactive content to consumers' phones was emphasized because it is what ad executives believe their consumers have come to expect in Asia and elsewhere.

Smartphone-based marketing technologies in use when I completed my field research in 2012 were the use of Bluetooth devices that could pick up an image for a real-time coupon, Foursquare and other location-based applications that could offer discounts to consumers in certain locations, and QR codes (barcodes) that could be scanned and redeemed for a gift or discount in a specified location. Andrea, the digital executive, spoke of the popularity of this type of marketing in Asia. She remarked that location-based services are becoming more common in the United States, especially Facebook and Foursquare, an application that asks people to "check in" at specific locations to redeem rewards. "We want to put this technology in place for retail and encourage people to check in more," she said. Possible venues she named include department stores, grocery stores, clothing and apparel retailers, gyms, salons, and spas—basically everywhere. In a campaign for a department store in a greater Los Angeles–area mall in a major Chinese American suburb, place-based promotions were designed to take effect the instant a consumer entered the general shopping area. Inside the store there would be a kiosk where consumers could scan a QR code from their phones that would generate a coupon for a certain percentage off. Checking in at a restaurant could result in certain promotions as well.

The notion of zapping things through the air to someone's Bluetooth-ready device in a neighborhood or suburban mall takes marketing to a whole new level, one that marks the landscape in invisible yet significant ways from an advertising standpoint. Assemblages of this sort offer new possibilities for branding places and circulating messages, as well as marking landscapes of ethnoracial diversity in previously unseen ways. Since I completed my research, in 2014 these discussions have expanded to include purchasing ad space in apps and smartphone-based email interfaces. New communicative platforms emerge on an ongoing basis, leaving ad executives to innovate ways to incorporate them. For instance, major brands are expected to have a large social media presence, which can include a Facebook page, a Twitter feed, a blog, and numerous other digital ways of connecting with consumers.

I better understood how ad executives were aspiring to use these new platforms when I was invited by one of the Los Angeles Asian American agencies I visited to attend an industry event in a media lab. I accompanied Ramesh, one of the agency's vice presidents, to the late afternoon event. The turnout was modest but engaged, with about thirty attendees and five presenters. The scene was a mix of the advertising world and the tech world: women in the LA chic of short skirts, blouses, bare legs, and heels, and men in the Silicon Valley casual of Oxford shirts, jeans, and Converse sneakers. As we entered we were given name tags and a sticker was placed on our backs for an icebreaker game; each of us was a social media platform, and we were to guess our identity by asking others questions, ideally prompting people to talk to those they did not know. It took two questions each for Ramesh and me to guess that we were Facebook and Twitter, respectively, after which we found seats for the presentation.

The presenters focused on how to utilize social media to promote brands as well as manage negative publicity. The panel of two women and a man sitting on a stage, plus a third woman via video feed, expected the audience to be familiar with social media lingo and offered their best practices to the group. One remarked that she relied on social media for her news, claiming, "Facebook status update is my NPR." Another recommended scripting a daily slate of tweets up to a week in advance, to reduce the pressure of generating content during busy work days. Attributing his large Twitter following to this well-tested approach, he quickly dismissed a fellow panelist who suggested this would ruin spontaneity. A third advised against creating a "social cemetery" by posting words without pictures. All the presenters offered "tactical" suggestions about trends in "social" (short for social media, I learned), via social "strike teams" that can help with marketing and PR. It was above all critical to protect oneself from "badvocates," people who "trash your brand." This advice was of course important for product and service brands but could also include "your personal brand," reflected in one's Twitter feed, blog, Facebook page, or any other social media platform. Remarks such as these serve as a reminder that social media is anything but incidental when brand is concerned; indeed it has moved into the mainstay of discussion about how branding should happen and how to do damage control. As they struggled to master the communicative nuances of these new mediums, advertising executives kept the message central to what they sought to accomplish. Events such as this one underscore the industry-wide emphasis on digital platforms and also draw attention to the work they do as mediums for promoting brands.

Public Relations, Corporate Sponsorship, and Promotions

Assemblages of ethnoracial diversity, as several of the examples given previously note, are more than simply an advertisement placed in broadcast media. Public relations, corporate sponsorship, and promotions aimed at Asian American consumers also play important supporting roles through which ad executives promote their clients' brands to existing and intended consumers. Sometimes these categories blend into one another, such as when managing brand identity involves media messaging, grassroots outreach, and corporate sponsorship (fig. 4.11). Sometimes one method best suits a client's needs and budget. Public relations is, broadly defined, a process of managing and protecting the public image of an individual, corporation, or brand. Similar to how public figures such as politicians have public relations agents and teams who arrange events and schedule their appearances to boost their image in the media, so too does nearly every brand, corporation, university, and other commercial as well as nonprofit entity utilize PR on an as-needed or ongoing basis. Public relations is so intimately linked to brand management that some consider it a foundational element of the advertising process and include it in media plans alongside broadcast media buys and digital whenever possible. Ramesh, the Asian American ad executive with whom I attended the social media event, worked on all aspects of client business. He explained that his work

4.11 Promotion for E*Trade at a Chinese American festival. Photo by agency (2009).

was "less about message and more about finding the right [consumer]. We need to find the right Asian target audience, foster and continue that relationship, and continue to keep the brand relevant." Imparting to brands the power that others might credit to advertising executives or consumers, Ramesh contended, "You can have great brands without doing advertising because they get to know customers and never take them for granted. Some will come quickly into that mode, others will come kicking and screaming." Ramesh and others at his agency considered PR crucial to managing brand, an approach to which many advertising executives subscribe.

In fact the advertising industry itself does a good deal of PR work to promote their own image, values, and standards of excellence. They promote themselves to clients on an ongoing basis but also emphasize their importance to the broader public via publications, events, and awards. Awards are technically a different category from public relations, but the advertising industry at times bundles them with the broader aim of promoting their work through different channels. The most prestigious advertising award is the CLIO, which is awarded primarily in general market advertising. It serves the dual purpose of acknowledging superlative creative and production and bolstering the image of the agency that handled the account. Likewise the Asian American Advertising Federation sponsors its own award contest for this niche market, while others, like the Advertising Education Foundation, sponsor awards to acknowledge and promote multicultural advertising and diversity more broadly. All of these work to create a positive public image for the advertising industry and maintain the relevance of multicultural agencies and their work. In Asian American advertising, public relations often includes grassroots efforts to find consumers, to manage tensions between consumers and a brand, and to keep a community invested in a particular brand. PR is an area where Asian American advertising executives are able to showcase their expertise, social networks, and knowledge of Asian populations and regional geographies. At his agency Ramesh did PR work for Hollywood films and network television programs with major Asian American actors as a way to broaden appeal and draw Asian American viewers who might not otherwise consume English-language media.

Other ad executives noted the vital role of public relations in crisis management, especially to rebuild brand identities after small- or large-scale public incidents. (Recall the series of ads after the 2010 BP oil spill in the Gulf of Mexico, for instance.) Sammy, a PR manager in an Asian American ad agency in Los Angeles, told me in 2011 that his team does "everything! Crisis communication, supermarket labor strikes, public affairs, grassroots lobbying work, and cultural sensitivity training."[24] Sammy's PR interests developed during the Los Angeles riots that erupted after the Rodney King verdict was announced in 1992. He was hired by an insurance agency in desperate need of bilingual Korean-English speakers to process insurance claims for damages to their businesses—people who could also be "a sympathetic face to Korean families whose businesses had been burned and decimated," as Sammy put it. "Out of three thousand employees, I was the only one in the area who spoke Korean," he recalled. Working as a claims agent, he identified other community issues that he thought his company should address: "Due to money and politics, relief money went to African American businesses that weren't even damaged. Not a single aid dollar went to the Korean community even though they had the majority of ruined businesses. I brought this to the regional VP, who told me to get out there and see what we can do to help the Korean community. That's how I got more involved in the PR and community relations aspect of the business and spearheaded an Asian American outreach initiative." Proudly recalling the success of this initiative, Sammy credited his understanding of the Korean American community as vital to bringing about this aid. He resigned when management changed and much of his business was given to a non-Korean. He decided he could make a greater impact working directly in a PR position at an Asian American agency.

For Sammy and others, public relations has a positive social impact but does not necessarily protect everyday citizens. Rather PR is fundamentally about promoting brand, regardless of how that positions some individuals. For example, Sammy told me about other campaigns he had worked on, where he had to go against labor organizers and small businesses in the service of a major department store. Emphasizing the vital role he and his firm played in managing community opposition to a corporate client, he stated, "People may not think that Asian Americans have a role, but we do. When we served [department store] as political consultants, we helped them by arranging meetings with people who are against [brand]. We tracked media to understand what was said about them. Before launching the [brand] campaign, we did strictly grassroots and media, six months in advance, with no advertising. We did that because seventy percent of media coverage of [brand] was negative, thirty percent was positive in the general market news." He further explained that by meeting with community leaders and other consumers, they were able to shift perception and eventually begin a marketing campaign. Sammy emphasized the value of PR in paving the way for advertising: "For us, PR is as if not more important than marketing. If they don't trust you or your brand, why would they buy from you just because you tell them to? All you're left with is a price and a product." The interpersonal work he and his team accomplished was due in large part to their connections and visibility in the Asian American community in the greater Los Angeles area. This large chain store was eventually able to successfully enter their desired region with a dense Asian American population, thanks to this well-executed PR campaign.

When done effectively, PR and ads created for broadcast media blend into one another and strengthen brands in unexpected ways. In a grassroots PR campaign by an LA-based agency promoting an insurance company to the region's large Korean American population, account executive Henry carried out a "user-generated" campaign: "We went to Korean churches and videotaped children singing a popular Korean song, one that is sung by kids to their hardworking fathers, which is basically about 'See,

I'm there for you.' Our client **loved** it, it was a perfect expression of their brand, being there for you, but not like a big company." Due to the very low cost involved, the agency produced nine fifteen-second spots for television and established their presence in the community. They accomplished the latter by installing temporary video booths and uploading all the performances to a website for people to see. They also sent branded DVDs of the performances to all the participants and their extended families. "Brand awareness rose by ten percent from this campaign," Henry added. PR opportunities are not always easily found, however, and for small agencies that do not specialize in producing events, managing PR can be challenging. Doing Asian American PR well requires in-language, in-culture "brand advocates" who can travel, do a media tour with the brand, and speak to potential consumers in-language. Not having an in-language speaker for PR events may "cause a disconnect," as Alan, the Asian Ads account director, put it, and events can do more brand damage than promotion. While most clients do not allocate a budget to hire a celebrity as a brand ambassador for Asian American markets, at least having a brand advocate who can answer questions and promote a brand in-language enables a deeper connection with intended consumers.

Corporate sponsorship plays a role in building brand and extending public relations efforts, especially when ad executives act as the intermediaries between clients and the ethnic communities they wish to reach. According to Sammy and others, clients doing PR signals a deeper level of "investment" in the community and greater recognition of these individuals as consumers. Grassroots marketing, combined with public relations, works to promote brand. Ad executives emphasized their position as "community insiders" who could bring corporate clients into otherwise closed spaces. "Diwali mela (Diwali festival), Holi, Rakhi, Pooram (Hindu holidays), whatever. We get face time for our clients," explained Mr. Hali, a media and marketing executive at his own firm. Asian American agencies act as gatekeepers for these events, using their social and business networks and connections to promote corporate clients and their brands, and do so in ways that are possible only because of their intimate knowledge of these events. As Mr. Hali put it, "You could be living next door to an Indian American and not even know who he or she is." He stressed that without his firm, there would be many missed opportunities for corporate clients. Once in, opportunities for branding abounded: "The marketing teams make banners and tents and wear nice T-shirts and give out literature, run raffles, and give away gifts to people who give them their email and contact info."

Mr. Hali told me that his network of regional retail stores, restaurants, and entrepreneurs was so vast that he sometimes planned his own large events for brand promotion rather than waiting for ethnic festivals and holidays.

Bringing brands into events that were once solely for community members does the vital work of racial naturalization, introducing mainstream corporate culture into otherwise private spaces. This approach can be especially attractive to clients who are looking to launch their brand to Asian ethnic communities in specific regions of the country. PR can take the form of a "go-to-market" plan, which is generally based on focus group data that indicate low brand awareness among a target population. Timing is essential here, and partnering with major community festivals and events can provide easier entry into a community. In developing a go-to-market plan for his insurance client trying to reach the Asian Indian segment, Asian Ads account executive Sunil identified community dance competitions as ideal sites to build brand presence. Offering sponsorship and receiving recognition and ad space in return made dance competitions "a very good opportunity." He mentioned numerous dance competitions in several East and West Coast locations, including the greater New York City area, Houston, the Bay Area, and Los Angeles, which would be excellent designated market areas for his clients to launch their brands. Pairing with regional radio to make announcements and run promos for their listeners prior to the event and having a "street team" to approach attendees with branded giveaway items onsite are ways that ad executives diversify their media plans to cover many bases with a unified brand message.

Planning community events for promotional purposes can be a major undertaking in terms of cost and logistics, but they can be very effective if done well. A highly successful example of such a promotion is the South Asian Spelling Bee, developed and promoted by Touchdown Media, an advertising and media company based in New Jersey. Currently sponsored by MetLife, the event is a series of regional spelling competitions for children of South Asian parentage in fourteen different locations nationwide, the winners of each competing in a nationally televised final in New Jersey. The founder and CEO Rahul Walia emphasized the ideal match with South Asian Americans, who, he observed, already excel at the National Spelling Bee organized by Scripps. To allow for adequate promotional time, he follows the National Spelling Bee format, which requires spellers to take a preliminary written test, and uses this time to have parents attend an insurance presentation by regional representatives. As a result, the MetLife brand has seen a great boost in visibility among South Asian Americans.

Corporate sponsorship of particular community events is an important type of promotion, especially for ad executives who expect it to continue on an ongoing basis. These include experiential promotions like inviting celebrities to promote brands in certain communities or sponsoring a long-running competition like the South Asian Spelling Bee. Most promotions, however, are "for a limited time" or "while supplies last" and are based on in-store or Internet participation. Direct mailers—promotional pieces of mail sent via the U.S. Postal Service—are often used to announce promotions, but this kind of targeted marketing is a bit more difficult to execute in niche markets. Accessing Asian American consumers' mailing addresses is quite challenging; telecommunications and cable companies sometimes compile and sell lists of possible Asian American subscribers, but for the most part such lists are difficult to obtain. In-store promotions in select designated market areas promise a more viable way to reach consumers; these generally involve some kind of discount or free item, a gift card, or a gift that is mailed after a customer registers for a product or service. Store-based promotions include small items timed to celebrate Asian festivals such as Lunar New Year. In 2010 Lunar New Year coincided with Valentine's Day, offering a set of creative possibilities. For a campaign for Send Cash, the money-transfer service, one creative suggested the Chinese copy "Sweet sweet, Love love," which An Rong promised sounded more interesting in-language than in English. The conceit was that loved ones in Asia would be sent chocolates or other sweets when the U.S. consumer used the service. "Either way, this candy should elevate the consumer experience with Send Cash." Jun Yi pointed out that many people get married right before Chinese New Year, so the tie-in with Valentine's Day was very promising. Other promotions for this campaign included partnering with local Chinese American businesses, including hair salons, massage parlors, and cell phone retailers.

To sell clients on the value of promotions, Asian American ad executives reiterated the overall work they did to build brand and generate consumer spending data. For instance, in one promotion-planning session I observed for a department store I call Zephyr, ad executives reminded their client that gift cards cost something only when customers redeem them, and that the numbers on the card could enable them to track Asian American purchases and better understand consumer trends. Ad executives suggested using the in-culture theme of family and linking with the upcoming Mother's Day holiday. They could market Zephyr gift cards in a variety of ways that would not look commercial. In this meeting suggestions to the client included a gift-card holder that a child could decorate and an entire series of events constituting "afterschool fun," including essay contests that would culminate in corporate-sponsored scholarships. One ad executive quipped, "Asians have a smart gene that others don't have!," to which the client happily responded, "Keep those ideas coming!" Several ad executives put forth additional ideas: sponsoring events at Chinese-language schools that children attend on weekends; offering a branded back-to-school kit with a gift card and coupon, for which Zephyr would give some of the proceeds to the child's school; holding contests in which schools compete to amass the most Zephyr donations. As one account executive voiced it, "We need to get a gift card in Mommy's hand, so she will drive herself to [Zephyr], or when she is already at the mall, she will say 'Oh! I have a [Zephyr] gift card from my children.'" The only idea that was decidedly not a good fit was a spelling competition for Chinese and Korean American children, perhaps because the lack of an in-language component would make it difficult for older generations to remain engaged. Shifting the conversation away from this, one creative stated, "I think the concept of 'style watch' is something we can leverage and use [Zephyr] clothing to do a fun fashion show in the language schools." As the conversation wore on, the account team assured the client that any promotions the client liked could be paired with significant events, including Mother's Day, Father's Day, Moon Festival, and Lunar New Year, all of which promised great brand promotion potential.

Thus clients look to niche ad agencies to design giveaways that will appeal to their Asian American customers while increasing sales, both in a cost-effective way. Ad executives and clients engage in an ongoing struggle to come up with appealing promotions that do not seem too traditional or too expensive. In a meeting at Asian Ads before a client call with a liquor client, the account team generated a list of potential items to brand and give away in a limited edition gift set along with a bottle of cognac. "Maybe chopsticks? Is bone considered valuable? What is prestigious? What would get people to buy the cognac?" were some of the questions raised during this brainstorming session. As the team continued to mull it over, account executive Tina realized it was time for the call and dialed the number. After pleasantries were exchanged and Tina confirmed that the client had received the presentation she had sent over, the team began to present their ideas for in-store items to draw consumers to the product, followed by ideas of what they could package with the product to increase sales. Asian Ads suggested shiny, dangling things that would draw consumers to this area of the store, including a lenticular, which is similar to a hologram, with images of the bottle that turn into a dragon as it catches the light. The client was momentarily excited but declined when she learned the cost per item. Other ideas included an LCD monitor mounted in the store to screen promotional imagery, but the client voiced concern about maintenance. Another creative suggested metal detector covers with the brand name and logo to grab consumers' attention as they entered the store. The client politely remarked that metal detector covers were too costly and, moreover, not right for the brand. At that point a senior account executive and company VP offered two ideas: a "shelf talker," or a pop-up card that juts out of the shelf to promote a product, and satin banners that could be hung throughout the store. When the client heard that cost, she exclaimed, "Price point!," suggesting that even this would be too expensive. He reminded her that the promotional materials should convey "premiumness" and that she would see excellent return on investment for them.

Asian American ad executives often spoke about the notion of "premium" with clients, emphasizing it as the brand identity called for it. Indexing the upward mobility of this population with the use of this term, they suggested that Chinese Americans and Vietnamese Americans would be even more willing to purchase cognac, for instance, when it came with a limited edition keepsake. For the liquor company promotion Asian Ads suggested that such items as candles, a decorative plate with a stand, or a mirror would be "very premium." Boxed chopsticks were another suggestion, but the client reported feedback she had received from her own Asian American coworkers: "All the Chinese people over here are saying that they wouldn't use them, and that's what we need to hear!" Momentarily stunned that their ideas were being dismissed because coworkers did not care for them (though this routinely occurred in creative work), the account team quickly recovered and continued their presentation. Alex reminded the client that she thought the "rat bottle stopper" for the Year of the Rat "looked cute" and suggested doing an ox this year: "A twelve-zodiac collection would be interesting, something that the competition doesn't have. Can we produce one that would be really premium?" Opting to pursue this instead of a paperweight, especially because there could be motivation to purchase one annually, the client raised concerns about the bottle stopper sufficiently promoting the brand: "Branding should be stronger with [brand] on the stopper. You want to use it and put it back into the bottle of the [brand]." Assuring the client that this was easily remedied, the account team worked with her to develop a product that would appeal to an Asian American consumer while also communicating premiumness as a central aspect of brand identity. In this promotion Chinese and Vietnamese American consumers were appealed to as upwardly mobile liquor drinkers who would remain loyal to the brand via keepsake bottle stoppers. Notably there was no overt discussion about how the notion of premium might differ for consumers in lower-income neighborhoods with in-store metal detectors. This did not seem to matter, as the assumption was that the specialized promotions would appeal to Asian Americans due to their deluxe, premium messaging.

Asian American agencies often worked to develop promotions even with those clients that already had in-house ethnic marketing specialists. To promote their brand to Chinese Americans, one bank's multicultural marketing team partnered with Asian Ads. The goal was to improve business in the "Asian market," and the promotion would be an MGM (member-get-member) scheme. In this approach, often used in fitness centers and other account-based service centers, existing members are rewarded for successfully recruiting new members. Account executive Tina remarked that consumers responded very well to this approach in Asia, especially when incentivized with small luxury items or cash. The plan for Asian Americans, beginning with Chinese Americans, was to "use existing customers to tap their social networks of families and friends, aiming for an overall increase of twenty-five percent in our premium-level customers." This last detail was important, as the launch was to begin in the twenty bank locations with the highest populations of Asian Americans who also had the highest savings account balances. The promotion involved members calling the bank on a dedicated phone line or visiting a bank agent at a participating branch to refer a new member and eventually collect a cash bonus or a high-end crystal figurine worth one and a half times as much. Tina emphasized the importance of sending samples of the crystal to each of the branches: "We know you like it when your customers can touch and feel premium items and see what they look like." Stressing the materiality of the items as something vital for their consumers, Tina explained that the agency would also furnish a small display unit so that branch bankers "can do a little Vanna White presentation!" Tina's charming delivery elicited a warm round of laughter from her clients. Their Chinese American in-house ethnic promotions manager remarked, "I am confident that we will knock this one out of the park!," and the rest agreed enthusiastically.

Another effective promotion involved partnering with a regional business and giving away coupons for popular Asian food items. Customers reaching a certain quota of transactions with the money-transfer service Send Cash received a gift card for a popular Hawaiian food store chain. Linking Send Cash with free food products like Spam tinned meat was a way for the campaign to give an internationally recognized brand local relevance and roots. Featuring regional favorites like Spam had worked well for past promotions, and giving it away for a limited time would lead to positive associations with the brand. Ad executives began to outline the steps to put this promotion in place, including setting up tables outside the store to emphasize the promotion, have the store provide the promotional items at cost, and establishing a time frame for the giveaway. Remarking that most stores appreciate the additional customer traffic the promotion would drive, ad executives conveyed to their client that this would be a straightforward and likely successful promotion. Other clients recognized that their product or service already drew Asian American consumers and partnered with Asian American agencies to draw in even more consumers. Casinos, especially in the Northeast, are frequented by significant numbers of Chinese Americans, to the extent that there are free, dedicated buses running from Chinatowns in New York, Boston, and other East Coast cities to facilitate visitation. Some have catered to Asian American guests by building themed retail and dining areas, such as Sunrise Square in the Mohegan Sun Casino in Connecticut. Promotional gift cards to spend in these restaurants and shops designed for Asian Americans draw consumers to a distinctive space that explicitly caters to them, and frequent promotions ensure regular visits.

TOWARD AUDIENCE TESTING

"Casting for diversity," as general market executives described it, reveals the contemporary politics of diversity in the neoliberal imagination as envisaged by advertising executives. General market advertising is clear about its intentions for diversity: diversity is profitable, and clients want ads to be diverse. This plays out in several ways, ranging from the deliberate inclusion of distinguishable ethnic or racial groups, to the selection of "ethnically ambiguous" actors and the careful curating of ads that avoid miscegenation. Assemblages of diversity convey what ad executives consider "normal," a seemingly neutral term that is steeped in ideologies of whiteness. In casting, normal is premised on a complex set of ideas about what people should look like, how they should sound, what affect they are able to convey, and how they look when placed alongside others in an ad. In a different space, higher education, Sara Ahmed has remarked that persons of color "embody diversity" because they provide "an institution of whiteness with color."[25] In advertising, talent that embodies diversity does the postracial work of overwriting ethnic and racial inequality and prejudice by creating attractive tableaux of minority actors that ultimately further a normative whiteness. The reception of assemblages of diversity is difficult to predict but can be carefully controlled with PR, though it can be disastrous when PR fails. The question remains as to whether this approach does much more than reproduce a concept of diversity that reinforces racially naturalized ideas about difference rather than interrogating and expanding them.

Casting talent is equally important for Asian American advertising, but other production-based cultural and linguistic details are also vital to shaping the overall authenticity of an ad. The ideologies that underpin corporate American notions of normal and where diversity stands in relation to it leave much unspoken. General market ad executives balance entertainment value and what "feels real" and "normal" with representing diversity so that it "does not feel like advertising."

Advertising and branding for multicultural audiences are transforming aspects of urban and suburban America. Advertising and marketing have long been a part of ethnically saturated neighborhoods and retail corridors and for at least the past few decades have featured smaller scale versions of corporate sponsorship and promotions. Yet the role of social media is only beginning to be understood in terms of linking brand to ethnicity and language and creating assemblages that link broadcast ads, public relations, digital, and place-based technologies. Ad executives use digital media to interact with consumers for marketing and promotion in designated market areas in ways that publicly showcase ethnic difference to support consumption. As generational preferences shift and digital technology becomes even more ubiquitous, Asian Americans will be appealed to through multiple media simultaneously, and perhaps continuously. The increasingly sophisticated ways that data are collected result in marketers tracking consumers' every move in ways that exceed consumption trends and spending habits reportable from other metrics. For instance, analyzing monthly credit card purchases, conducting focus groups about how people shop, and other measurements that track consumption do not produce real-time, location-specific results, as GPS-based technologies do. Corporate sponsorship is inescapably tied to everything from civic centers to sporting arenas and educational events and is an indelible part of the urban landscape. Promotions large and small make in-store, public appeals to Asian American consumers, thus increasing their visibility in the retail sphere and further legitimating Asian American advertising.

Digital platforms for communication, consumption, and knowledge production are hallmarks of the new economy and illustrate the complex web of individuals, agendas, and capital that have been brought together in previously unseen ways. Such assemblages are temporally and spatially finite and generate and circulate social meaning in ways that include consumers as well as advertising executives, marketers, and clients. Place-based as well as social media brand promotions allow ad executives to map Asian Americans onto their urban and suburban neighborhoods and regions in ways that complicate the politics of visibility, especially as the use of digital increases. Through media placement and other types of marketing, assemblages are actually located somewhere and are part of certain locations in deliberate ways. The expectation is that consumers will make sense of these assemblages in ways that resonate with them, in their landscape. In these ways Asian American ad executives are using digital media not only to market and promote brands but also to offer new types of experiential consumerism in ethnic enclaves. New media, which is so often not linked to actual places in the physical world, is here reliant on place in order to be meaningful. Brand is being communicated specifically and invisibly according to ethnicity. These media give urban neighborhoods added markers of ethnic identity and language and serve to differentiate particular ethnic groups from others who may also share this urban space. In these assemblages of diversity, major retail outlets recognize ethnic consumers as important to that location and that neighborhood. Digital marketing builds brand recognition among Asian ethnic groups and also rebrands those neighborhoods and creates a shift in racialization that makes Asian Americans a more naturalized part of the landscape through consumption. These approaches provide a range of ways to think about how diversity has become an emblem for branding in cities and suburbs and how brand is extended and made more pervasive through digital and social media in ethnic, location-specific ways.

Audience Testing

Having launched Allied Country's brand in several segments of the Asian American market, Asian Ads made
a strong case to justify targeting consumers through
niche advertising. Even though the brand's general market
messaging began to feature more diverse talent, the client still
believed that Asian American consumers were worth targeting through multicultural advertising. In fact the client liked
aspects of the Asian American creative so much that they considered using select visual elements in their general market
campaign. Such a move would not only underscore the value
of Asian Ads' creative work but would also keep multicultural
advertising relevant. Creative director An Rong reiterated this
point to his client after the successful brand launch: "We are
different from the general market. The Chinese market has
never had this advertising before. And this is the first phase,
where they will learn about Allied Country, what kind of company it is. Every aspect of this, including placing your logo in
the layout, is seen here." With the client in appreciative agreement, Asian Ads chalked this campaign up as a success—
something that was never taken for granted in the competitive world of advertising. Helpful here was their reflective and
engaged client George, who self-identified as a minority and
invoked his Hispanic heritage to show his alignment with
Asian Ads and empathize about the challenges of making
in-culture and in-language creative for his company's mostly
white marketing department. Although not Asian American
himself, George made the intercultural spaces of the adver-

tising process vastly more navigable. Even so, the struggle over diversity and which sectors of the advertising industry could best represent it was far from resolved. General market and multicultural agencies struggled to control this dynamic aspect of advertising in a shrinking industry, each vying for the opportunity to demonstrate their expertise and convince clients of the efficacy of their approach.

In this conclusion I consider the significance and impact of assemblages of ethnoracial diversity on multicultural advertising, the "new normal" of white corporate America, and how both come to bear on racialization for Asian Americans. Census-based categories of race and ethnicity and statistics about the growing minority population have elicited new advertising agendas about diversity. These biopolitical concerns took center stage after the 2010 U.S. Census and other projections predicted that diversity will only become more important for advertising in the decades to come. Multicultural and general market executives each promoted their own approaches to advertising diversity, how it should be conceptualized, and the extent to which it matters. General market executives tried to include more diversity in their version of "normal," while multicultural executives set about remaking this definition altogether. How racism and whiteness take new forms and how Asian American advertising maps onto a broader twenty-first-century U.S. landscape hang in the balance.

ASSEMBLAGES AND DIVERSITY

Using the concept of assemblages of diversity has allowed me to present the struggle to control the process of knowledge production about race and ethnicity—specifically whether multicultural or general market advertising, or some combination, is best positioned to represent diversity. Throughout *Advertising Diversity* I have utilized the concept of assemblage to discuss the contingent, contentious process of advertising development and production. Looking at the process of assembling that occurs among ad executives, between them and clients, and the placement and circulation of brands through media, public relations, and promotions, my discussion has offered less-heard perspectives on defining and representing diversity. I have considered how assemblages capture the tension and overlaps between biopolitical measures designed to count and classify individuals according to racial and ethnic categories (the U.S. Census); capitalists who seek to maximize profit through consumption (corporate clients); advertising executives who see themselves as artful storytellers in promoting brand (creatives and agencies); and the variety of media in which they are placed to reach consumers (broadcast, place-based, and promotions). Assemblages can take material form and be marked by evocative elements, and are accordingly useful for thinking about how language and materiality operate in the same semiotic frame to communicate diversity in advertisements. General market agencies, multicultural agencies, and clients understand qualisigns of diversity differently, interpreting these values according to their own cultural and linguistic knowledge. In these spaces of corporate America, diversity is meted out in the creative work of agencies and in the intercultural spaces of making sense of racial and ethnic difference.

Through these assemblages of ethnoracial diversity that consider the semiotics of brands, their promoters, and their consumers in the same frame, ethnoracial difference is given market value and message is circulated through numerous modalities. Such assemblages are products of the new economy in which data and expertise are highly valued. Considering processes of producing and circulating the assemblage has allowed me to emphasize the varied, often competing agendas and ideologies about ethnicity and language held by the different constituencies involved and that signal further unpredictability through circulation and consumption. Consumers can derive different brand meanings than producers intended and that also differ from one another, and such consumption can have an impact on how the advertising industry addresses diversity in its agencies and its creative.

The tension between data about ethnoracial diversity in the United States today and the extent to which advertising agencies wish to substantively engage with race and ethnicity draw attention to the temporal and spatial limitations of assemblages of diversity. As I have illustrated throughout this book, diversity is articulated and operationalized in a variety of ways, erring on the side of ambiguous or culturally and linguistically marked. While the latter could be seen as more progressive and therefore forwarding an agenda about diversity and equality, ultimately they too are advertisements, intended to sell something. In a thought-provoking examination of what this type of work might accomplish, Evelyn Alsultany analyzes how citizenship and national belonging are reconfigured through public service announcements since 9/11, with the Ad Council's "I am an American" campaign. She deconstructs how American Muslims in these ads sell a newly reconstructed vision of multicultural America. Contrasting the good American Muslim with the antifreedom, antidiversity Arab Muslim, she points out the limits of diversity discourse in accomplishing meaningful change because it is already in the service of the state. Tolerance, then, extended only to those thought to sympathetically fit within the state visually, culturally, and even linguistically; for instance, English was the only language spoken by American Muslims in this campaign.[1]

Scholarly discussions concerning meanings and implementations of diversity have been predictably critical of corporate rhetoric about difference and how it should be acknowledged. In the introduction I discussed the relevance of Sara Ahmed's conceptions of diversity and inclusion to what I observed in advertising worlds.[2] Ultimately, like Ahmed's study, definitions of diversity and what they are meant to accomplish are about power and resources and which voices get heard in largely white institutional spaces. Corporate America poses different challenges of whiteness and has agendas different from those of the state or educational institutions. A growing body of critical scholarship has offered analyses of how *diversity* and *multiculturalism* have become empty catch-all phrases in institutional and corporate contexts, and I highlight only a few here. Often employed to create the illusion of inclusion of minority groups, corporate policies about diversity are steeped in rhetoric about tolerance and cultural appreciation. Many of these critiques draw attention to the bounds of terms such as *diversity* and *multiculturalism* by pointing to the limits of the notion of tolerance itself. Stanley Fish calls such an approach to diversity "boutique" multiculturalism and contrasts it to "strong" multiculturalism; the former promotes and furthers a superficial appreciation for cultural diversity with very limited cultural tolerance, to the extent that political beliefs are not disrupted.[3] Douglas Hartmann and Joseph Gerteis offer a similar position by considering multiculturalism as a series of responses to diversity. Building on Fish's critique of boutique multiculturalism, they identify cosmopolitan multiculturalism as claiming to be more tolerant but ultimately reaching a limit to tolerance for pluralistic difference.[4] Jan Blommaert and Jef Verschueren go so far as to contend that in Belgium, modern debates surrounding diversity may actually be the root of diversity-related problems rather than diversity itself.[5] Especially when applied to questions of immigration in Belgium, they argue, the societal preoccupation with cultural, ethnic, and racial diversity has turned diversity itself into a social tension. The uneven power hierarchies that allow some voices to be heard over others, however, do suggest that what is at stake is something larger than the debates themselves, namely social power and opportunities for upward mobility. All of these models are helpful for fleshing out the particulars of diversity in corporate American settings—a space largely dominated by marketing and human resources literature ultimately forwarding a version of boutique multiculturalism. Still none is an ideal fit for the work of advertising, which does not debate diversity in terms of citizenship, sovereignty, rights, or equality; rather diversity matters in terms of brand, consumers, and profit. Attending to what Robert Stam and Ella Shohat discuss as decolonizing knowledge production in the context of "corporate managed multiculturalism,"[6] I have looked at how proponents of diversity operationalize the agenda of color blindness and the postracial and how it can make ethnoracial differences seem irrelevant when ethnic ambiguity is doing the work of making America look diverse. Asian American advertising executives' moves for legitimacy through multicultural advertising in a largely white advertising world, their management of cultural and linguistic marginalization and occasionally ridicule, and the limited entrée for first-generation Asian American advertising executives in general market advertising underscore that this industry is certainly not color-blind. These dynamics have an impact on racial naturalization for Asian Americans in mass media and in corporate America, and also on how general market advertising may be slowly shifting its notions of normal.

Using the concept of assemblages of diversity to understand advertising and diversity leaves the means of representing ethnic and racial difference open to further contest. In the corporate worlds of clients and ad agencies, knowledge drawn from heritage languages and cultures is as valued as expertise formulated from data, research, and other means. This equation reveals the essentialist notions that underpin diversity and the racialized labor that is relied on to provide this expertise. Marilyn Strathern cautions against certain conceptions of diversity that rarely address anything substantive about difference. Situating discussions about diversity in "the knowledge economy," she remarks that it comes from a reductive place of people speaking for their cultures and echoes the type of essentialism that anthropology and other social sciences have long eschewed.[7] Yet this conception fits exceedingly well with corporate culture, and as I illustrated in chapter 3, ethnic and linguistic difference is conveyed in welcoming, inviting ways by those who can claim lived experience. Ad hoc focus groups comprising people of a specific ethnic or racial background, token employees who serve as intended audiences for creative work, and heritage-language speakers who are asked to judge copy are experts in corporate America today, whether or not they wish to be considered so. This trend benefits Asian American ad executives when it bolsters their credibility and expertise but can be a stumbling block when clients expect their expertise to be comprehensive or easily contradicted by their own coworkers of the same ethnic group. At the same time, general market agencies promote their own ideas about diversity that focus less on specific ethnic and linguistic details and more on visible differences that create versions of an essential sameness. In keeping with boutique multiculturalism, this general market approach further disengages representations from political economic and linguistic difference, as bodies of different hues, voices of different tenors, and sound bytes from various language varieties are put together in ways that further the postracial social climate. Such ambiguity offers new avenues for inviting brand identification among a broad range of minority consumers, while Asian American advertising narrows this scope by fostering brand identification in highly specific ways to what they believe to be elite, model consumers. In this contentious process clients are invited to choose how to effectively reach the same minority consumers and best promote their brand.

CONTESTS OF DIVERSITY

General and multicultural market ad executives define and manipulate diversity to index their own agendas and concerns. Concerned with what some marketers have dubbed "the new mainstream," ad executives have sought to rethink what they believe to be America's new ethnic and racial composition, but not necessarily the social and economic differences that may be included in this shift. Multicultural advertising, a presence in the American advertising landscape for at least the past three decades in its current configuration of African American, Asian American, Latino, and emerging markets of consumers, has fought to maintain its legitimacy and relevance. The 2010 U.S. Census both justified its cause and created the conditions that invite intense competition from the general market. For Asian American executives, representing diversity efficiently is an ongoing challenge because of the limited media platforms and viewership data. The Asian Ads media buyer Chris explained, "General market TV is vastly cheaper than any other way of talking," in terms of the number of people who can be reached at a time. He conceded that general market advertising's inclusion of more minorities is smart and cost-effective: "If you had unlimited money, then you could get really, really specific with your targeting, both in terms of age breakdown and geography and ethnic groups. But since you don't really have that luxury, you need to find a message that works as broadly as possible." Other ad executives countered that general market representations are superficial, and minority talent in general market ads are "just a face, just an agenda to show that 'we have multiculturalism,'" as one Asian American CEO told me. Appearing to be concerned with diversity but not representing it in a way that indexes anything socially identifiable led one Asian American executive to conclude that such representations are "not done in a meaningful way."

When asked, some Asian American executives admitted their concern about the increased inclusion of minorities in general market ads, for they wondered whether this would gradually reduce their overall advertising work. Most recognized that the general market is producing a greater number of ads featuring what they called "multicultural talent," which seems to address demands for more diverse ads. Even if they do not reach consumers through in-language and in-culture messaging, they still create the conditions for intense competition. As account executive Joyce put it to me, "Of course, multicultural agencies like us need to justify our existence," regardless of the quality of their work. Multicultural executives aimed to control these segments of the advertising industry to position themselves as indispensable so that they could claim a unique and irreproducible niche in advertising worlds. This was accomplished in part through the organization and self-promotion of agencies, a process that is most visibly and effectively achieved through conferences and workshops about multicultural marketing aimed at clients. Some events of this kind are held by the Asian American Advertising Federation, the member-driven organization that promotes Asian American advertising agencies, media companies, public relations firms, and their major corporate clients. In addition to their annual Marketing Summit, preceded by a marketing Boot Camp for those desiring a primer of the Asian American market, 3AF periodically offers marketing and training events for clients interested in reaching this market. Held every few months in a major designated market area for Asian American advertising, such as Los Angeles, San Francisco, New York, or Chicago, these events offer networking opportunities as well as informational sessions. As I discussed in chapter 1, doing ongoing education for clients and drawing in new clients is important for Asian American agencies to demonstrate legitimacy and relevance.

The legitimacy of this work was further boosted by awards and recognitions. Few things seemed to be as fetishized in neoliberal corporate culture as awards—a seemingly objective affirmation of one's merit and intrinsic value. On a small scale 3AF held its own award competition for best Asian American ad in each category. This low-profile competition nonetheless provided bragging rights among Asian American agencies for the year to come. On a far larger scale awards recognizing multiculturalism and diversity in general market advertising are more prestigious affairs. When I attended the 2009 Mosaic awards in New York City, the Association of American Advertising Agencies, in conjunction with the Advertising Education Foundation, was honoring excellence in multicultural marketing and diversity, which I mentioned in chapter 4. One award was given in each multicultural category of African American, Asian American, and Latino advertising, and additional commendations were bestowed upon general market agencies, corporations, and other firms that had excelled in promoting diversity. InterTrend, the Los Angeles–based agency that won in the Asian American category that year, had done a visually stunning print and television campaign for J. C. Penney. The campaign made Asian American consumers approachable and contemporary through themes of modern gift giving and consumption. In their presentation, InterTrend skillfully illustrated for their nonspecialist audience how targeted their work is but how accessible Asian American diversity can be. With similar awards for Latino and African American marketing, as well as recognition of diversity in general market agencies, the Mosaic awards contribute to the legitimacy of multicultural marketing. Assuring that such targeted efforts can be accomplished without causing "brand fracture" or otherwise opposing a general market brand, their visibility is an important reminder to the broader advertising world that minority groups are not monolithic and that avoiding stereotypes remains an ongoing challenge. Indeed such award ceremonies bring multicultural marketing into the center of advertising worlds by conferring prestige and enabling, as one female African American award winner put it, "running with the big boys."

Throughout the ceremony diversity was treated as a commodity and an asset, possessed by some for the consumption of all. For instance, a human relations firm specializing in diversity promoted itself as doing "diversity training from our CEO to our janitorial staff" and suggested that no one should be exempt from this important education. Indeed, as another presenter put it, diversity should be taken seriously as a business objective that can be profitable rather than simply undertaken for morale or publicity: "It has to make business sense, and your top executives have to be on board. So, diversity means good business, and the most important step

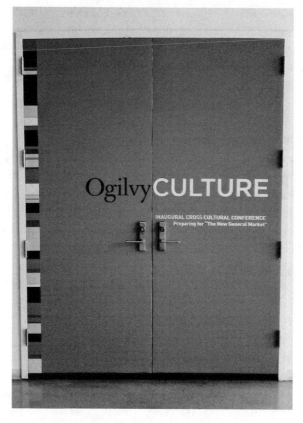

C.1 Doors painted in the Ogilvy, NY, building featuring the launch of a new unit, Ogilvy Culture. Photo by author (2011).

is encouragement from clients, which then impresses top management." Such a perspective does not, however, address *how* diversity should be conceptualized and represented, as was evident in the great variation of general market approaches I observed.

Unlike the hyperspecific, targeted advertising multicultural market executives make, general market executives see themselves as being experts of diversity broadly conceived. Major multinational agencies have honed in on "culture," using this term as code for "race and ethnicity." As I completed my fieldwork, the term they used for addressing diversity was *cross-cultural advertising*. Agencies promote their own version of expertise about diversity, such as BBDO's department of "cultural discoveries" or the "Ogilvy Culture" division (fig. C.1). Such approaches enable these multinational giants to signal to clients that they too are able to address a more diverse America. When I spoke to one multicultural ad executive in 2014, she informed me that the newest term was *total market*, an approach that involves the collaboration of general and multicultural agencies on all aspects of creative and production. Despite differences in terminology, diversity in general market advertising relies on broadly rendered notions of difference as intrinsic to humanity and to be celebrated. Arguing that people share more commonalities than differences, brands are credited with the power to bring consumers together. A 2014 spot for Coca-Cola, which first aired during the Super Bowl, exemplifies this approach (fig. C.2). In it a series of individuals of different racial, ethnic, and religious backgrounds each sing a line of "America the Beautiful" in their heritage language. The ad predictably received negative feedback from xenophobes, while some ad executives thought it was reductive of the company's past campaigns. Regardless, it signals a new approach to general market diversity that does, at least occasionally, venture beyond ambiguity to represent ethnoracial differences in more culturally and linguistically recognizable ways.

C.2 Coca-Cola Super Bowl spot featuring the song "America the Beautiful" with each line sung in a different language (2014).

For the most part, however, cross-cultural approaches to diversity mirror the culture of corporate America that pervades the workspaces of clients as well as general market agencies, where conceptions of normal are still steeped in whiteness. A separate division or at least a department in which minorities are hired with the explicit purpose of making cross-cultural messaging only underscores this point as well as the challenges of getting diversity right. Douglass Alligood, a general market agency veteran, identified the potential pitfalls of general market agencies undertaking cross-cultural messaging.[8] Drawing on his earlier work experience in African American advertising, he described the predicament: "How can you talk to minorities if all of your message creators are young white guys, twenty-seven-year-olds who think the world has always been like this? And don't know our history, and don't know what we're sensitive to." Yet he added that it is important for advertising executives to understand how people "identify themselves" in order to create messages that will reach them. Contending that people are identifying themselves increasingly by ethnicity and race, he said, "We're going to **have to do diversity** in order to keep up with what's going on." While others in general market advertising were less certain that ethnic and racial identification were on the rise, they nonetheless recognized that representing diversity was essential. The bottom line, as several general market ad executives put it, is that diversity is profitable and should be divested from broader social agendas. Mr. Alligood expressed it like this: "You don't have to pretend to love us because you don't! We don't need love, we need respect as consumers. Diversity is important for survival. As an agency, we want to be around in ten years, in fifteen years. . . . It's guaranteed you're going to fail if you're not diversified in the next several years. Starting now." Few are as blunt about this commercial agenda as Mr. Alligood, but they nonetheless promote the mission of diversity by making messaging for "the new mainstream." The new mainstream promotes a vision of America in which diversity is a foregone conclusion, and a corporate world in which missing that fact will lead to a quick demise. The extent to which clients and ad executives agree with this vision varies, but most seem to be well aware of the shift in diversity that the new mainstream underscores.

Part of this new mainstream, Asian American market executives noted, is second-generation Asian American and Latino youth—the children of those who immigrated in the 1960s and 1970s. It was especially important for multicultural executives to consider how to appeal to them in ways that differ from messaging created for their parents. Especially because

C.3 Web-based campaign by AT&T aimed at second-generation Asian American youth (2012).

Asian youth markets are booming, Asian American advertising executives grasp for meaningful ways of reaching second-generation Asian American youth in the United States. Digital media and interactive campaigns were two options. For example, for "Away we happened," a successful campaign for AT&T, the Asian American ad agency InterTrend created a short film featuring a budding romance and a website in which viewers could vote on what should happen to the couple in upcoming installments (fig. C.3). This highly successful digital campaign featuring attractive, stylish, second-generation Asian American talent offers one model of how to continue to reach these consumers through multicultural advertising. Asian American ad executives realize how different second-generation Asian Americans of various ethnic groups are, and that not all of them may identify with the broader category of Asian American. They acknowledge the difficulty of reaching youth outside of densely populated DMAs, where they can live in large ethnic communities. In *Desi Land* I argued that South Asian American and other minority youth who grew up in places like Silicon Valley had a very strong identification with their ethnoracial heritage, but the same may not be true in less diverse places.[9] Demographers predict that other regions may become similarly diverse over the next few decades, but also that Asian American youth will more easily be reached through general market media rather than the ethnic media outlets that cater primarily to their parents. Susan, the CEO of an Asian American agency, described second-generation youth as far more "global," in that they are attracted to more international foods and cultural traditions. She emphasized the difference from when she was younger: "The Asian American psyches have changed, so the way that we are reaching this market shouldn't be the same as twenty years ago." She also admitted that in some ways Asian American advertising has not sufficiently kept pace with these changes. Her coworker Andrea contextualized this difficulty, suggesting that reaching the second generation in more modern ways was often done in English, but that clients were less inclined to commission English-based messaging, especially if it was not an explicitly in-culture transcreation.

Some Asian American ad executives, themselves second generation, disagree with the notion that second-generation youth cannot be reached through multicultural advertising. Asian Ads media buyer Chris drew a comparison with African American and gay markets, which he described as "targeting a mind-set, not just a language." Others contend that English is not the only index of the second generation, who might identify with "enculturated" Asian American talent because of shared experiences of being Asian in the United States. This identity-based argument is likewise difficult to sell to clients, however, as general market ads already feature enculturated Asian Americans. Yet what Chris and others emphasized, and thought that clients underestimated, is the positive and willing identification of second-generation youth with their ethnic communities and with Asian Americans more broadly. Still others who have third-generation children find this less likely. Alex, a second-generation Chinese American ad executive with a first-generation wife from Hong Kong, believes that the third generation "won't marry into our segment." He laughed about his "old school" commitment to "making sure my children have a better life than me. Its all about their happiness." Sharing his hope that his children will "retain a lot of the values in our culture," he suggested that they would want "marketers addressing them as who they are as well as a mix of what their culture represents." Thus even if this means the in-language work is gradually replaced by in-culture ads in English, there will "always be a place for 'cultural advertising,' let's call it," Alex said. Apart from placing ads in the handful of periodicals aimed at Asian American youth of specific ethnicities, or utilizing digital and social media technologies, ad executives do not seem to attend to this area explicitly.

This may be the case because of the complete absence of pan-Asian media outlets. Asian Ads CEO Yang, who has given much thought to in-language versus simply in-culture messaging for second-generation youth, contended that language was still the hallmark of multicultural marketing. Chinese Americans who once needed in-language messaging are increasingly comfortable with Chinglish or simply English in-culture messaging, he noted, especially because many of the websites Chinese Americans access are in English. There is no English-language media aimed at a pan-Asian American audience to which they could transition. Media outlets that have attempted to reach specific Asian American youth or to promote a pan-Asian channel have barely gotten off the ground before being pulled off the air. Perhaps the most ambitious was "MTV World," which was to feature MTV Desi, MTV Korean, and MTV Chinese. One ad executive recounted in a 2011 interview, "**Every** attempt at launching pan-Asian media has failed, be it print, online, and television, and that has not been productive from an advertising perspective." Yang remarked that the lack of a major televised event like the Super Bowl, which drives American advertising innovation, contributes to this problem.

Digital platforms and social media offer alternatives to traditional broadcast media. Niche ad executives are hopeful about websites, social media, and viral marketing. Yang believes these media will achieve the audience concentration that is difficult to build elsewhere. Such options are considered newer and mirror a split between first- and second-generation immigrants. For example, some media buyers regarded digital cable platforms as skewed toward the older South Asian American generation, such as STAR TV and Zee TV. By contrast, MTV Desi and other MTV imprint channels are "the new generation," as are a number of matrimonial websites that cater to the second generation, although one media buyer predicted that many second-generation youth would just as likely "find their own matches." Still there are other considerations, such as second-generation youth trying to "rediscover" their Asian ethnic heritage, that could shift this balance, though most likely not in a major way. Yang reiterated the power of social media for advertising and offered this illustration: "You're South Asian, Indian, you use Facebook. I would guess that sixty to seventy percent of your Facebook network is also South Asian." He added that this would be a cost-effective and otherwise productive way to target second-generation audiences. Since Yang gave me this example in 2009, Facebook and other social media platforms have implemented exactly this model and welcomed targeted ads, to be placed alongside or right in the midst of users' newsfeeds. Such innovation suggests that we are in the fairly early stages of reconfiguring what will be considered "ethnic" media moving forward, especially digitally.

RACIAL NATURALIZATION AND NEW NORMALS

Debates over the significance of race, in confluence with the election of a black president, the 2010 U.S. Census reporting previously unseen numbers of minorities, and neoliberal ideologies that render ingrained socio-economic differences and prejudice underpinning racial formation as potentially inconsequential, all contribute to the current speculation about whether race matters, how it matters, and what to do about representing it. As the makers of racialized representations, advertising executives have considerable power over shaping the aim and reach of their communications. Through biopolitics and other processes of knowledge production, ad executives produce and circulate racial meanings about Asian Americans. These processes, in which ethnic and racial categories are named, defined, and operationalized to promote brands by linking particular characteristics to them, contribute to processes of racialization. In 1966 the Human Rights Commission report took Madison Avenue agencies to task for their striking lack of hiring diversity. In 2007, after the release of the Commission's follow-up report, New York Democratic senator Charles Schumer spoke at a breakfast hosted by Jesse Jackson's Rainbow Coalition / Wall Street Project. As part of his message of change, Schumer took up the issue of minority representation in the advertising industry's senior-most ranks with the comment, "We're saying to the ad industry, 'We're waiting for you.'" While this book has not investigated how the advertising industry has responded, I have identified how some minorities fare in multicultural agencies and how those in general market agencies as well as corporations are trying to make sense of diversity. I have also considered how diversity in advertisements is linked to broader matters of racialized labor and media production in the twenty-first century.

Despite all this work focused on diversity, advertising worlds still remain fundamentally steeped in whiteness. Ways of conjuring what normal looks like, everyday conversational and interactional norms, ways of speaking English, comportment and dress are all still governed by routine practices of whiteness. One Asian American ad executive carefully explained it to me like this: "This has nothing to do with racism, but [general marketing advertising] is still **a very** Anglo-Saxon way of looking at the world. . . . So if a client is truly committed to this market, we still think they should be retaining a specialist to do it, and do it well." Even in light of the changes with the new mainstream, this ad executive did not believe it was a meaningful priority:

> If you look at advertising trends right now, it's controversial in discussing what multicultural means. A lot of clients are saying that they want to consolidate it into the so-called **mainstream** agencies, the really **good** agencies like the Leo Burnetts, the Young and Rubicams, the J. Walter Thompsons, Ogilvy, Wieden and Kennedy, who are really great agencies. I could understand the business reason why they do that, but I have never seen a mainstream agency with [a] so-called multicultural division do well. And it's not because, it's not that they're, you know, there's any ill will against multicultural marketing, but ((sigh)) from a priority standpoint it's never going to be their priority, it **cannot** be their priority. It's going to take a while for any advertising agencies to look at the landscape of America right now and say that multicultural is really the mainstream.

One emerging approach that hints at such a reprioritization is the "total market" strategy I mentioned earlier. In this model clients expect each of their three multicultural agencies, those for African Americans, Asian Americans, and Latinos, to collaborate with their general market agency at every step of the process. The imbalances of power and budget are evident in this model, in which the general market agency overshadows the others, but it is a nod toward a more collaborative approach to creative than simply having multicultural agencies transcreate general market campaigns. It remains to be seen how the predominantly white world of general market advertising will welcome the niche insights of multicultural advertising. Yet there seems to be real potential in these collaborations, in that new versions of normal could emerge that may shift the otherwise white, middle-class notions of language and culture that prevail in general market advertising.

Multicultural advertising has the greater potential to create these new normals themselves, and this is what I observed. I have illustrated the work of postracial ideologies and their linkages to racialized capitalism through a process I have termed racial naturalization and analyzed representational shifts from Asian Americans as alien and foreign to how they are becoming selectively included in the American consumer landscape. One of the outcomes of racial naturalization is the legitimate place it is making for Asian Americans among U.S. citizenry. Whereas legislation of earlier eras denied citizenship and later ones involved legal inclusion but social exclusion, we are at a moment of Asian American visibility and prestige through advertising and consumption. Notably Asian American ad executives do not construct non–Asian Americans negatively, and note them only as points of contrast for certain cultural insights they wish to convey to clients. Rather they are far more concerned with depicting upwardly mobile, model consumers, making the difference about class rather than about race alone. It is part of the creation of a world, and a version of that world can be seen in advertising.

Selective inclusions and exclusions reframe Asian American consumers and, by extension, Asian Americans more broadly, as central to the United States in previously unseen ways. In the recovery from a difficult economic recession, Asian Americans can be part of the solution to overall financial growth. Their acculturated, well-positioned inclusion in general market ads as legitimate consumers rather than racially marked comedic foils shifts racism's gaze to those who also appear Asian American but are otherwise ridiculed for their way of speaking, dress, comportment, or lack of proficiency in consumer culture. Paradigms of consumerism forwarded by Asian American advertising have significantly narrowed the category of Asian American, effectively backgrounding if not altogether erasing those who are not easily framed as model consumers. These could include those whose income level excludes them from being upwardly mobile and willing to spend.

New normals are still normative, but newness does have some positive connotations. At the start of this book I raised James Ferguson's "politics of the anti-" and the blanket critique it entails as something I aimed to avoid. Similarly considering how to progress, Bonnie McElhinny differently frames a similar concern: "How do progressive scholars use the analytic lens of affect to think toward a better future?"[10] Throughout my discussion of corporate America, advertising worlds, and profit making, I have aimed to show the potential for antiracism that these ads hold, even while they sometimes reproduce racist notions of normal that remain unchanged. Especially when these ads circulate and are taken up by consumers in un-

Make Love. GAP

Waris Ahluwalia & Quentin Jones **make art.**
#makelove

c.4 Gap "Make Love" print ad campaign featuring Waris Ahluwalia and Quentin Jones (2013).

expected and unpredictable ways, they have great potential for social activism and raising awareness among new generations using previously unavailable social media channels to create grassroots responses to racism. For instance, a 2013 print ad for Gap featuring a Sikh actor and model and a white filmmaker that was located on a Bronx subway platform was tagged with racist graffiti. Seemingly instantly, it was photographed, tweeted, and retweeted widely by several antiracist bloggers and web personalities, resulting in Gap's proud affirmation of the diverse talent it had cast (fig. c.4). This small bit of graffiti mobilized an antiracist campaign, emphasizing the unforeseen potential of ads that push the parameters of normal when they represent diversity.

The new economy never stops inventing the need for improved forms of expertise based on data and innovation. This cycle pushes the notion of normal to incorporate innovative ways of conceiving of diversity and can change what advertising diversity should look and sound like. Creating multiple versions of normal can complicate the singular version of diversity prevalent in general market advertising. A range of representational choices that engage more substantively with visible and audible elements of cultural and linguistic variation can contribute to making minorities part of normal without necessarily erasing difference. For Asian Americans this could include qualisigns of diversity from multicultural advertising that, over time, become more familiar to broader audiences, thereby naturalizing a more substantive set of differences than simply making them interchangeable with white talent. The hope, then, is that these diverse new versions of normal will someday become simply "normal."

ACKNOWLEDGMENTS

Research for this book was generously sponsored by the National Science Foundation (BCS 0924472) and by Northwestern University. It is with heartfelt thanks that I acknowledge the advertising agencies that allowed me to visit, conduct interviews and observations, and better understand their work, including the following agencies in New York: Ad Asia, Admerasia, A Partnership, ASB Communications, BBDO, Cinemaya Media, Kang and Lee, Ogilvy, and Young and Rubicam; in other locations: Dae (San Francisco), Euro RSCG (Chicago), InterTrend (Long Beach), IW Group (Los Angeles), and Touchdown Media (Metuchen). Several individuals were especially instrumental in helping me gain access to agencies and ongoing account activities; special thanks go to the Advertising Education Foundation, the Asian American Advertising Federation, Douglass Alligood, Neeta Bhasin, Ed Chang, Rita Denny, Sharmila Fowler, Belle Franks, Genny Hom-Franzen, Saul Gitlin, Julia Huang, Bill Imada, Tom Kraemer, Jeff Lin, Bob Morais, Jane Nakagawa, Navin Narayanan, Tommy Ng, Zan Ng, Jenny Russo-Novak, Sangeet Pillai, Rekha Radhakrishnan, Lisa Skriloff, Nita Song, Patricia Sunderland, Aarti Thiagarajan, Nimesh Trivedi, and Rahul Walia.

It has been a pleasure to work with Duke University Press on this book. I am grateful to Ken Wissoker for his enthusiasm for this project from the first time I mentioned it, to Elizabeth Ault, Amy Ruth Buchanan, Christine Riggio, Liz Smith, and the production team. Portions of this book benefited greatly from presentations and interactions with colleagues at the American Anthropological Association annual meetings, the Association for American Studies meetings, the Association for Asian American Studies meetings, the American Ethnological Society meetings, Emory University, The Graduate Center–CUNY, New York University, Northwestern University, University of California at Irvine, University of California at Los Angeles, University of Chicago, and the University of Illinois at Urbana-Champaign.

I am immeasurably grateful to generous colleagues who offered feedback and suggestions during various stages of presentation and writing: Don Brenneis, Summerson Carr, Arlene Davila, Tejaswini Ganti, Faye Ginsburg, Jessica Greenberg, Angelique Haugerud, Monica Heller, Doug Holmes, Daniel Hosang, Aisha Khan, Setha Low, Lisa Lowe, Martin Manalansan, Purnima Mankekar, Jeff Maskofsky, William Mazzarella, Laura Miller, Fred Myers, Elinor Ochs, Kent Ono, Junaid Rana, Bambi Schieffelin, Min Song, and Stan Thangaraj. At Northwestern I benefited from conversations with numerous colleagues, including Carolyn Chen, Micaela di Leonardo, Mark Hauser, Barnor Hesse, Katherine Hoffman, Jinah Kim, Helen Schwartzman, Nitasha Sharma, Jessica Winegar, and Ji-Yeon Yuh. I am indebted especially to Mark Hauser for reading this entire manuscript, and to Jillian Cavanaugh for reading the entire manuscript twice; the substantial improvements that have come from their comments are evident throughout. Last but not least, several fantastic students helped me with research, transcription, and data organization—thank you so much, Ronen Bay, Sonya Bearden, Corrine Ellis, Christine Hazday, Sarah Jeong, Faith Kares, Akhilesh Pant, Becky Raffensperger, and Sam Rolfe.

I am so fortunate to have a wonderful family that has been encouraging and supportive in every way. Without them this research and book would simply not have been possible. Huge thanks to Ratnaswamy and Shyamala Shankar for all their help and support; to Ravi Shankar for being a great brother, friend, and interlocutor; to my extended family in India for all their curiosity and inquiries, and to the Mueller family—Linda Mueller, Karen Mueller-Sparacino, Mark Sparacino, Lili Rosano-Mueller, Michelle Brooks, and Dan Mueller—for their ongoing interest in and excitement about my work. To my late father-in-law, Dr. James Mueller, I know you would have read every page of this book and had so many smart questions and comments—I wish we could have had that conversation. Finally, to my two sweet *ladoos*, Roshan and Anisha, to whom this book is dedicated, thank you for asking me daily if it was finished yet—it finally is! I love you with all my heart and look forward to much more time with you, away from my computer. And to my unconditionally supportive, thoughtful, funny, and wonderfully original husband, Kurt, you make me happy about what I do and who I am and helped make this research and book what it is.

APPENDIX 1

Transcription Key

Transliterations of Hindi into the Roman alphabet are nearly all drawn from advertising copy or use those conventions. The following key features symbols used to represent speech, sound, and gesture in the conversational excerpts featured throughout the book.

TABLE A1.1

Symbol	Meaning	Example
[ ]	Overlap	Jack: [Well]
		Jane: [Or is it]
bold	Emphasis	Jack: **Transcreated**
=	Latching	Jack: by the=
		Jane: =label company
(2.2)	Pause in seconds and tenths	
?	Raising intonation	Jane: It's so happy, right?
,	Slight pause	Jane: what the song is singing about, and
"	Quoted speech	Jack: "It really worked!"
!	Strong emotion	Jack: Oh!
(( ))	Some action	((laughter))
(↑)	Uptick in prosody	George: my English-speaking brain (↑)
( )	Contextual information	Esther: (to Paul) Why don't you go first?

Asian American Populations in the United States

TABLE A2.1

	Chinese	Vietnamese	Korean	Asian Indian	Filipino	Japanese
Population in the United States	4,010,114	1,737,433	1,706,822	3,183,063	3,416,840	1,304,286
Limited English proficiency (percent by population)[1]	42	51	41	23	19	18
Education level: % completing high school[1]	82	72	92	n/a	92	94
Education level: % completing college[1]	50	27	52	68[2]	46	46
Languages spoken (top 2–3, excluding English)[1]	n/a	Vietnamese	Korean	Hindi, Urdu, Gujarati	Tagalog	Japanese
Unemployment (% of group population)[3]	6.5	7.6	6.4	6.6	8.5	4.6
Median household income (USD)[4]	67,350	55,132	53,154	86,130	76,954	66,433

	Chinese	Vietnamese	Korean	Asian Indian	Filipino	Japanese
Three states of highest geographic concentration, ordered highest to lowest	California, New York, Hawai'i	California, Texas, Washington	California, New York, New Jersey	California, New York, New Jersey	California, Hawai'i, Illinois	California, Hawai'i, Washington
Percentage of population growth since 2000 Census	40	42	38.9	67.6	44.5	13.5
Percentage of total Asian American population	23.2	10	9.9	18.4	19.7	7.5
Percentage of population reporting single racial ancestry (out of total Asian American population)	22.8	10.6	9.7	19.4	17.4	5.2
Percentage of population reporting multiple racial ancestry (out of total Asian American population)	12.6	3.5	8.2	9.1	24.4	13.9
U.S. geographic areas with highest concentrations	West, South, Northeast	West, South, Northeast	West, South, Northeast	West, South, Northeast	West, South, Northeast	West, South, Northeast

Source: Hoeffel et al. 2012, U.S. Department of Commerce.

1. Asian American Center for Advancing Justice 2011.

2. Le 2014.

3. U.S. Department of Labor n.d.

4. Numbers from populations reported single racial ancestry or combined racial ancestry.

TABLE A2.2

Percentage of Asian American population reporting single racial ancestry	84.7
Percentage of Asian American population reporting multiple racial ancestry	15.3
U.S. geographic areas with highest concentrations of Asian Americans	West, South, Northeast
Average household income among Asian Americans	$78,600
Expenditures/year among Asian Americans	$61,400
Percentage of Asian American population who know English "very well"	61
Percentage of Asian American population who speak a second language at home	77

Source: Nielsen 2013.

INTRODUCTION: THE PITCH

1. Lipsitz 2011.

2. Throughout the book, I toggle between terms currently in use in social science, such as *Asian American*, *African American*, and *Latino*, and those used in the ad industry according to time period. While the category "black" has been replaced by "African American," "Asian" and "Hispanic" are still widely used to refer to Asian Americans and Latinos, respectively.

3. Povinelli 2011, 133.

4. Welker et al. 2011.

5. Ferguson 2010.

6. Hesse 2011, 172.

7. See the Kochhar et al. (2011) Pew Research Center report on Asian American poverty.

8. Alcoff 2005; Goldberg 1993; Koshy 2001; Montoya 2007.

9. Deleuze and Guattari 1987, 156.

10. Anderson et al. 2012, 177; Puar 2007.

11. Marcus and Saka 2006, 103.

12. Assemblages are not altogether different from other analytics that have been used to identify cultural production, including montage, collage, pastiche, bricolage, and formations. For my purposes, assemblage allows me to ethnographically consider the multiparty production of mass-circulated representations in ways that connect anthropology with other fields interested in similar questions, especially American studies, critical ethnic studies, and cultural studies. About anthropology and American studies, Faye Ginsburg has written that ethnography is "particularly well suited to track the impact of global capital in everyday life, the increasing flows of bodies and information, and the accelerating transformations in biomedicine, media, and information technology" (2006, 492). Linking these levels, I use assemblage to signal the multimodal, multimaterial process of meaning making that is temporally and perspectivally limited.

13. Shankar and Cavanaugh 2012.

14. Shankar 2006; Shankar 2012.

15. Miller 2005, 4.

16. Interview with Douglass Alligood, New York, January 29, 2011.

17. Fisher and Downey 2006.

18. Callon et al. 2002.

19. Olds and Thrift 2005, 271.

20. Fisher and Downey 2006.

21. Ho 2009, 37.

22. Harvey 2005.

23. Povinelli 2011, 134.

24. Povinelli 2011, 19.

25. Marable 2000.

26. McElhinny 2010, 315.

27. Goodwin 1994.

28. See Urciuoli 2008 for a similar discussion in university settings.

29. Ahmed 2012, 80–81. In a similar vein, Roderick Ferguson (2012) looks at minorities in the institutional life of the university, focusing on complex relationships between institutionality and textuality in the civil rights movement.

30. Urciuoli 2009.

31. Munn 1986, 74.

32. Munn 1986, 20.

33. Ahmed 2012, 4.

34. Lipsitz 2011, 5.

35. Excerpt from email from general market ad executive to author, July 2011.

36. Melamed 2006.

37. Davila 2008.

38. Davila 2001, 69.

39. For further illustration of this point with Arab Americans in media, see Alsultany 2012.

40. Hosang 2010.

41. For different illustrations of this point, see Fabian 2006; Hesse 2011; Holland 2012.

42. Cited in Holland 2012, 2.

43. See Ahmed 2012; Strathern 2006.

44. Ahmed 2012, 150.

45. Lipsitz 2001, 124.

46. Cited in Alsultany 2012, 27. To denote this culture of whiteness in her ethnography of Latino advertising, Arlene Davila (2001) uses *Anglo*, a term used by Hispanic advertising executives as a counterpoint to *Latino*.

47. Campbell and Sitze 2013, 3. Melissa Fisher and Greg Downey (2006) bring together a range of perspectives on how the new economy can be understood in terms of biopolitics and technopolitics, emphasizing quite usefully how biopoli-

tics is linked to other forces of change. Manuel Castells (2000) has delved into the connections between technology, economic change, and social change, while David Harvey's post-Fordist critique has been integral to understanding cultural foundations of postmodernity (1989) as well as economic and social formations of neoliberalism (2005). Foucauldian biopolitics are also evident in Michael Hardt and Antonio Negri's influential work *Empire* (2001), and these arguments have shaped a broader discussion about biopolitics and geopolitics (see Fisher and Downey 2006, 23).

48. Lefebvre 1991. See also de Certeau 2004; Foucault 1986.

49. Smith and Low 2013.

50. Zukin 2004.

51. Grewal 2005.

52. Shankar 2013b.

53. Kim 1999; Tuan 1998.

54. Rana 2011; Werbner 2001.

55. Carbado 2005, 651.

56. Carbado 2005, 651.

57. Goldberg 2009; Hesse 2011.

58. Ginsburg et al. 2002.

59. Ginsburg 2006; Naficy 1993.

60. Agha 2011; Eisenlohr 2006; Shankar 2008; Spitulnik 1996.

61. Dornfeld 1998; Ganti 2012; Himpele 2008.

62. Kemper 2001; Malefyt and Moeran 2003; Mazzerella 2003; Moeran 1996a; Sunderland and Denny 2007.

63. Burke 1996.

64. For discussions of branding, see Arvidsson 2006; Lury 2006; Schroeder and Salzer-Mörling 2006. On commodity consumption in an era of neoliberal globalization, see Foster 2007; Liechty 2003; Lukose 2009; West 2012.

65. Shankar 2006, 2008.

66. Naficy 1993; Schein 2013; Shankar 2008.

67. Mankekar 2013.

68. Mankekar and Schein 2013, 15.

69. Stam and Shohat 2012, 84.

70. Myers 2004b, 5–6.

71. Poole 2005, 160.

72. Ono and Pham 2009, 2.

73. Rana 2011, 27.

74. See also Mamdani 2002.

75. Farquhar 2012.

76. For examples, see Pieraccini and Alligood 2007; Chin 2001; Kern-Foxworth 1994.

77. Lee and Joo 2005; Paek and Shah 2003; Taylor and Stern 1997. For additional perspectives, see Okihiro 1994; Palumbo-Lu 1999; Prashad 2000.

78. Hannerz 2010, 544.

79. Fisher and Downey 2006, 18.

80. See, for instance, Malefyt and Morais 2012; Sunderland and Denny 2007.

81. Holmes and Marcus 2006, 251.

82. Holmes and Marcus 2005, 36.

83. Holmes and Marcus 2005, 36.

84. For a review of the Frankfurt School's theories of media and repression, as exemplified in the work of Theodore Adorno, Max Horkheimer, and Herbert Marcuse, see, for instance, Jay 1996.

85. Geertz 1973.

1. ACCOUNT PLANNING

1. Davila 2008; Pieraccini and Alligood 2007; Rubin and Melnick 2007.

2. Olds and Thrift 2005, 271.

3. Olds and Thrift 2005, 273.

4. Olds and Thrift 2005, 274. See also Greenhouse 2010; Strathern 2006.

5. Clough 2008, 19.

6. Campbell and Sitze 2013, 19.

7. Most notably these would be the end of affirmative action and the rise of whiteness as an ideology. See Võ 2010 for the former and Lipsitz 2011 for the latter.

8. Omi 2010. For other seminal perspectives on the postracial, see Bonilla-Silva 2009; Hesse 2011; Hill 2008; Lacy and Ono 2011.

9. Comaroff and Comaroff 2001, 13.

10. R. Kim 2002, cited in Ono and Pham 2009.

11. Lyon 2011.

12. Shin 2010.

13. Hao 2011.

14. Bankston 2010a.

15. Fox 1984, 40.

16. Fox 1984, 40.

17. *Mad Men* fans, Pete Campbell epitomizes the account executive, especially in early seasons of the show.

18. Fox 1984, 41–42.

19. Sivulka 1998, 94.

20. Fox 1984, 66–67; Sivulka 1998, 118. Notably Upton Sinclair's *The Jungle* is largely remembered for its prompting of this act in an ethnically segmented Chicago.

21. Beckman 1996, 8; Jackson 1992.

22. Matsukawa 2009, 60.

23. President and Fellows of Harvard College 1931; see also Garvey 1996.

24. Haddad 2008, 236.

25. Kim 2006, 379.

26. Chan 2005, extract from web essay.

27. Beckman 1996.

28. Fox 1984, 79.

29. This period, known as the Roaring Twenties, also ushered in new spending habits among women, who now had their own disposable income due to wartime earnings. Advertising thus began targeting female consumers as it never had before, and the automobile industry quickened its pace to meet the increasing demands of the market of women and men they had created earlier, who now craved new automobile models (Sivulka 1998, 137).

30. Fox 1984, 63–64.

31. Karen Leonard (1992) has chronicled the intermarrying of Sikh men with Mexican American women, both to procreate and to entrust their land and property in their wives' names.

32. Sivulka 1998, 200.

33. Fox 1984, 150.

34. Sivulka 1998, 232.

35. Fox 1984, 183.

36. Fox 1984, 172.

37. See also Sivulka 1998, 245.

38. Sivulka 1998, 261–63.

39. Fox 1984, 218.

40. Fox 1984, 262. See also Sivulka 1998, 308.

41. Fox 1984, 179.

42. See Fox 1984, 273–84.

43. Sivulka 1998, 318; Cortese 2004, 87.

44. Barde et al. 2010.

45. Lutz 2010.

46. See Sivulka 1998, chapter 8.

47. Sivulka 1998, 359–64.

48. Sivulka 1998, 366–76.

49. Sivulka 1998, 380.

50. Sivulka 1998, 388.

51. Cortese 2004, 101.

52. For discussion of these points in television and Hollywood films, see Iwamura 2011; Lee 1999.

53. Interview with author, January 2011.

54. Davila 2001.

55. Interview with author, 2011.

56. I regard this as a version of a postracial argument that Asian American advertising executives seemed to apply to African Americans but not to Latinos or Asian Americans.

57. Interview with author, March 2011. To my knowledge there is no comprehensive history of the niche agencies that create messaging for Asian American audiences, and I do not attempt that here. I visited the offices of eight agencies; of these I visited two twice, once for interviews in 2008 and again in 2011; I visited two others for several days each; and one for four continuous months. During this time I attempted to contact other Asian American agencies but was not successful in arranging interviews and observations. Given the partial nature of this picture, I outline several trends and commonalities that together offer a fairly detailed picture of how Asian American agencies emerged, the ways they are structured and managed, changes they have undergone during major economic shifts, and how they are altering in their foci and personnel. Overall these agencies were friendly and welcoming, and those that allowed me to observe were especially hospitable and generous with their space and time.

58. Interview with author, December 2009.

59. Interview with author, December 2009.

60. Interview with author, November 2012.

61. Interview with author, June 2008.

62. Interview with author, June 2008.

63. Tu 2011.

64. Interview with author, November 2009.

65. Interview with author, June 2008.

66. Interview with author, November 2012.

67. Interview with author, November 2012.

68. Interview with author, June 2011.

69. Interview with author, November 2007.

70. Interview with author, May 2008.

71. Interview with author, November 2009.

72. Interview with author, March 2011.

73. Interview with author, June 2008.

74. Interview with author, December 2009.

75. Interview with author, March 2011.

76. Interview with author, March 2011.

77. Interview with author, April 2011.

78. Interview with author, March 2011.

79. Miller 1997.

80. Miller 1997, 86.

81. Hong 2011.

82. Interview with author, June 2008.

83. Interview with author, June 2008.

84. Farrao 2010.

85. Bhalla 2011.

86. Lee and Nadeau 2011.

87. Um 2010.

88. Chang and Kim 2010.

89. Shankar 2013a; Tuan 1998.

90. Kim 1999.

91. Niiya 2010.

92. Chen and Yoo 2010.

93. Standard and Poor's produced "Advertising" industry surveys through August 2007; from mid-2008 onward they produced "Publishing and Advertising" surveys.

94. Peters and Donald, 2007a.

95. See also Wang 2008.

96. Wang 2008.

97. Agnese 2009.

98. Agnese 2011.

99. For examples of tailoring multicultural ads to specific audiences, see chapter 2; Cavanaugh and Shankar 2014.

100. Notably, almost 60 percent of the net increase in AAPI poverty was in the native-born segment of the population, suggesting that not all second- and third-generation immigrants are able to achieve the upward mobility of their parents. These dramatic increases in poverty have not been in reflected in the overall AAPI poverty rate because of large increases in their population base, which include large numbers of highly skilled and highly educated immigrants.

101. "Asian-Americans: Smart, High Incomes and . . . Poor?," National Public Radio, May 20, 2013, http://www.npr.org/templates/story/story.php?storyId =185534666 (accessed August 29, 2013).

102. In the NPR story Austin contended that the official poverty rate from the U.S. Census Bureau does not account for geographic cost-of-living differences, and so he draws from an alternative poverty measure supplied by the National Academy of Sciences (NAS). With the cost-of-living adjustment, the NAS Asian poverty rate is 5.7 percentage points higher, nearly double the unadjusted difference.

103. Interview with author, June 2011.

104. Interview with author, June 2011.

105. See Chávez 2001.

106. Davila 2001, 229.

107. Iwamura 2011, 9.

108. For examples and analysis, see Feng 2002; Marchetti 1993; Okihiro 1994.

109. For Asian Americans in independent media, see Hamamoto and Liu 2000; for general media, see Feng 2002. Okihiro (2001), Palumbo-Liu (1999), and Wu (2002) offer further analyses of yellow peril and its racializing impact.

110. Pinney 2005, 265.

111. Miyazaki and Riles 2005, 326–27.

2. CREATIVE

1. Profitability of language, Alexandre Duchêne and Monica Heller (2012) contend, results from nation-states having lost their stronghold on meanings and glosses of "pride" to neoliberal processes of profit making that no longer rely on the nation-state in their ideological work. The expansion of profit making beyond the nation-state by capitalist projects that transcend locality precisely by commodifying that which indexes the local and circulating it beyond its original context (see Cavanaugh and Shankar 2014) illustrates how global capitalism has transformed linkages between language and political economy.

2. Foster 2007, 708.

3. Peirce 1955.

4. Munn 1986, 74.

5. Keane 2003.

6. Marcus and Saka 2006.

7. Arvidsson 2006; Foster 2007; Lury 2006; Schroeder and Salzer-Mörling 2006.

8. Interview with author, June 2008.

9. Foster 2007.

10. Interview with author, March 2011.

11. Interview with author, April 2011.

12. Shankar 2013b.

13. Interview with author, June 2008.

14. Interview with author, March 2011.

15. Latino advertising executives in Arlene Davila's (2001) study seemed to face a similar conundrum. They want to find ways to represent Latino life in America, but if their creative presentations do not sound "cultural enough," they "run the risk of losing their relevance" (2001, 85). This was sometimes handled through the insertion of stock images such as kitchen scenes, grandmothers, mustachioed men, and family life.

16. Shankar 2012.

17. Interview with author, November 2012.

18. Conversation with author, November 2009.

19. Interview with author, December 2009.

20. It was far more difficult for me to answer these questions than I had expected, primarily because it made me realize that I really do not know the values and beliefs of their intended audience. As a South Indian who was raised Hindu in the New York area, seeing women in saris without *bindis* was perhaps unusual but not offensive; I have been to Hindu weddings where there are invitees of all religious faiths, and I know for a fact that I am not the only South Indian who loves Bollywood.

21. Interview with author, November 2012.

22. Myers 2004b, 5–6.

23. Myers 2004b, 5–6.

24. Schieffelin et al. 1998; Woolard 1998.

25. Cavanaugh and Shankar 2014; Shankar 2012.

26. Bakhtin 2004.

27. Barthes 1972.

28. Coupland 2001.

29. Davila 2001, 71.

30. Jakobson 1960.

31. Interview with author, March 2011.

32. See Lippi-Green 2012.

33. Interview with author, March 2011.

34. Interview with author, March 2011.

35. Cavanaugh 2005; Cavanaugh and Shankar 2014; Moore 2011.

36. Parmentier 1994.

37. Wang 2008.

38. In a different advertising context, Robert Moore (2003) has observed the ubiquity of certain brands and the "genericide" they can undergo as they become so much a part of the everyday lexicon that they are no longer considered a brand name. Q-Tip, Xerox, and Kleenex are good examples from the United States.

39. See Coombe 1998 for trademark.

40. See Manning 2010; also Arvidsson 2005; Mazzerella 2003.

3. ACCOUNT SERVICES

1. As in other settings in which expertise is collective, different individuals inhabit specialized roles. E. Summerson Carr (2010b) shows how rehabilitation counselors each bring a different skill set to the project of helping clients at a center, and Peter Redfield (2005, 16) identifies Doctors without Borders as dispersed individuals who form a collective that can bear witness to conditions and predicaments requiring attention and intervention. For agency executives, each in the collective must be able to successfully perform his or her role in creative, production work, media buying, and so on.

2. Myers 2004b.

3. In this "economy of affect," to apply Analiese Richard and Daromir Rudnyckyj's phrase, "affect serves as a means of conducting conduct and thus forming subjects" (2009, 57). They offer this as a way of providing "analytic purchase" between economic transformations and affective transformations. They call attention to two forms of affect: *affect* as a noun, as in an embodied disposition to be performed, and *affect* as a transitive verb, as in its purpose in advertisements themselves. Economies of affect thus draw attention to the work affect does in certain economic and social formations; as a medium for subject formation, it is, as Brian Massumi has argued, "an intrinsic variable of the late capitalist system" (quoted in Richard and Rudnyckyj 2009, 73).

4. See Berlant 2007; Hardt 1999; Harvey 1989; Massumi 2002. About the post-Fordist workplace, Andrea Muehlebach has remarked, "The economy of good feeling is more than an ideological smoke screen or a psychological palliative. Rather it is a profoundly indeterminate space of both love and loss, pleasure and pain, compassion and exclusion" (2011, 75).

5. Hardt 1999, 90.

6. Mazzerella 2009.

7. Cavanaugh and Shankar 2014.

8. Clough 2008, 2.

9. Berlant 2007, 224.

10. Anderson et al. 2012, 173.

11. Sunderland and Denny 2007.

12. See Goodwin 1994. Also useful to this discussion is how Michael Montoya (2007, 95) distinguishes between ethnic and racial (he jointly calls them "ethnoracial") classifications and those that attribute characteristics to these categories. While the former is a question of naming the groups, the latter is about linking particular characteristics to them, noting that attribution can lead to racialization. What executives are doing is twofold, classifying as well as assigning attributes. In chapter 2 I analyze the complex process by which executives reflect on and select those values and attributes that will best exemplify a group for advertising purposes.

13. I borrow Carr's phrase "enactments of expertise" to discuss how expertise is operationalized. Carr describes expertise as "inherently interactional because it involves the participation of objects, producers, and consumers of knowledge" (2010a, 18).

14. Malefyt 2009, 204; see also Moore 2003.

15. For additional illustrations of this point, see Mazzerella 2003; Miller 1997.

16. Goodwin 1994.

17. Aaron Cicourel (1999) underscores the various ways language is used to authenticate status between novice and experts. Michael Silverstein (2006) and

Bonnie Urciuoli (2008) both identify the role of specialized language or "registers" in constructing authority in expert displays. "Skills discourses" (Urciuoli 2008) and other discursive strategies individuals master to excel in neoliberal workplaces underscore how expertise may be constructed as a cultural and linguistic object.

18. Urciuoli 2008, 212, citing Silverstein.

19. Interview with author, June 2008.

20. Shankar 2013a.

21. Maria Sanniniatelli, "Specialist Advertising Agencies Target the Asian American Market," *International Herald Tribune*, October 9, 1995.

22. Collier and Ong 2005, 4.

23. Giddens cited in Collier and Ong 2005, 11.

4. PRODUCTION AND MEDIA

1. Deleuze and Guattari 1987.

2. Marcus and Saka 2006, 104.

3. See my discussion in the introduction, especially of Mankekar and Schein 2013 and Stam and Shohat 2012.

4. Interview with author, June 2008.

5. Interview with author, March 2011.

6. Interview with author, June 2008.

7. Interview with author, June 2008.

8. Interview with author, March 2011.

9. Interview with author, April 2011.

10. Entwistle and Wissinger 2012.

11. Interview with author, August 2011.

12. Interview with author, June 2008.

13. Hill 2008.

14. Katia Hetter, "Jamaica 'Gets Happy' with Post–Super Bowl Buzz," CNN, February 5, 2013, http://www.cnn.com/2013/02/05/travel/vw-get-happy -jamaica-commercial/ (accessed October 17, 2013).

15. Lefebvre 1991; Low and Smith 2013; Zukin 2004.

16. For an analysis of how Internet businesses are gaining much of their revenue through advertising on their search result pages, see Wilson 2011.

17. Sarah Perez correlates the increased possibilities for viewership in households with broadcast TV and broadband Internet, emphasizing that people watch on multiple platforms; "Nielsen: Cord Cutting and Internet TV Viewing on the Rise," techcrunch.com, February 9, 2012, http://techcrunch.com/2012/02/09 /nielsen-cord-cutting-and-internet-tv-viewing-on-the-rise/ (accessed November 19, 2013).

18. For an elaboration of this argument, see Erick Schonfeld, "Mobile Passes Print in Time Spent, but Doesn't Get the Ad Dollars," techcrunch.com, December 12, 2011, http://techcrunch.com/2011/12/12/time-spent-mobile-print/.

19. Castells 2000.

20. Ingrid Lunden discusses the specific possibilities of Facebook advertising, which has already been put into effect; "Analyst: Facebook Will Make $1.2 Billion Annually from Mobile Ads," techcrunch.com, February 17, 2012, http://techcrunch.com/2012/02/17/analyst-facebook-will-make-1-2-billion-annually-from-mobile-ads/ (accessed November 18, 2013). Other sites for advertising, including search engines such as Google (Meghan Kelly, "96 Percent of Google's Revenue Is Advertising, Who Buys It?," venturebeat.com, January 29, 2012, http://venturebeat.com/2012/01/29/google-advertising/) and online newspapers (De Waal et al. 2005), are still evolving in terms of potential, and research in this area confirms that location and placement are still important, even on the Internet.

21. Interview with author, March 2011.

22. Interview with author, June 2008.

23. Interview with author, March 2011.

24. Interview with author, March 2011.

25. Ahmed 2012, 4.

CONCLUSION: AUDIENCE TESTING

1. Alsultany 2007.

2. Ahmed 2012.

3. Fish 1997.

4. Hartmann and Gerteis 2005.

5. Blommaert and Verschueren 1998.

6. Stam and Shohat 2012, 85.

7. Strathern 2006.

8. Interview with author, January 2011.

9. Shankar 2008.

10. McElhinny 2010, 320.

GLOSSARY

account executive   An advertising executive responsible for overseeing the coordination of development and production and liaising with a client for a campaign.

advertiser   An entity (individual or corporation) that pays to promote a good or service. Ad executives also refer to them as "clients."

advertising executive   A general industry term for those working on the advertisement and development process.

Chinglish   A niche advertising term referring to a language variety that combines Chinese and English.

client   An entity (individual or corporation) that pays to promote a good or service. Ad executives also refer to them as "advertisers."

copy   Text that is printed or spoken in an advertisement.

creative   (1) A portion of the advertising development process in which concepts, copy, and other aspects of the ad's conceit are developed. (2) An advertising executive responsible for generating ideas and copy.

cross-cultural   An industry term used by general market agencies to refer to an emphasis on ethnic and racial diversity in advertising strategy.

EMEASA   A niche advertising acronym that refers to emerging areas of multicultural marketing, specifically Eastern Europe, the Middle East, Africa, and South Asia.

ethnoracial   An academic term that refers to matters of ethnicity and race.

general market   An industry term used to refer to agencies that do not specialize in targeting any one population and create advertising for mainstream audiences.

Hinglish   A niche advertising term referring to a language variety that combines Hindi and English.

in-culture   A niche advertising term that refers to ethnically specific cultural elements in an ad that differ from mainstream depictions.

in-language   A niche advertising term that refers to non–American English elements in an ad.

Konglish   A niche advertising term referring to a language variety that combines Korean and English.

media An industry term that refers to the medium into which an ad is placed, usually print, television, radio, or digital.

multicultural advertising An industry term that refers to advertising and ad agencies that specialize in reaching African American/black, Latino/Hispanic, and Asian American audiences. These can also include other minorities, such as Native Americans, as well as LGBTQ consumers.

niche advertising An industry term that refers to targeting advertising at a specific subsection of the population. In the United States, the term is sometimes used interchangeably with *multicultural advertising*.

production A portion of the advertising process in which the creative is photographed, filmed, recorded, or digitally made for media.

Taglish A niche advertising term referring to a language variety that combines Tagalog and English.

total market An industry term referring to commissioned collaboration between general market and multicultural agencies on the development and production of campaigns.

transcreation A multicultural advertising term referring to the process of adapting a general market ad or campaign for a specific Asian American ethnic audience.

Vinglish A niche advertising term referring to a language variety that combines Vietnamese and English.

REFERENCES

Agha, Asif. 2007. *Language and Social Relations*. New York: Cambridge University Press.

Agha, Asif, ed. 2011. Mediatized Communication in Complex Societies. Special issue, *Language and Communication* 31(3).

Agnese, Joseph. 2009. Current Environment: Publishers, Advertisers Chase the Digital-Savvy Consumer. *Publishing and Advertising*, October 22. Standard and Poor's Industry Surveys. Accessed September 10, 2013.

Agnese, Joseph. 2010a. Current Environment: Advertising Trends Turn More Favorable, Though Contraction Continues. *Publishing and Advertising*, November 24. Standard and Poor's Industry Surveys. Accessed September 10, 2013.

Agnese, Joseph. 2010b. Current Environment: Electronic Readers Offer Opportunity as Advertising Market Fragments. *Publishing and Advertising*, May 27. Standard and Poor's Industry Surveys. Accessed September 10, 2013.

Agnese, Joseph. 2011. Current Environment: Newspapers Move to Paid Online Models. *Publishing and Advertising*, April 28. Standard and Poor's Industry Surveys. Accessed September 10, 2013.

Ahmed, Sara. 2012. *On Being Included: Racism and Diversity in Institutional Life*. Durham, NC: Duke University Press.

Alcoff, Linda M. 2005. *Visible Identities: Race, Gender, and the Self*. New York: Oxford University Press.

Alsultany, Evelyn. 2007. Selling American Diversity and Muslim American Identity through Nonprofit Advertising Post-9/11. *American Quarterly* 59(3): 593–622.

Alsultany, Evelyn. 2012. *Arabs and Muslims in the Media: Race and Representation after 9/11*. New York: New York University Press.

Anderson, Ben, M. Kearnes, C. McFarlane, and D. Swanton. 2012. On Assemblages and Geography. *Dialogues in Human Geography* 2(2): 171–89.

Aquino, Allan. 2010. Filipino Americans. In *Encyclopedia of Asian American Issues Today*, edited by Edith Wen-Chu Chen and Grace J. Yoo, 1:25–32. Santa Barbara, CA: Greenwood Press. Gale Virtual Reference Library. Accessed August 19, 2013.

Arvidsson, Adam. 2006. *Brands: Meaning and Value in Media Culture*. London: Routledge.

Asian American Center for Advancing Justice. 2011. A Community of Contrasts: Asian Americans in the United States: 2011. http://napca.org/wp-content/uploads/2012/11/AAJC-Community-of-Contrast.pdf. Accessed September 10, 2013.

Austin, Algernon. 2013. The Impact of Geography on Asian American Poverty. Economic Policy Institute. May 2. http://www.epi.org/publication/impact-geography-asian-american-poverty/. Accessed August 29, 2013.

Bakhtin, Mikhail. 2004. *The Dialogic Imagination: Four Essays*. Edited by Michael Holquist. Translated by Caryl Emerson and Michael Holquist. Austin: University of Texas Press.

Bankston, Carl L., III. 2010a. Filipino Immigrants. In *Encyclopedia of American Immigration*, edited by Carl L. Bankston III, 1:68–373. Pasadena, CA: Salem Press. Gale Virtual Reference Library. Accessed August 19, 2013.

Bankston, Carl L., III, ed. 2010b. Foreign-Born Population, by Country of Birth: 1850–1990. In *International Migration. Historical Statistics of the United States: Millennial Edition Online*. New York: Cambridge University Press. Accessed August 28, 2013.

Barde, Robert, Susan B. Carter, and Richard Sutch, eds. 2010. Foreign-Born Population, by Country of Birth: 1850–1990. In *International Migration: Historical Statistics of the United States: Millennial Edition Online*. New York: Cambridge University Press. Accessed August 28, 2013.

Barratt, David. 2010. Pakistani Immigrants. In *Encyclopedia of American Immigration*, edited by Carl L. Bankston III, 2:823–24. Pasadena, CA: Salem Press. Gale Virtual Reference Library. Accessed August 27, 2013.

Barthes, Roland. 1972. *Mythologies*. New York: Noonday Press.

Bauman, Richard, and Charles L. Briggs. 1992. Genre, Intertextuality, and Social Power. In *Language, Culture, and Society*, edited by Ben G. Blount, 567–91. New York: Waveland.

Beckman, Thomas. 1996. Japanese Influences on American Advertising Card Imagery and Design, 1875–1890. *Journal of American Culture* 19(1): 7–20.

Berlant, Lauren. 2007. Nearly Utopian, Nearly Normal: Post-Fordist Affect in *La Promesse and Rosetta*. *Public Culture* 19(2): 273–301.

Berlant, Lauren. 2011. *Cruel Optimism*. Durham, NC: Duke University Press.

Bhalla, Shereen. 2011. Indian Americans: Vernacular Language, Speech, and Manner. In *Encyclopedia of Asian American Folklore and Folklife*, edited by Jonathan H. X. Lee and Kathleen M. Nadeau, 2:512–13. Santa Barbara, CA: ABC-CLIO.

Bhatia, T. K. 1992. Discourse Functions and the Pragmatics of Mixing: Advertising across Cultures. *World Englishes* 11(1): 195–215.

Blommaert, Jan, and Jef Verschueren. 1998. *Debating Diversity: Analysing the Discourse of Tolerance*. London: Routledge.

Bonilla-Silva, Eduardo. 2009. *Racism without Racists: Color-Blind Racism and the Persistence of Racial Inequality in America*. 3rd ed. New York: Rowman and Littlefield.

Burke, Timothy. 1996. *Lifebuoy Men, Lux Women: Commodification, Consumption, and Cleanliness in Modern Zimbabwe*. Durham, NC: Duke University Press.

Callon, Michel, Cécile Méadel, and Vololona Rabeharisoa. 2002. The Economy of Qualities. *Economy and Society* 31(2): 194–217.

Campbell, Timothy C., and Adam Sitze, eds. 2013. Biopolitics: An Encounter. In *Biopolitics: A Reader*, edited by Timothy Campbell and Adam Sitze, 1–40. Durham, NC: Duke University Press.

Carbado, Devon. 2005. Racial Naturalization. *American Quarterly* 57(3): 633–58.

Carr, E. Summerson. 2010a. Enactments of Expertise. *Annual Review of Anthropology* 39: 17–32.

Carr, E. Summerson. 2010b. *Scripting Addiction: The Politics of Therapeutic Talk and American Sobriety*. Princeton, NJ: Princeton University Press.

Castells, Manuel. 2000. *The Rise of the Network Society*. Vol. 1 of *The Information Age: Economy, Society, and Culture*. Malden, MA: Wiley-Blackwell.

Cavanaugh, Jillian. 2005. Accent Matters: Material Consequences of Sounding Local in Northern Italy. *Language and Communication* 25: 127–48.

Cavanaugh, Jillian R., and Shalini Shankar. 2014. Producing Authenticity in Global Capitalism: Language, Materiality, and Value. *American Anthropologist* 116(1): 51–64.

Chan, James. 2005. "Rough on Rats": Racism and Advertising in the Latter Half of the Nineteenth Century. *Daniel K.E. Ching Collection — Conference Excerpt*. Chinese Historical Society of America. March 5. http://chsa.org/2005/03/daniel-k-e-ching-collection-conference-excerpt/. Accessed September 17, 2014.

Chan, Sucheng. 1991. *Asian Americans: An Interpretive History*. Boston: Twayne.

Chang, Edward Taehan, and Barbara W. Kim. 2010. Korean Americans. In *Encyclopedia of Asian American Issues Today*, edited by Edith Wen-Chu Chen and Grace J. Yoo, 1:41–50. Santa Barbara, CA: Greenwood Press. Gale Virtual Reference Library. Accessed August 17, 2013.

Chávez, Leo. 2001. *Covering Immigration: Popular Images and the Politics of the Nation*. Berkeley: University of California Press.

Chen, Edith Wen-Chu, and Grace J. Yoo. 2010. Chinese Americans. In *Encyclopedia of Asian American Issues Today*, edited by Peter Kwon and Edith Wen-Chu Chen, 1:15–23. Santa Barbara, CA: Greenwood Press. Gale Virtual Reference Library. Accessed August 2, 2013.

Chen, Tina. 2002. Dissecting the "Devil Doctor": Stereotype and Sensationalism in Sax Rohmer's *Fu Manchu*. In *Re-collecting Early Asian America: Essays in Cul-*

tural History, edited by Josephine Lee, Imogene Lim, and Yuko Matsukawa, 218–37. Philadelphia: Temple University Press.

Chin, Elizabeth. 2001. *Purchasing Power: Black Kids and American Consumer Culture*. Minneapolis: University of Minnesota Press.

Cicourel, Aaron. 1999. Expert. *Journal of Linguistic Anthropology* 9(1–2): 72–75.

Clough, Patricia. 2008. The Affective Turn: Political Economy, Biomedia, and Bodies. *Theory, Culture, and Society* 25(1): 1–22.

Collier, Stephen J., and Aihwa Ong. 2005. Global Assemblages, Anthropological Problems. In *Global Assemblages: Technology, Politics, and Ethics as Anthropological Problems*, edited by Aihwa Ong and Stephen J. Collier, 3–21. Malden, MA: Wiley-Blackwell.

Comaroff, John L., and Jean Comaroff. 2001. First Thoughts on a Second Coming. In *Millennial Capitalism and the Culture of Neoliberalism*, edited by Jean Comaroff and John L. Comaroff, 1–58. Durham, NC: Duke University Press.

Comaroff, John L., and Jean Comaroff. 2009. *Ethnicity, Inc.* Chicago: University of Chicago Press.

Coombe, Rosemary. 1998. *The Cultural Life of Intellectual Properties: Authorship, Alterity, and the Law*. Durham, NC: Duke University Press.

Cortese, Anthony J. 2004. *Provocateur: Images of Women and Minorities in Advertising*. Oxford: Rowman and Littlefield.

Coupland, Nikolas. 2001. Dialect Stylization in Radio Talk. *Language in Society* 30: 345–75.

Davé, Shilpa. 2005. Apu's Brown Voice: Cultural Inflection and South Asian Accents. In *East Main Street: Asian American Popular Culture*, edited by Shilpa Davé, LeiLani Nishime, and Tasha G. Oren, 313–36. New York: New York University Press.

Davé, Shilpa S. 2013. *Indian Accents: Brown Voice and Racial Performance in American Television and Film*. Champaign: University of Illinois Press.

Davila, Arlene. 2001. *Latinos Inc.: The Marketing and Making of a People*. Berkeley: University of California Press.

Davila, Arlene. 2008. *Latino Spin: Public Image and the Whitewashing of Race*. New York: New York University Press.

de Burgh-Woodman, Helene, and Janice Brace-Govan. 2010. Vista, Vision and Visual Consumption from the Age of Enlightenment. *Marketing Theory* 10(2): 173–91.

de Certeau, Michel. 2004. "Making Do": Uses and Tactics. In *Practicing History: New Directions in Historical Writing after the Linguistic Turn*, edited by Gabrielle M. Spiegel. New York: Routledge, 2005.

Deleuze, Gilles, and Félix Guattari. 1987. *A Thousand Plateaus: Capitalism and Schizophrenia*. Minneapolis: University of Minnesota Press.

Del Percio, Alfonso, and Alexandre Duchene. 2012. Commodification of Pride and Resistance to Profit: Language Practices as Terrain of Struggle in a Swiss Football Stadium. In *Language in Late Capitalism: Pride and Profit*, edited by Alexandre Duchene and Monica Heller, 43–72. New York: Routledge.

De Waal, E., K. Schönbach, and E. Lauf. 2005. Online Newspapers: A Substitute or Complement for Print Newspapers and Other Information Channels? *Communications* 30: 55–72.

Dhingra, Pawan. 2007. *Managing Multicultural Lives: Asian American Professionals and the Challenge of Multiple Identities*. Stanford: Stanford University Press.

Di Leonardo, Micaela. 2008. Introduction: New Global and American Landscapes of Inequality. In *Landscapes of Inequality: Neoliberalism and the Erosion of Democracy in America*, edited by Jane Collins, Micaela di Leonardo, and Brett Williams, 3–20. Santa Fe, NM: School of Advanced Research Press.

Dornfeld, Barry. 1998. *Producing Public Television, Producing Public Culture*. Princeton, NJ: Princeton University Press.

Duchêne, Alexandre, and Monica Heller, eds. 2012. *Language in Late Capitalism: Pride and Profit*. Routledge Critical Studies in Multilingualism. New York: Routledge.

Dwyer, Claire, and Philip Crang. 2002. Fashioning Ethnicities: The Commercial Spaces of Multiculture. *Ethnicities* 2(3): 410–30.

Eisenlohr, Patrick. 2006. As Makkah Is Sweet and Beloved, So Is Medina. *American Ethnologist* 33(2): 230–45.

Entwistle, Joanne, and Elizabeth Wissinger, eds. 2012. *Fashioning Models: Images, Text, and Industry*. New York: Bloomsbury Academic.

Espiritu, Yen Le. 1992. *Asian American Panethnicity: Bridging Institutions and Identities*. Philadelphia: Temple University Press.

Fabian, Johannes. 2006. The Other Revisited: Critical Afterthoughts. *Anthropological Theory* 6(2): 139–52.

Farquhar, Judith. 2012. For Your Reading Pleasure: Self-Health (*Ziwo Baojian*) Information in Beijing in the 1990s. In *Media, Erotics, and Transnational Asia*, edited by Purnima Mankekar and Louisa Schein, 53–74. Durham, NC: Duke University Press.

Farrao, R. Benedito. 2010. Pan–South Asian Identity. In *Encyclopedia of Asian American Issues Today*, edited by Edith Wen-Chu Chen and Grace J. Yoo, 1:445–49. Santa Barbara, CA: Greenwood Press. Gale Virtual Reference Library. Accessed August 27, 2013.

Feng, Peter, ed. 2002. *Screening Asian Americans*. New Brunswick, NJ: Rutgers University Press.

Ferguson, James. 2010. The Uses of Neoliberalism. *Antipode* 41(s1): 166–84.

Ferguson, Roderick. 2012. *The Reorder of Things: The University and Its Pedagogies of Minority Difference*. Minneapolis: University of Minnesota Press.

Fish, Stanley. 1997. Boutique Multiculturalism, or Why Liberals Are Incapable of Thinking about Hate Speech. *Critical Inquiry* 23(2): 378–95.

Fisher, Melissa, and Greg Downey, eds. 2006. *Frontiers of Capital: Ethnographic Reflections on a New Economy*. Durham, NC: Duke University Press.

Foster, Robert. 2007. The Work of the New Economy: Consumers, Brands and Value Creation. *Cultural Anthropology* 22(4): 707–31.

Foucault, Michel. 1986. Of Other Spaces. *Diacritics* 16(1): 22–27.

Fox, Stephen. 1984. *The Mirror Makers: A History of American Advertising and Its Creators*. New York: Morrow.

Ganti, Tejaswini. 2012. *Producing Bollywood: Inside the Contemporary Hindi Film Industry*. Durham, NC: Duke University Press.

Garvey, Ellen. 1996. *Adman in the Parlor: Magazines and the Gendering of Consumer Culture, 1880s to 1910s*. New York: Oxford University Press.

Gee, James Paul, Glynda Hull, and Colin Lankshear. 1996. *The New Work Order: Behind the Language of the New Capitalism*. Boulder, CO: Westview Press.

Geertz, Clifford. 1973. *The Interpretation of Cultures: Selected Essays*. New York: Basic Books.

Ginsburg, Faye. 2006. Ethnography and American Studies. *Cultural Anthropology* 21(3): 487–95.

Ginsburg, Faye D., Lila Abu-Lughod, and Brian Larkin, eds. 2002. *Media Worlds: Anthropology on New Terrain*. Berkeley: University of California Press.

Goldberg, David. 1993. *Racist Culture: Philosophy and the Politics of Meaning*. Oxford: Blackwell.

Goldberg, David. 2009. *The Threat of Race: Reflections on Racial Neoliberalism*. Malden, MA: Wiley-Blackwell.

Goodwin, Charles. 1994. Professional Vision. *American Anthropologist* 96(3): 606–33.

Greenhouse, Carol, ed. 2010. *Ethnographies of Neoliberalism*. Philadelphia: University of Pennsylvania Press.

Grewal, Inderpal. 2005. *Transnational America: Feminisms, Diasporas, Neoliberalisms*. Durham, NC: Duke University Press.

Haddad, John R. 2008. *The Romance of China: Excursions to China in U.S. Culture, 1776–1876*. New York: Columbia University Press.

Hamamoto, Darrell, and Sandra Liu, eds. 2000. *Countervisions: Asian American Film Criticism*. Philadelphia: Temple University Press.

Hannerz, Ulf. 2010. Diversity Is Our Business. *American Anthropologist* 112(4): 539–51.

Hao, Richie Neil. 2011. Filipino Americans: History, People, and Culture. In *Encyclopedia of Asian American Folklore and Folklife*, edited by Jonathan H. X. Lee and Kathleen M. Nadeau, 1:331–36. Santa Barbara, CA: ABC-CLIO. Gale Virtual Reference Library. Accessed August 19, 2013.

Hardt, Michael. 1999. Affective Labor. *boundary 2* 26(2): 89–100.

Hardt, Michael, and Antonio Negri. 2001. *Empire*. Cambridge, MA: Harvard University Press.

Hartigan, John. 2009. What Are You Laughing At? Assessing the Racial in U.S. Public Discourse. *Transforming Anthropology* 17: 4–19.

Hartmann, Douglas, and Joseph Gerteis. 2005. Dealing with Diversity: Mapping Multiculturalism in Sociological Terms. *Sociological Theory* 23(2): 218–40.

Harvey, David. 1989. *The Condition of Postmodernity*. Malden, MA: Wiley-Blackwell.

Harvey, David. 2005. *A Brief History of Neoliberalism*. New York: Oxford University Press.

Heller, Monica. 2003. Globalization, the New Economy, and the Commodification of Language and Identity. *Journal of Sociolinguistics* 7(4): 473–92.

Hesse, Barnor. 2011. Self-Fulfilling Prophecy: The Postracial Horizon. *South Atlantic Quarterly* 110: 155–78.

Hill, Jane. 2000. Ideological Complexity and the Overdetermination of Promising in American Presidential Politics. In *Regimes of Language*, edited by Paul V. Kroskrity, 259–91. Santa Fe, NM: School of American Research Press.

Hill, Jane. 2008. *The Everyday Language of White Racism*. Malden, MA: Wiley-Blackwell.

Himpele, Jeff. 2008. *Circuits of Culture: Media, Politics, and Indigenous Identity in the Andes*. Minneapolis: University of Minnesota Press, 2008.

Ho, Karen. 2009. *Liquidated: An Ethnography of Wall Street*. Durham, NC: Duke University Press.

Hoeffel, Elizabeth M., Sonya Rastogi, Myoung Ouk Kim, and Hasan Shahid. 2012. *The Asian Population. 2010 Census Brief*. March. U.S. Department of Commerce.

Holland, Sharon. 2012. *The Erotic Life of Racism*. Durham, NC: Duke University Press.

Holmes, Douglas. 2014. *Economy of Words*. Princeton, NJ: Princeton University Press.

Holmes, Douglas R., and George E. Marcus. 2005. Cultures of Expertise and the Management of Globalization: Toward the Re-functioning of Ethnography. In *Global Assemblages: Technology, Politics, and Ethics as Anthropological Problems*, edited by Aihwa Ong and Stephen J. Collier, 235–52. Malden, MA: Wiley-Blackwell.

Holmes, Douglas R., and George E. Marcus. 2006. Para-ethnography and the Rise of the Symbolic Analyst. In *Frontiers of Capital: Ethnographic Reflections on the New Economy*, edited by Melissa S. Fisher and Greg Downey, 33–57. Durham, NC: Duke University Press.

Hong, Jun Sung. 2011. Korean Americans: Vernacular Language, Speech, and Manner. In *Encyclopedia of Asian American Folklore and Folklife*, edited by

Jonathan H. X. Lee and Kathleen M. Nadeau, 2:710–11. Santa Barbara, CA: ABC-CLIO. Gale Virtual Reference Library. Accessed August 17, 2013.

Hosang, Daniel. 2010. *Racial Propositions: Ballot Initiatives and the Making of Postwar California*. Berkeley: University of California Press.

Hwang, Young Suk. 2011. Korean Americans: Religion. In *Encyclopedia of Asian American Folklore and Folklife*, edited by Jonathan H. X. Lee and Kathleen M. Nadeau, 2:701–4. Santa Barbara, CA: ABC-CLIO. Gale Virtual Reference Library. Accessed August 17, 2013.

Iwamura, Jane. 2011. *Virtual Orientalism: Asian Religions and American Popular Culture*. New York: Oxford University Press.

Jackson, Anna. 1992. Imagining Japan: The Victorian Perception and the Acquisition of Japanese Culture. *Journal of Design History* 5(4): 245–56.

Jakobson, Roman. 1960. Closing Statement: Linguistics and Poetics. In *Style in Language*, edited by Thomas A. Sebeok, 350–59. Cambridge, MA: MIT Press.

Jameson, Fredric. 1991. *Postmodernism or, the Cultural Logic of Late Capitalism*. Durham, NC: Duke University Press.

Jay, Martin. 1996. *The Dialectical Imagination: A History of the Frankfurt School and the Institute of Social Research 1923–1950*. Berkeley: University of California Press.

Jhally, Sut. 1987. *The Codes of Advertising: Fetishism and the Political Economy of Meaning in the Consumer Society*. New York: St. Martin's Press.

Jun, Helen. 2011. *Race for Citizenship: Black Orientalism and Asian Uplift from Pre-Emancipation to Neoliberal America*. New York: New York University Press.

Kamal, Rabia. 2011. Pakistani Americans: History, People, and Culture. In *Encyclopedia of Asian American Folklore and Folklife*, edited by Jonathan H. X. Lee and Kathleen M. Nadeau, 3:55–60. Santa Barbara, CA: ABC-CLIO. Gale Virtual Reference Library. Accessed August 28, 2013.

Keane, Webb. 2003. Semiotics and the Social Analysis of Material Things. *Language and Communication* 23(3–4): 409–25.

Kelly-Holmes, Helen. 2005. *Advertising as Multilingual Communication*. Basingstoke, UK: Palgrave-Macmillan.

Kemper, Steven. 2001. *Buying and Believing: Sri Lankan Advertising and Consumers in a Transnational World*. Chicago: University of Chicago Press.

Kern-Foxworth, Marylin. 1994. *Aunt Jemima, Uncle Ben, and Rastas*. Westport, CT: Greenwood Press.

Kim, Claire. 1999. The Racial Triangulation of Model Minorities. *Politics and Society* 27(1): 105–38.

Kim, Minjeong, and Angie Chung. 2005. Consuming Orientalism: Images of Asian/American Women in Multicultural Advertising. *Qualitative Sociology* 28(1): 67–91.

Kim, Thomas. 2006. Being Modern: The Circulation of Oriental Objects. *American Quarterly* 58(2): 379–406.

Knobloch-Westerwick, Silvia, and Brendon Coates. 2006. Minority Models in Advertisements in Magazines Popular with Minorities. *Journalism and Mass Communication Quarterly* 83(3): 596–614.

Kochhar, Rakesh, Richard Fry, and Paul Taylor. 2011. *Wealth Gaps Rise to Record Highs between Whites, Blacks, Hispanics.* Washington, DC: Pew Research Center.

Koshy, Susan. 2001. Morphing Race into Ethnicity: Asian Americans and Critical Transformations of Whiteness. *boundary 2* 28(1): 153–94.

Kwon, Soo Ah. 2013. *Uncivil Youth: Race, Activism, and Affirmative Governmentality.* Durham, NC: Duke University Press.

Lacy, Michael G., and Kent A. Ono, eds. 2011. *Critical Rhetorics of Race.* New York: New York University Press.

Le, C. N. 2014. 14 Important Statistics about Asian Americans. Asian-Nation: The Landscape of Asian America. http://www.asian-nation.org/14-statistics.shtml. Accessed July 16, 2014.

Le, Long S. 2011. Vietnamese Americans: Vernacular Language, Speech, and Manner. In *Encyclopedia of Asian American Folklore and Folklife*, edited by Jonathan H. X. Lee and Kathleen M. Nadeau, 3:1216–18. Santa Barbara, CA: ABC-CLIO. Gale Virtual Reference Library. Accessed August 20, 2013.

Lee, Benjamin. 1997. *Talking Heads: Language, Metalanguage, and the Semiotics of Subjectivity.* Durham, NC: Duke University Press.

Lee, Jonathan H. X., and Kathleen M. Nadeau. 2011. Chinese Americans. In *Encyclopedia of Asian American Folklore and Folklife*, edited by Jonathan H. X. Lee and Kathleen M. Nadeau, 1:223–28. Santa Barbara, CA: ABC-CLIO. Gale Virtual Reference Library. Accessed August 2, 2013.

Lee, Ki-Young, and Sung-Hee Joo. 2005. The Portrayal of Asian Americans in Mainstream Magazine Ads: An Update. *Journalism and Mass Communication Quarterly* 82(3): 654–71.

Lee, Robert. 1999. *Orientals: Asian Americans in Popular Culture.* Philadelphia: Temple University Press.

Lee, Stacey. 1996. *Unraveling the "Model Minority" Stereotype: Listening to Asian American Youth.* New York: Teachers College Press.

Lefebvre, Henri. 1991. *The Production of Space.* Vol. 30. Oxford: Blackwell.

Lefkowitz, Daniel. 2003. Investing in Emotion: Love and Anger in Financial Advertising. *Journal of Linguistic Anthropology* 13(1): 71–97.

Leonard, Karen. 1992. *Making Ethnic Choices: California's Punjabi Mexican Americans.* Philadelphia: Temple University Press.

Leslie, Deborah. 1995. Global Scan: The Globalization of Advertising Agencies, Concepts, and Campaigns. *Economic Geography* 71(4): 402–26.

Liechty, Mark. 2003. *Suitably Modern: Making Middle-Class Culture in a New Consumer Society*. Princeton, NJ: Princeton University Press.

Ling, Huping. 2010. Chinese Immigrants. In *Encyclopedia of American Immigration*, edited by Carl L. Bankston III, 1:197–202. Pasadena, CA: Salem Press. Gale Virtual Reference Library. Accessed August 2, 2013.

Lippi-Green, Rosina. 2012. *English with an Accent: Language, Ideology, and Discrimination in the United States*. 2nd ed. London: Routledge.

Lipsitz, George. 2011. *How Racism Takes Place*. Philadelphia: Temple University Press.

Liu, Cynthia. 2000. When Dragon Ladies Die, Do They Come Back as Butterflies? Re-imagining Anna May Wong. In *Countervisions: Asian American Film Criticism*, edited by Darrell Hamamoto and Sandra Liu, 23–39. Philadelphia: Temple University Press.

Low, Setha, and Neil Smith, eds. 2013. *The Politics of Public Space*. New York: Routledge.

Low, Setha M., and Denise Lawrence-Zúñiga, eds. 2003. *Anthropology of Space and Place: Locating Culture*. Malden, MA: Wiley-Blackwell.

Lukose, Ritty. 2009. *Liberalization's Children: Gender, Youth, and Consumer Citizenship in Globalizing India*. Durham, NC: Duke University Press.

Lury, Adam. 1994. Advertising: Moving beyond the Stereotypes. In *The Authority of the Consumer*, edited by Russell Keat, Nicholas Abercrombie, and Nigel Whitley, 91–101. London: Routledge.

Lury, Celia. 2006. *Brands: The Logos of the Global Economy*. London: Routledge.

Lutz, R. C. 2010. Vietnamese Immigrants. In *Encyclopedia of American Immigration*, edited by Carl L. Bankston III, 3:1036–41. Pasadena, CA: Salem Press. Gale Virtual Reference Library. Accessed August 20, 2013.

Lyon, Cherstin M. 2011. Japanese Americans: History, People, and Culture. In *Encyclopedia of Asian American Folklore and Folklife*, edited by Jonathan H. X. Lee and Kathleen M. Nadeau, 2:569–76. Santa Barbara, CA: ABC-CLIO. Gale Virtual Reference Library. Accessed August 13, 2013.

Malefyt, Timothy de Waal. 2009. Understanding the Rise of Consumer Ethnography: Branding Technomethodologies in the New Economy. *American Anthropologist* 111(2): 201–10.

Malefyt, Timothy, and Brian Moeran, eds. 2003. *Advertising Cultures*. Oxford: Berg.

Malefyt, Timothy, and Robert Morais. 2012. *Advertising and Anthropology: Ethnographic Practice and Cultural Perspectives*. London: Berg.

Mamdani, Mahmood. 2002. Good Muslim, Bad Muslim: A Political Perspective on Culture and Terrorism. *American Anthropologist* 104: 766–75.

Manalansan, Martin F. 2012. Wayward Erotics: Mediating Queer Diasporic Return. In *Media, Erotics, and Transnational Asia*, edited by Purnima Mankekar and Louisa Schein, 33–52. Durham, NC: Duke University Press.

Mankekar, Purnima. 2013. Dangerous Desires: Erotics, Public Culture, and Identity in Late Twentieth-Century India. In *Media, Erotics, and Transnational Asia*, edited by Purnima Mankekar and Louisa Schein, 173–202. Durham, NC: Duke University Press.

Mankekar, Purnima, and Louisa Schein. 2013. Introduction: Mediations and Transmediations. In *Media, Erotics, and Transnational Asia*, edited by Purnima Mankekar and Louisa Schein, 1–32. Durham, NC: Duke University Press.

Manning, Paul. 2010. The Semiotics of Brand. *Annual Review of Anthropology* 39: 33–49.

Marable, Manning. 2000. *How Capitalism Underdeveloped Black America*. Cambridge, MA: South End Press.

Marchetti, Gina. 1993. *Romance and the "Yellow Peril": Race, Sex, and Discursive Strategies in Hollywood Fiction*. Berkeley: University of California Press.

Marcus, George E., and Erkan Saka. 2006. Assemblage. *Theory, Culture and Society* 23(2–3): 101–6.

Massumi, Brian. 2002. *Parables for the Virtual: Movement, Affect, Sensation*. Durham, NC: Duke University Press.

Matsukawa, Yuko. 2002. Representing the Oriental in Nineteenth-Century Trade Cards. In *Re-collecting Early Asian America: Essays in Cultural History*, edited by Josephine Lee, Imogene Lim, and Yuko Matsukawa, 200–217. Philadelphia: Temple University Press.

Matsukawa, Yuko. 2009. "Vain Imaginings about Place and Power": Mikado Trade Cards, Gender, Race, and Leisure. *The Seijo Bungei: The Seijo University Arts and Literature Quarterly* 208: 58–82.

Mazzerella, William. 2003. *Shoveling Smoke: Advertising and Globalization in Contemporary India*. Durham, NC: Duke University Press.

Mazzerella, William. 2009. Affect: What Is It Good For? In *Enchantments of Modernity: Empire, Nation, Globalization*, edited by Saurabh Dube, 291–309. New Delhi: Routledge.

McElhinny, Bonnie. 2010. The Audacity of Affect: Gender, Race, and History in Linguistic Accounts of Legitimacy and Belonging. *Annual Review of Anthropology* 39: 309–28.

Melamed, Jodi. 2006. The Spirit of Neoliberalism: From Racial Liberalism to Neoliberal Multiculturalism. *Social Text* 89(24): 1–26.

Metrick-Chen, Lenore. 2007. The Chinese in the American Imagination: 19th Century Trade Card Images. *Visual Anthropology Review* 23(2): 115–36.

Miller, Daniel. 1997. *Capitalism: An Ethnographic Approach*. London: Berg.

Miller, Daniel. 1998. *A Theory of Shopping*. Ithaca, NY: Cornell University Press.

Miller, Daniel. 2005. Materiality: An Introduction. In *Materiality*, edited by Daniel Miller, 1–50. Durham, NC: Duke University Press.

Miyazaki, Hirokazu, and Annelise Riles. 2005. Failure as an Endpoint. In *Global Assemblages: Technology, Politics, and Ethics as Anthropological Problems*, edited by Aihwa Ong and Stephen J. Collier, 320–31. Malden, MA: Wiley-Blackwell.

Moeran, Brian. 1996a. *A Japanese Advertising Agency: An Anthropology of Media and Markets*. Honolulu: University of Hawai'i Press.

Moeran, Brian. 1996b. The Orient Strikes Back: Advertising and Imaging in Japan. *Theory, Culture, and Society* 13(3): 77–112.

Montoya, Michael. 2007. Bioethnic Conscription: Genes, Race, and the Mexicana/o Ethnicity in Diabetes Research. *Cultural Anthropology* 22(1): 94–128.

Moore, Robert. 2003. From Genericide to Viral Marketing: On Brand. *Language and Communication* 23(3–4): 331–58.

Moore, Robert. 2011. "If I Talked Like That I'd Pull a Gun on Myself": Accent, Avoidance, and Moral Panic in Irish English. *Anthropological Quarterly* 84(1): 41–64.

Muehlebach, Andrea. 2011. On Affective Labor in Post-Fordist Italy. *Cultural Anthropology* 26(1): 59–82.

Munn, Nancy. 1986. *The Fame of Gawa: A Symbolic Study of Value Transformation in a Massim (Papua New Guinea) Society*. Cambridge: Cambridge University Press.

Murguia, Salvador Jimenez. 2011. Japanese Americans: History, People, and Culture. In *Encyclopedia of Asian American Folklore and Folklife*, edited by Jonathan H. X. Lee and Kathleen M. Nadeau, 2:637–38. Santa Barbara, CA: ABC-CLIO. Gale Virtual Reference Library. Accessed August 13, 2013.

Myers, Fred R. 2004a. Introduction: The Empire of Things. In *The Empire of Things: Regimes of Value and Material Culture*, edited by Fred R. Myers, 3–63. Santa Fe, NM: School of American Research Press.

Myers, Fred R. 2004b. Ontologies of the Image and Economies of Exchange. *American Ethnologist* 31(1): 5–20.

Naficy, Hamid. 1993. *The Making of Exile Cultures*. Minneapolis: University of Minnesota Press.

Nakasone, Ronald Y., and Sayaka Inaishi. 2011. Japanese Americans: Vernacular Language, Speech, and Manner. In *Encyclopedia of Asian American Folklore and Folklife*, edited by Jonathan H. X. Lee and Kathleen M. Nadeau, 3:892. Santa Barbara, CA: ABC-CLIO. Gale Virtual Reference Library. Accessed August 13, 2013.

National Coalition for Asian Pacific American Community Development. 2013. Spotlight on Asian American and Pacific Islander Poverty: A Demographic Profile. National Coalition for Asian Pacific American Community Develop-

ment. June. http://nationalcapacd.org/sites/default/files/u12/aapi_poverty
_report-web_compressed.pdf. Accessed August 29, 2013.

Nielsen. 2013. "Significant, Sophisticated, and Savvy: The Asian American Consumer 2013 Report." http://www.nielsen.com/content/corporate/us/en
/insights/reports/2013/significant-sophisticated-and-savvy-the-asian
-american-consumer-report-2013.html. Accessed December 3, 2013.

Niiya, Brian. 2010. Japanese Americans. In *Encyclopedia of Asian American Issues
Today*, edited by Edith Wen-Chu Chen and Grace J. Yoo, 1:33–40. Santa
Barbara, CA: Greenwood Press. Gale Virtual Reference Library. Accessed
August 13, 2013.

Ochs, Elinor. 1992. Indexing Gender. In *Rethinking Context*, edited by Alessan-
dro Duranti and Charles Goodwin, 335–58. Cambridge: Cambridge University
Press.

Okihiro, Gary Y. 1994. *Margins and Mainstreams: Asians in American History and
Culture*. Seattle: University of Washington Press.

Okihiro, Gary Y. 2001. *Common Ground: Reimagining American History*. Princeton,
NJ: Princeton University Press.

Olds, Kris, and Nigel Thrift. 2005. Cultures on the Brink: Reengineering the Soul
of Capitalism—on a Global Scale. In *Global Assemblages: Technology, Politics
and Ethics as Anthropological Problems*, edited by Aihwa Ong and Stephen J.
Collier, 270–90. Malden, MA: Wiley Blackwell.

Omi, Michael. 2010. "Slippin' into Darkness": The (Re)Biologization of Race. *Journal of Asian American Studies* 13: 343–58.

Ono, Kent, and Vincent Pham. 2009. *Asian Americans and the Media*. Malden, MA:
Polity.

Paek, Hye Jin, and Hemant Shah. 2003. Racial Ideology, Model Minorities, and
the "Not-So-Silent Partner": Stereotyping of Asian Americans in U.S. Magazine Advertising. *Howard Journal of Communication* 14(4): 225–43.

Palumbo-Liu, David. 1999. *Asian/American: Historical Crossings of a Racial Frontier*.
Stanford: Stanford University Press.

Parmentier, Richard J. 1994. *Signs in Society: Studies in Semiotic Anthropology*.
Bloomington: Indiana University Press.

Peché, Linda Ho. 2011. Vietnamese Americans: Domestic Religious Practices. In
Encyclopedia of Asian American Folklore and Folklife, edited by Jonathan H. X.
Lee and Kathleen M. Nadeau, 3:1171–74. Santa Barbara, CA: ABC-CLIO. Gale
Virtual Reference Library. Accessed August 20, 2013.

Peirce, Charles S. 1955. *Philosophical Writings of Peirce*. Edited by Justin Buchler.
New York: Dover.

Peters, James. 2008a. Current Environment: Publishers Face Myriad Challenges.
Publishing and Advertising, March 6. Standard and Poor's Industry Surveys.
Accessed September 7, 2013.

Peters, James. 2008b. Current Environment: Publishers Face Myriad Challenges. *Publishing and Advertising*, August 21. Standard and Poor's Industry Surveys. Accessed September 7, 2013.

Peters, James, and William H. Donald. 2007a. Current Environment: Agencies Look Abroad for Growth. *Advertising*, February 8. Standard and Poor's Industry Surveys. Accessed September 7, 2013.

Peters, James, and William H. Donald. 2007b. Current Environment: U.S. Advertising Spending Momentum Slows. *Advertising*, August 9. Standard and Poor's Industry Surveys. Accessed September 7, 2013.

Peterson, Robin. 2007. Consumer Magazine Advertisement Portrayals of Models by Race in the U.S.: An Assessment. *Journal of Marketing Communications* 13(3): 199–211.

Pieraccini, Cristina, and Douglass Alligood. 2007. *Color Television: Sixty Years of African American and Latino Images on Prime-Time Television*. Dubuque, IA: Kendall Hunt.

Piller, Ingrid. 2001. Identity Constructions in Multilingual Advertising. *Language in Society* 30: 153–86.

Pinney, Christopher. 2005. Things Happen: Or, from Which Moment Does That Object Come? In *Materiality*, edited by Daniel Miller, 256–72. Durham, NC: Duke University Press.

Poole, Deborah. 2005. An Excess of Description: Ethnography, Race, and Visual Technologies. *Annual Review of Anthropology* 34: 159–79.

Povinelli, Elizabeth. 2011. *Economies of Abandonment: Social Belonging and Endurance in Late Liberalism*. Durham, NC: Duke University Press.

Prashad, Vijay. 2000. *The Karma of Brown Folk*. Minneapolis: University of Minnesota Press.

President and Fellows of Harvard College. 1931. A Short History of Trade Cards. *Bulletin of the Business Historical Society* 5(3): 1–6.

Puar, Jasbir. 2007. *Terrorist Assemblages: Homonationalism in Queer Times*. Durham, NC: Duke University Press.

Purkayastha, Bandana, and Ranita Ray. 2010. South Asian Americans. In *Encyclopedia of Asian American Issues Today*, edited by Edith Wen-Chu Chen and Grace J. Yoo, 1:51–63. Santa Barbara, CA: Greenwood Press. Gale Virtual Reference Library. Accessed August 27, 2013.

Rana, Junaid. 2011. *Terrifying Muslims: Race and Labor in the South Asian Diaspora*. Durham, NC: Duke University Press.

Reddy, Chandan. 2011. *Freedom with Violence: Race, Sexuality, and the U.S. State*. Durham, NC: Duke University Press.

Redfield, Peter. 2005. Doctors, Borders, and Life in Crisis. *Cultural Anthropology* 20(3): 328–61.

Richard, Analiese, and Daromir Rudnyckyj. 2009. Economies of Affect. *Journal of the Royal Anthropological Institute* 15: 57–77.

Rubin, Rachel, and Jeffrey Melnick. 2007. *Immigration and American Popular Culture: An Introduction*. New York: New York University Press.

Schein, Louisa. 2013. Homeland Beauty: Transnational Longing and Hmong American Video. In *Media, Erotics, and Transnational Asia*, edited by Purnima Mankekar and Louisa Schein, 203–32. Durham, NC: Duke University Press.

Schieffelin, Bambi, Kathryn Woolard, and Paul Kroskrity. 1998. *Language Ideologies: Practice and Theory*. New York: Oxford University Press.

Schroeder, Jonathan E. 2009. The Cultural Codes of Branding. *Marketing Theory* 9(1): 123–26.

Schroeder, Jonathan E., and Miriam Salzer-Mörling, eds. 2006. *Brand Culture*. New York: Routledge.

Scranton, Philip, ed. 2001. *Beauty and Business: Commerce, Gender, and Culture in Modern America*. New York: Routledge.

Shankar, Shalini. 2006. Metaconsumptive Practices and the Circulation of Objectifications. *Journal of Material Culture* 11(3): 293–317.

Shankar, Shalini. 2008. *Desi Land: Teen Culture, Class, and Success in Silicon Valley*. Durham, NC: Duke University Press.

Shankar, Shalini. 2012. Creating Model Consumers: Producing Ethnicity, Race, and Class in Asian American Advertising. *American Ethnologist* 39(3): 578–91.

Shankar, Shalini. 2013a. Affect and Sport in Asian American Advertising. *South Asian Popular Culture* 11(3): 231–42.

Shankar, Shalini. 2013b. Racial Naturalization, Advertising, and Model Consumers for a New Millennium. *Journal of Asian American Studies* 16(2): 159–88.

Shankar, Shalini, and Jillian Cavanaugh. 2012. Language and Materiality in Global Capitalism. *Annual Review of Anthropology* 41: 355–69.

Shever, Elana. 2008. Neoliberal Associations: Property, Company, and Family in the Argentine Oil Fields. *American Ethnologist* 35: 701–16.

Shin, Ji-Hye. 2010. Korean Immigrants. In *Encyclopedia of American Immigration*, edited by Carl L. Bankston III, 2:627–31. Pasadena, CA: Salem Press. Gale Virtual Reference Library. Accessed August 17, 2013.

Silverstein, Michael. 1993. Metapragmatic Discourse and Metapragmatic Function. In *Reflexive Language: Reported Speech and Metapragmatics*, edited by John A. Lucy, 33–58. Cambridge: Cambridge University Press.

Silverstein, Michael. 2003. Indexical Order and the Dialectics of Sociolinguistic Life. *Language and Communication* 23(3–4): 193–229.

Silverstein, Michael. 2006. Old Wine, New Ethnographic Lexicography. *Annual Review of Anthropology* 35: 481–96.

Silverstein, Michael, and Greg Urban. 1996. The Natural History of Discourse.

In *The Natural Histories of Discourse*, edited by Michael Silverstein and Greg Urban, 1–17. Chicago: University of Chicago Press.

Siu, Lok, and Rhacel Parreñas, eds. 2006. *Asian Diasporas: New Formations, New Conceptions*. Stanford: Stanford University Press.

Sivulka, Juliann. 1998. *Soap, Sex, and Cigarettes: A Cultural History of American Advertising*. Belmont, CA: Wadsworth.

Smith, Neil, and Setha Low. 2013. Introduction to *The Politics of Public Space*, edited by Setha Low and Neil Smith, 1–18. New York: Routledge.

Spitulnik, Deborah. 1996. The Circulation of Media Discourse and the Mediation of Communities. *Journal of Linguistic Anthropology* 6(2): 161–87.

Stam, Robert, and Ella Shohat. 2012. *Race in Translation: Culture Wars around the Postcolonial Atlantic*. New York: New York University Press.

Steele, Jeffery. 2000. Reduced to Images: American Indians in Nineteenth-Century Advertising. In *The Gender and Consumer Culture Reader*, edited by J. Scanlon, 109–28. New York: New York University Press.

Strathern, Marilyn. 2006. A Community of Critics? Thoughts on New Knowledge. *Journal of the Royal Anthropological Institute* 12(1): 191–209.

Sunderland, Patricia, and Rita Denny. 2007. *Doing Anthropology in Consumer Research*. Walnut Creek, CA: Left Coast Press.

Taylor, Charles R., and Barbara B. Stern. 1997. Asian-Americans: Television Advertising and the "Model Minority" Stereotype. *Journal of Advertising* 26(2): 47–61.

Thorndike, Jonathan L. 2010. Japanese Immigrants. In *Encyclopedia of American Immigration*, edited by Carl L. Bankston III, 2:607–13. Pasadena, CA: Salem Press. Gale Virtual Reference Library. Accessed August 13, 2013.

Tu, Thuy Linh. 2011. *The Beautiful Generation: Asian Americans and the Cultural Economy of Fashion*. Durham, NC: Duke University Press.

Tuan, Mia. 1998. *Forever Foreigners or Honorary Whites? The Asian Ethnic Experience Today*. New Brunswick, NJ: Rutgers University Press.

Um, Khatharya. 2010. Southeast Asian Americans. In *Encyclopedia of Asian American Issues Today*, edited by Edith Wen-Chu Chen and Grace J. Yoo, 1:65–80. Santa Barbara, CA: Greenwood Press. Gale Virtual Reference Library. Accessed August 20, 2013.

Urban, Greg. 2001. *Metaculture: How Cultures Move through the World*. Minneapolis: University of Minnesota Press.

Urciuoli, Bonnie. 2008. Skills and Selves in the New Workplace. *American Ethnologist* 35(2): 211–28.

Urciuoli, Bonnie. 2009. Talking/Not Talking about Race: The Enregisterments of Culture in Higher Education Discourses. *Journal of Linguistic Anthropology* 19(1): 21–39.

U.S. Census Bureau. 2010. *The Asian Population: 2010*. 2010 Census Briefs. U.S. Cen-

sus. http://www.census.gov/prod/cen2010/briefs/c2010br-11.pdf. Accessed
August 2, 2013.

U.S. Census Bureau. 2011a. American Community Survey 1-Year Estimates.
American Fact Finder. Accessed August 28, 2013.

U.S. Census Bureau. 2011b. American Community Survey 3-Year Estimates.
American Fact Finder. Accessed August 28, 2013.

U.S. Department of Labor. N.d. *The Asian-American Labor Force in the Recovery.*
http://www.dol.gov/_sec/media/reports/asianlaborforce/. Accessed August
28, 2013.

Valentine, Tamara M. 2010. Asian Indian Immigrants. In *Encyclopedia of American Immigration,* edited by Carl L. Bankston III, 1:77–80. Pasadena, CA: Salem
Press. Gale Virtual Reference Library. Accessed August 23, 2013.

Võ, Linda Trinh. 2010. Beyond Color-Blind Universalism: Asians in a "Postracial
America." *Journal of Asian American Studies* 13: 327–42.

Wang, Jing. 2008. *Brand New China.* Cambridge, MA: Harvard University Press.

Welker, Marina, Damani J. Partridge, and Rebecca Hardin. 2011. Corporate Lives:
New Perspectives on the Social Life of the Corporate Form. *Current Anthropology* 52(S3, supplement to April 2011): S3–16.

Werbner, Pnina. 2001. The Limits of Cultural Hybridity: On Ritual Monsters,
Poetic Licence, and Contested Postcolonial Purifications. *Journal of the Royal
Anthropological Institute* 7(1): 133–52.

West, Paige. 2012. *From Modern Production to Imagined Primitive: The Social World
of Coffee from Papua New Guinea.* Durham, NC: Duke University Press.

Wilson, C. 2011. Advertising, Search and Intermediaries on the Internet: Introduction. *Economic Journal* 121: F291–96.

Winant, Howard. 2001. *The World Is a Ghetto: Race and Democracy since World
War II.* New York: Basic Books.

Winant, Howard. 2004. *The New Politics of Race: Globalism, Difference, Justice.*
Minneapolis: University of Minnesota Press.

Woolard, Kathryn. 1998. Introduction: Language Ideology as a Field of Inquiry.
In *Language Ideologies: Practice and Theory,* edited by Bambi Schieffelin,
Kathryn Woolard, and Paul Kroskrity, 3–47. New York: Oxford University
Press.

Wu, William. 2002. *Yellow: Race in America beyond Black and White.* New York: Basic
Books.

Zukin, Sharon. 2004. *Point of Purchase: How Shopping Changed American Culture.*
New York: Psychology Press.

INDEX

Page numbers in *italics* indicate figures.

Celluloid Collar and Cuff advertisement, 46

Census, U.S.: categories, 1, 10, 21, 22–23, 39, 61, 73–74, 87, 160, 251; minority data, 4–5, 38, 54, 152–54; multicultural advertising use of, 38, 40, 50, 54, 71–80, 83–85, 150, 152, 157, 255

Chang, Ed, 61, 64, 82, 83

character sketches. *See* consumer sketches

Cheerios advertisement, *208*, 208–9

Chinese Americans: accents in advertisements, 138–39, 141–42; in advertising, 7, 46, 52, 53, 54, 60, 123–24, *124*, 137, *161*, 199, *238*; as consumer segment, 59; immigration, 42–43, 45, 48–49, 50–51; as model minority, 53; population statistics, 73; representations of, 44

Chinese Exclusion Act (1882), 42–43

Choi, Jake, 5, 219–20

Chou, Rosalind, 83

Cicourel, Aaron, 284n17

Citibank advertisements, *169*, *172*

citizenship, 23, 45, 47, 252

class, cultural insight and, 107

CLIO awards, 239

Clough, Patricia, 40, 150

Coca-Cola advertisement, 259

Collier, Stephen J., 189

color blindness, 19, 20, 41, 254

Comaroff, Jean, 41

Comaroff, John, 41

community events, 242–43

consumer insights, 103, 110, 162–64, 167, 173

consumer sketches, 97, *109*, 109–10, 112–13

consumption, 25–26

copyright, 143, 226

corporate America: on Asian Americans, 42, 78; belonging and, 158; casting in, 202–3; diversity in, 11, 15, 17–18, 24, 66, 140–41, 149–50, 203, 252–55, 260; intercultural affect in, 150, 174, 180, 189; "normal" in, 5, 7, 188–89, 201, 205–6, 248, 251; racialized capitalism in, 4–5, 19, 95; use of term, 10

creative(s), 87–88; affect, 92, 94, 96, 120,

146, 149, 195; as normal, 99; strategy, 95–97; use of term, 90

cultural insights, *100*, 100–106, 159. *See also* transcreation

culture, use of term, 17, 154, 258–59. *See also* intercultural spaces

Dae (ad agency), 57, 61

Davila, Arlene, 19, 25, 56, 65, 72, 282n15

Deleuze, Gilles, 11, 193

designated market areas (DMAs), 79–80, 154, 164–65, 261–62

desire: brand identity and, 87, 130; capitalism and, 16; in multicultural advertising, 72

diasporas and consumption, 26

difference: brand identity and, 3; management of, 18; in multicultural advertising, 10, 71

diversity: approaches, Asian American market, 99–101; approaches, general market, 94, 98–99; assemblages of, 11–14, 17, 91, 94, 150, 167, 189–90, 193–222, 251–55; capitalism and, 15–17; casting for, 150, 201–22, 247–49, 256; contests of, 255–64; in corporate America, 11, 15, 17–18, 24, 66, 140–41, 149–50, 203, 252–55, 260; embodying, 194; emergence in advertising, 54–55; expertise on, 22, 50, 61, 74, 105, 148–49, 151–56, 166; indexical icons of, 93; neoliberalism and, 15–17, 155, 166, 190, 247; as normal, 4–7, 207; as profitable, 260; qualisigns of, 17–20, 40, 93, 94, 98, 102, 110, 130, 187, 194, 201; use of term, 4, 10, 17, 154. *See also* ethnicity; race

Diwali Times Square event, 84, *85*

DMAs. *See* designated market areas

Domino's pizza ad campaign, 214

Dornfeld, Barry, 25

Downey, Greg, 29, 276n47

Duchêne, Alexandre, 282n1

Eastern Europeans, 55

Ebony (magazine), 50, 205

EBT. *See* English back-translation

miscegenation, 47–48, 207–9

Miyazaki, Hiro, 87

model minority stereotype, 28, 53, 78, 86, 122

modernity, 19, 103–4

Montoya, Michael, 284n12

Moore, Robert, 283n38

Mosaic awards, 257

MTV World (television program), 263

Muehlebach, Andrea, 284n4

multicultural advertising, 55–71; aesthetics in, 87; census data, 38, 40, 50, 54, 71–80, 83–85, 150, 152, 157, 255; consumer sketches, 97, *109*, 109–10, 112–13; difference and, 10, 20, 36; expertise on diversity, 22, 50, 61, 74, 105, 148–49, 151–56, 166; foundations of, 21, 25, 54–55, 87; indexical icons, 93–94, 101–6, 154; intercultural affect, 173–88; investment strategies, 224; legitimacy of, 255; market approaches to, 99–101; media plans for, 222, 227; neoliberal ideologies in, 41; as niche, 3–4, 64, 66, 228–29; in 1960s–1990s, 50–55; racial stereotypes in, 6, 20, 28, 38–39, 41, 44–48, 94–95, 148–50, 167; during recession, 82; register formation in, 154; second-generation, 62–63, 129, 140, 157, 227, 231, 260–63; selling it in, 156–67; synchronized launches in, 198; as thriving, 41; total market strategy, 259, 265; transcreation in, 92, 109–10, 114–16, 125, 181; in 2000s, 80–85. *See also* Asian American advertising agencies

multiculturalism, boutique, 253–55

Multicultural Marketing Resources, 64

multicultural talent. *See* casting for diversity

Munn, Nancy, 17, 93

Muslim Americans, 76–68, 167–68; in advertising, 77, 252–53

Myers, Fred, 27, 36, 115–16, 149, 150

Naficy, Hamid, 26

Nakagawa, Jane, 70

narrative structure, 116–20

National Broadcasting Corporation (NBC), 48

National Bureau of Economic Research, 83

National Coalition for Asian Pacific American Community Development, 83

Nationwide South Asian advertisement, 76–78, 77, 122, 138, 229

Native Americans: representations of, 44; as target audience, 55

Negri, Antonio, 277n47

neoliberalism: diversity and, 15–17, 155, 166, 190, 247; and intellectual labor, 152; in multiculturalism, 16, 19, 41, 155; and profit making, 15, 282n1; and racial formation, 41, 264; use of term, 16–17

New York Times (newspaper), 53, 84

Ng, Tommy, 62, 63–64, 70

Ng, Zan, 57, 61, 64, 70

niche advertising, 3–4, 64, 66, 160, 186. *See also* multicultural advertising

Nielsen ratings, 224, *225*

Nissan, 95; advertisement, 7, *80*, 123–24, *124*

Niu, Max, 63–64, 69–70

normal (term), 7; in corporate America, 5, 7, 188–89, 201, 205–6, 248, 251; definitions, 101, 194; diversity as, 4–7; racial naturalization and, 201–3, 209, 211, 254, 264–68; racism and, 5, 18; whiteness as, 18, 150, 201, 203, 205–6, 247–48, 260, 264–65

North Africans, 55

Obama, Barack, 19, 41

Ogilvy, David, 50

Ogilvy Culture, 258, 258–59

Olds, Kris, 15, 39–40

Omi, Michael, 41

Ong, Aihwa, 189

Ono, Kent, 27

Oriental stereotype, 44–45

Ozawa, Takao, 47

pan-Asian, use of term, 213

Parmentier, Richard, 144–45

Peerless Wringer advertisement, *46*

Peirce, Charles Sanders, 17, 93

Perez, Sarah, 285n17

Pew Research Center, 83

Pham, Vincent, 27

Pinney, Christopher, 87

Poehler, Amy, 5, 219–20

poetics, 133–40, 141

politics of anti-, 7, 24, 266

Polk data, 82, 226

Poole, Deborah, 27

Popchips advertisement, 216–17, 217

post-Fordism, 149, 284n3

postracial era, 4, 19, 27–28, 41, 201, 254–55

Povinelli, Elizabeth, 5, 16

production: as art, 197; assemblages of diversity in, 193–222; brand identity and, 194–97; politics of, 192–93; postproduction, 197, 199–200; preproduction, 197, 201; storyboards, 198, 199; time frames, 197–98

profit making: diversity and, 19, 94, 247, 254, 260; intercultural affect in, 151; neoliberal ideologies on, 15, 154–56, 282n1; norms in, 91; race and, 3, 15, 41, 42, 266–67

Progressive Era, 43–44

Psy ("Gangnam Style"), 91

Puar, Jasbir, 12

public relations, 221–22, 237–47

puffery, 144–45

Pure Food and Drugs Act (1906), 44

qualisigns of diversity, 40, 93, 94, 98, 102, 110, 130, 187, 194, 201

race: assemblages of, 251–55; in brand identity, 4, 41, 94, 242, 249; in capitalism, 4–5, 7, 9, 15, 16–17, 41, 95, 148, 150, 265–66; in casting, 202–9; census categories, 1, 10, 21, 22–23, 39, 61, 73–74, 87, 160, 251; humor and, 214–15; importance of, 3; indexical icons, 94; media and, 24–29; neoliberalism and, 41, 264; representation of, 76, 85–86; self-identification by, 260; spatialization of, 20. See also diversity; ethnicity

racialization: assemblages of diversity and, 251; biopolitics and, 38–39; in capitalism, 16–17, 95, 148–49, 150, 265–66; ethnic/racial categorization in, 264, 284n12; intercultural affect in, 174; of Islam, 27; of labor, 254, 264; naturalization and, 249; neoliberalism and, 264; as racism, 23–24; semiotics of, 90–91; use of term, 10–11

racial naturalization, 7, 36, 40, 146, 148; assemblages of diversity and, 91, 167; biopolitics and, 21–24, 40, 264; in brand identity, 242, 249; in census data, 152, 160; intercultural affect and, 173–74, 190; normal and, 201–3, 209, 211, 254, 264–68; use of term, 78, 265–66

racial stereotypes, 6, 20, 28, 38–39, 41, 44–48, 50, 86, 94–95, 148–50, 167, 215–17, 257

racism: biomediation of, 40; in conversation/humor, 190, 215; as downplayed, 19–20; normalcy and, 5, 18; perpetuation of, 28–29; politics of, 6–7; in visual anthropology, 27. See also racialization; racial naturalization

Rainbow Coalition, 264

Rana, Junaid, 23, 27

Red (firm), 29

register formation (enregisterment), 154

Richard, Analiese, 284n3

Riles, Annalise, 87

Rudnyckyj, Daromir, 284n3

Russian Americans in advertising, 169

Saka, Erkan, 12, 193, 194

Samsung advertisements, 211–12, 212

Sanjaya, 229–30

Schein, Louisa, 26–27, 31

Schumer, Charles, 264

Scripps National Spelling Bee, 242

second generation, 62–63, 76, 129, 140, 157, 166, 227, 231, 260–63, 261

semiotics, 12–13, 90–91

Shohat, Ella, 27, 28, 86, 254

Silicon India (magazine), 227

Silverstein, Michael, 11, 284–85n17
Sivulka, Juliann, 50
Six Flags advertisement, 215–16, *216*
Skriloff, Lisa, 64, 71, 82, 83–84
slogans, 133–34
Smith, Neil, 21
social media, 223–24, 231–37, 248, 263–64
social networks, 62, 164–65, 200
South Asian Americans, 59
South Asian Spelling Bee, 242–43
spaces: intercultural, 36, 149–51; social, 21–22
Stam, Robert, 27, 28, 86, 254
State Farm Insurance, 79
stereotypes. *See* racial stereotypes
Strathern, Marilyn, 254
subtitles, 123–24
Suburu, 95
Sullivan, Arthur, 44
Super Bowl ads, 2, 5, 91, 208, 219–21, *220*, 226, 259
surveillance, 21, 193

Tan (magazine), 50
Telemundo, 57
television: as advertising platform, 222–23; development of, 48
Teo, Sunny, 61, 64
Thompson, J. Walter, 45
3AF. *See* Asian American Advertising Federation
Thrift, Nigel, 15, 39–40
tonality, 105, 121, 141
Tong, Jimmy, 68
total market strategy, 259, 265
Touchdown Media (ad agency), 242
Toyama, Stan, 70
Toyota advertisement, *92*
trade cards, 44–45, *46*
trademarks, 133, 134, 143–46
transcreation, 88, 181; brand identity and, 92, 94, 101, 116, 120, 129–32, 140, 146; humor in, 121–22; in-culture, 56, 69, 93, 100, 101–14, 120, 122, *137*, *140*, *153*, 154, *161*, 195; in-language, 56, 69, 93, 100,

114–16, 120, 122, 124–32, 136–39, *137*, 140–42, 145–46, 154, *161*, 195; narrative structure, 116–20; poetics in, 133–40, 141; process of, 92–93, 111–12; tonality in, 105, 120–21, 141; use of term, 35, 92–93, 154, 156, 182
Tu, Thuy Linh, 62
Tuan, Mia, 23, 78

United Colors of Benetton advertisement, 98, *99*, 207
United States v. Bhagat Singh Thind, 47
Univision, 57
Urciuoli, Bonnie, 11, 17, 154, 285n17
U.S. News & World Report (magazine), 53

value: cultural, 13, 16, 93, 150–51, 171–72, 252; distinctions and, 152, 160; indexical, 95, 117, 125; linguistic materiality and, 149–50; qualisigns of, 17–18, 93; use of term, 15
Verschueren, Jef, 253
Vietnamese Americans: as consumer segment, 59; immigration, 43, 51; population statistics, 73
Volkswagen advertisement, 219–21, *220*

Walia, Rahul, 242
Wall Street Project, 264
Werbner, Pnina, 23
Western Union advertisement, *161*
whiteness: corporate policies and, 253; in general advertising, 4–5, 19–20, 53, 55, 158; as modernity, 18; as normal, 18–19, 150, 201, 203, 205–6, 247–48, 260, 264–65; target audience and, 205; use of term, 10
women, as target audience, 279n29
Wong, Vicky, 58

yellow peril imagery, 47–48, 86
Yi, Sid, 62
Yuen, Jeannie, 61

Zukin, Sharon, 21